SOUND AND SEMBLANCE

Books by Peter Kivy

Speaking of Art (1973)

The Seventh Sense: A Study of Francis Hutcheson's Aesthetics and Its Influence in Eighteenth-Century Britain (1976)

The Corded Shell: Reflections on Musical Expression (1980)

Osmin's Rage: Philosophical Reflections on Opera, Drama, and Text (1988)

Music Alone: Philosophical Reflections on the Purely Musical Experience (1990)

SOUND AND SEMBLANCE

Reflections on Musical Representation

With a New Afterword by the Author
Peter Kivy

CORNELL UNIVERSITY PRESS
Ithaca and London

First published, Cornell Paperbacks, 1991
by Cornell University Press.

International Standard Book Number 0-8014-9946-1
Library of Congress Catalog Card Number 91-55159
Printed in the United States of America
*Librarians: Library of Congress cataloging information
appears on the last page of the book.*

♾ The paper in this book meets the minimum requirements
of the American National Standard for Information Sciences—
Permanence of Paper for Printed Library Materials,
ANSI Z39.48-1984.

To the memory of Evelyn Kivy Rosenberg,
scientist and teacher.

Honegger, *Pacific* (231)

'Εποποιία δὴ καὶ ἡ τῆς τραγῳδίας ποίησις ἔτι δὲ κωμῳδία καὶ ἡ διθυραμβοποιητικὴ καὶ τῆς αὐλητικῆς ἡ πλείστη καὶ κιθαριστικῆς, πᾶσαι τυγχάνουσιν οὖσαι μιμήσεις τὸ σύνολον, διαφέρουσι δὲ ἀλλήλων τρισίν, ἢ γὰρ τῷ γένει[1] ἑτέροις μιμεῖσθαι ἢ τῷ ἕτερα ἢ τῷ ἑτέρως καὶ μὴ τὸν αὐτὸν τρόπον.

Aristotle, *Poetics* (1447a)

Contents

Preface to the Paperback Edition

As can be gathered from my Preface to the first edition of
Sound and Semblance, the work was intended as the second of a
matched pair, covering between them what I saw then to be the
two most philosophically tractable issues in music aesthetics,
namely, "expression" and "representation." The completion of
the second book was to put an end to the project, and I fully
intended thereafter to pursue more familiar philosophical
game. But that is not the way things have turned out.

Much to my surprise, what started out as a fairly self-contained study of two specific philosophical issues in music ex-
panded into a yet-to-be completed (and sometimes seemingly
open-ended) series of books on the "philosophy of music"
which now constitute a kind of "system." It is, therefore, most
gratifying to me to see a paperback edition of this "early" book
appear, since it will allow the system, as it is presently consti-
tuted, to remain intact—which is to say, in print.

One need not master the system, I hasten to add, in order
to comprehend *Sound and Semblance*. It is a fully autonomous
work. But to those who do read it as a part of the system, I beg
some indulgence. My ideas have developed over a period of
more than ten years. So I dare say one is bound to find incon-
sistencies, if one compares this work, originally published in
1984, with the latest in the series, *Music Alone*, published in
1990. Unlike Walt Whitman, I am not proud of my contradic-
tions; and I do not suggest they be applauded as evidence of a
large intellect, or overlooked as evidence of a careless yet profound one. What I do ask of the charitable reader is to look
past them to the larger whole, while I try to deal with them as
the work goes on.

PETER KIVY

New York City
January 1991

Preface

I look upon the present work as a companion piece to my previously published volume on music, *The Corded Shell: Reflections on Musical Expression* (Princeton: Princeton University Press, 1980). Between the two of them, they express my views on what I take to be the major claims of music to possess a "content" beyond its purely musical "syntax" and structure.

Like *The Corded Shell,* the present work pays its respects and is deeply indebted to the musical writers of the seventeenth and eighteenth centuries. But whereas in the former I built upon Enlightenment theories of musical "expression" that were, I thought then and do still think, basically correct, and mainly in need of refurbishing and defense, the present volume rejects (with the exception of Adam Smith's) the efforts of the period to explicate musical "representation" as basically misconceived. We owe, however, as much, if not more, to those thinkers whose speculations we take the time to refute, as to those whose views we accept. It is only those we ignore that we need feel no obligation to thank or embalm in our footnotes.

Again, as in *The Corded Shell,* I have relied heavily on musical examples to make my points. My arguments will scarcely convince anyone of the representational in music if the music will not itself. And very often, what may seem an extravagant or exaggerated claim about musical representation, arguments to the contrary notwithstanding, will, when the music is examined in score and attended to with an unbiased ear, quite convince the reader. I have come to the conclusions expressed here, first and foremost, through my experience of music, not by spinning out philosophical arguments. If my musical examples do not carry conviction, little else that I say will. So I must insist that they be seen as an integral part of my book, not merely an ornament.

Although the present work is, in the sense explained, a companion piece to my previous musical essay, familiarity with the earlier work is by no means required or assumed in the present one. Where I have made use here of conclusions reached in *The Corded Shell,* I have always taken the time to explain them as thoroughly as necessary, and although no author wishes to discourage readers from perusing *any* of his or her works, I certainly do not wish, on the other hand, to discourage readers from picking up the present volume because it places them under the necessity of picking up a previous one. A book in the hand, to an author if not to a librarian, is worth two on the shelf.

The general argument of the book was presented, in a somewhat primitive and highly condensed form, on two separate occasions, in talks at the University of Maryland, Baltimore County, and New York University. I wish to thank the auditors present on those two occasions for much lively discussion and valuable criticism. In particular, I am indebted to Raziel Abelson, Annette Barnes, Michael Broiles, Frances Kamm, Jerrold Levinson, Thomas Mark, John Titchener, Alan Tormey. I am again indebted to Wilson Coker for undertaking to read and criticize the entire manuscript. His tragic and untimely death stills a voice always for clarity and common sense in the philosophy of music. The same burdensome task was undertaken, much to my delight, by Kendall Walton, to whom I owe a really special debt for his careful, insightful, and always constructive philosophical observations. Mark Mueller took time off from more pressing matters to supply me with a dog in motion. I am indebted to Sarah Wilk for expert advice on the choice of illustrations. Margaret Cohen of Princeton University Press made numerous suggestions on style, as well as on substantive musical points, for all of which I am most grateful. And to Sandy Thatcher of the Press I am continually grateful for the truly professional help without which an author—at least this author—could never get around the publication board from "Go" to "Boardwalk." My thanks to all, none of whom is responsible in any way for the remaining mistakes.

New York City PETER KIVY
April 1983

SOUND AND SEMBLANCE

CHAPTER I

Music as Imitation

◇ 1 ◇ The eighteenth- and nineteenth-century English translators of Aristotle were remarkably consistent in their rendering of the Greek word μί/μησιζ as "imitation," at least where it is used in reference to the fine arts. Consider, for example, Thomas Twining's version (1789) of *Poetics* (1747a):

> Epic Poetry, Tragedy, Comedy Dithyrambics, as also, for the most part, the Music of the flute, and of the lyre—all these are in the most general view of them, IMITATIONS; differing, however, from each other in *three* respects, according to the different *means,* the different *objects,* or the different *manner,* of their imitation.[1]

Or compare Butcher's translation, over a century later, of the same passage (1894):

> Epic poetry and Tragedy, Comedy also and Dithyrambic poetry, and the music of the flute and of the lyre in most of their forms, are all in their general conception modes of imitation. They differ, however, from one another in three respects,—the medium, the objects, the manner or mode of imitation, being in each distinct.[2]

I am neither capable nor desirous of commenting on the propriety of such translations. But I will be concerned, in what directly follows, to point out the consequences they had for the theory of musical representation, which is the subject of my inquiry. More properly, I should say, I am concerned to repair the mischief that has been done to what should have been a theory of musical representation, but which started out life, in the eighteenth century, as a theory of musical imitation.

That there is a problem for the Aristotelian aesthetics of music, in translating μί/μησιζ as "imitation," was already quite apparent to Twining in 1789. He seems to have located the problem—although, as we shall see in a moment, it is only the tip of the iceberg—in Aristotle's claim, in, for example, *Politics* VII (1340a), that what music "imitates" is emotions and states of human character: "Rhythm and melody supply imitations of anger and gentleness, and also of courage and temperance, and of all the qualities contrary to these, and of the other qualities of character, which hardly fall short of the actual affections. . . ."[3]

But how, one wonders (and Twining wondered), can musical sounds *imitate* the emotions? The *Shorter Oxford English Dictionary* tells us: to imitate is to "copy," or "reproduce" (1590); and an imitation is a "copy," an "artificial likeness," a "counterfeit" (1601). But how can we copy or reproduce emotions or states of character in sound? How can sound be an artificial likeness, or a copy, or a counterfeit of anger, or grief, courage or temperance? It cannot, Twining concluded, "for between *sounds themselves,* and *natural affections,* there can be no resemblance."[4]

What then could Aristotle have meant by saying that music *imitates* emotions and states of character? Only, Twining thought, what his own century meant by "expresses."

> The ideas, and the language of the antients, on this subject, were different [from our own]. When *they* speak of Music as imitation, they appear to have solely, or chiefly, in view, its power over the affections. By *imitation,* they mean, in short, what *we* commonly distinguish from imitation, and oppose to it, under the general term of *expression.*[5]

And what Twining quite correctly thought was commonly (though by no means universally) meant in his own day by "expression" was "arousal": "power over the affections" being power to arouse them. Thus all that Aristotle could possibly have meant by music imitating the emotions and mental states of men, unless, of course, he was saying something absurdly false, was that music *arouses* such emotions and states in the listener.

> The resemblance [of music to emotions and mental states] can only be a resemblance of effect:—the *general emotions, tempers,* or *feelings* produced in us by certain sounds, are *like* those that accompany actual grief, joy, anger, &c.—And this . . . appears to be all that Aristotle meant.[6]

Now as I have said before, it is no part of my intention to pass judgment on the adequacy or inadequacy of this translation cum interpretation of Aristotle on imitation. What I am interested in is evaluating its plausibility, or lack of it, as an account of musical illustration in the modern era. And from that point of view, it is, as can readily be seen, woefully inadequate. I shall be adducing some deeper reasons for this adverse judgment later on in the present chapter. But for starters, and laying aside the obvious objections to construing musical "expression" as the arousal of emotions in the listener (I have dealt with that elsewhere),[7] an expression theory of musical illustration of the kind Twining is attributing to Aristotle can only get off the ground if emotions and states of mind are the only things that one wants to say music "imitates" or "illustrates." Twining, indeed, although he does not go so far as to deny to music all but emotions and states of mind as proper objects of imitation, goes a long way in that direction by playing down the nonexpressive objects. Thus:

> Music can raise ideas, immediately [that is, without the aid of expression], only by the actual resemblance of its *sounds* and *motions* to the sounds and motions of the thing suggested. Such Music we call *imitative*, in the same sense in which we apply the word to a similar resemblance of sound and motion in poetry. In both cases, the resemblance, though *immediate*, is so *imperfect*, that it cannot be seen till it is, in some sort, pointed out, and even when it *is* so, is not always very evident. Poetry, indeed, has here a great advantage; it carries with it, of necessity, its own explanation: for the same word that imitates by its *sound*, points out, or hints, at least, the imitation, by its *meaning*. With music it is not so. It must call in the assistance of language, or something equivalent to language, for its interpreter.[8]

But on any adequate account of musical illustration that does not simply beg the question in favor of an expressive theory from the start, it must be acknowledged that composers purport to illustrate far more than "mental" objects, that the *world* is their oyster as well.

That the problem here lies deeper than this, however, will best be seen by examining in a little detail an account of musical imitation from Twining's own time, one with which he himself was familiar, and one frequently mentioned in the aesthetic literature of the late eighteenth century. I refer to James Harris' *Discourse on Music, Painting, and Poetry* (1744). I shall argue that the problem for music which it raises is the result of the baleful influence of the notion of imitation that the translators of Aristotle cast like a pall over the musical speculations of the time having to do with what would more happily be called musical representation.

◊ 2 ◊   Harris is engaged in a philosophical parlor game peculiar to the Enlightenment and, fortunately, no longer popular: that of trying to prove, a priori, which of the fine arts is superior. This exercise involves, first, determining what the peculiar genius of each of the fine arts is (for it is the first premise of the game that such essences exist), and then demonstrating, on this basis, their individual order of merit. As Harris states his objective: "The Design of this Discourse is to treat of MUSIC, PAINTING, and POETRY; to consider in what they *agree,* and in what they *differ;* and WHICH UPON THE WHOLE, IS MORE EXCELLENT THAN THE OTHER TWO."[9]

I say this game has fallen from favor; but it would be more accurate to say that part of it still survives: that part, preliminary to the value judgment, where the essential nature of the respective arts is determined—what Lessing called in *Laokoön,* with respect to painting and poetry, their "limits."[10] Be that as it may, in the process of determining "in what they *agree,* and in what they *differ,*" Harris makes observations on the imitative nature of the fine arts in general, and music in particular, that can be separated from the Platonic search for essences and for what is better and what is worse and examined in isolation. It is his observations on imitative music that are, of course, our major concern.

That Harris was driven to his views on music as imitation by ancient views on the arts—notably Plato's and Aristotle's—and the translators' preference for "imitation" as the correct rendering of μί/μησιζ is beyond serious doubt. The views themselves broadcast their lineage; and if that were not enough to clinch the matter, Harris' writing is peppered with references to the Greek text of the *Poetics.*

Harris begins with the familiar enough assumption of his time that the fine arts are arts of imitation: that "by the several *Organs of the Senses* . . . these Arts exhibit to the Mind *Imitations,* and imitate either Parts or Affections of this *natural World,* or else the Passions, Energies, and other Affections of *Minds.*"[11] Readers of the more recent writings in aesthetics, starting perhaps with Collingwood, are likely to take this for what some contemporary philosophers have called, following Paul Ziff, the "traditional task of defining the work of art," by which they have meant providing necessary and sufficient conditions for arthood. That Harris does not see himself at this task (and that the task may not be the traditional task it is taken to be) is readily apparent from the fact that he by no means thinks all music to be imitative, or that any music is solely imitative. In other words, being an imitation, for Harris, is neither a necessary nor a sufficient condition for making sounds music, which is to say, art. The arts *"agree,* by being *all* MIMETIC, or IMITATIVE,"* Harris insists.[12] But given at least the nonimitative aspects of music, this can only be taken to mean that the fine arts—the "Arts of *Elegance,*" as Harris refers to them—"agree" in that they all at times can be imitative: imitation is not excluded from any of them, even music. It cannot be taken to mean that they all "agree" in being essentially imitative. To put it another way, they are essentially imitative in the sense that it is part of their essence to be capable of imitation.

As the elegant arts agree in their imitative capabilities, they disagree as to the mode and manner of the imitation. "THEY *differ*, as they imitate by *different Media*; PAINTING by *Figure* and *Colour*; MUSIC, by *Sound* and *Motion*; PAINTING and MUSIC, by *Media which are Natural*; POETRY, for the greatest PART, by a *Medium, which is Artificial.*"[13]

Embodied in this passage is one of two theses that follow, as I shall argue shortly, from Harris' assumption that music is an imitation of its object (when it has an object at all). I shall extract it here, but reserve my criticism of it until I have the other thesis before me as well. That thesis is simply that whereas poetry has as its medium a conventional material, that is, words and arbitrarily assigned semantic properties, meanings, the medium of music is a "natural" material, sound, which just happens to resemble—resemblance taken to be a "natural" relation—certain things in the world. (This is not to say that Harris thought there was no natural resemblance between words and sounds; he was quite familiar with the phenomenon of onomatopoeia, and exploited it in his account of poetic imitation.)

From this naturalistic thesis another seems directly to follow, namely, that music is capable of having as its objects only just those things which sounds, its medium, naturally resemble, which is to say, other sounds and "motions." (That sounds can literally sound like *motions* Harris, like many others, quite unreflectively assumes. Strictly speaking, they cannot; and that really is the thin edge of the wedge into Harris' imitation theory of music.) Harris writes, of the subjects (as he prefers to call them) accessible to music:

IN MUSIC, THE FITTEST SUBJECTS of IMITATION are all such THINGS and INCIDENTS, *as are most eminently characterised by* MOTION *and* SOUND.

MOTION may be either *slow* or *swift, even* or *uneven, broken* or *continuous*—SOUND may be either *soft* or *loud, high* or *low.* Wherever therefore any of these Species of *Motion* or *Sound* may be found in an *eminent* (not a *moderate* or *mean*) *degree*, there will be room for MUSICAL IMITATION.

Thus, in the *Natural* or *Inanimate World*, MUSIC may imitate the Glidings, Murmurings, Tossings, Roarings, and other *Accidents of Water*, as perceived in Fountains, Cataracts, Rivers, Seas, &c.—The

same of Thunder—the same of Winds, as well the stormy as the gentle.—In the *Animal World,* it may imitate the *Voice* of some Animals, but *chiefly* that of singing Birds.—It may also *faintly copy* some of their *Motions* and *Sounds;* and of Sounds those *most perfectly,* which are expressive of *Grief* and *Anguish.*

And thus much as to the Subjects, which Music imitates.[14]

If, now, we recall the core senses of "imitate" and "imitation" given by the *Shorter Oxford English Dictionary*—as well entrenched, it might be noted, in Harris' time as in our own—we can perceive immediately why Harris' theory had to take the form that it did. To imitate is to "copy" or "reproduce"; and an imitation is a "copy," an "artificial likeness," a "counterfeit." If, then, the relation of music to its objects (or subjects, as Harris prefers) is imitation, then what the composer must provide, like the counterfeiter, is an artifact that can be taken for the original: a substitute; a surrogate. That the relation must be imitation was, as we have seen, pretty much forced upon Harris and his contemporaries by the power and prestige of the Aristotelian and Platonic accounts of the fine arts, and the preference of the translators, rightly or wrongly, for rendering μίμησις "imitation." Add to this the notion that musical sound is a "natural" medium and all falls into place. The relation of music to its objects is like the happy circumstance of finding a stone on the beach just in the shape of a darning egg, a nearly perfect substitute for the real thing. That is not to say the composer must rely on accident and luck to make his imitations. For he can select from his repertoire of "natural" materials, just as I can choose the pebbles on the beach, rejecting the inappropriate, accepting the satisfactory. But, on Harris' view, the poet's medium is a conventional human artifact, whereas the composer's is a natural resource.

Given these constraints on the relation between music and its possible objects, it becomes altogether clear why the range of musical objects, on Harris' view, must be so narrow and circumscribed. For what else can satisfy the naturalistic thesis and the requirement that music be a copy, an artificial likeness, a counterfeit, but sounds, sounds which bear a resemblance to music independent of any linguistic or artistic convention? If I am to produce a successful copy, a convincing counterfeit of a dollar bill, I must produce an object that will satisfy all of the sense modalities normally involved in the perception of currency in ordinary life. The bill must look right and feel right. But music impinges upon only one of the senses: the sense of hearing. If, therefore, the composer is to present us with copies or counterfeits of objects in the natural world, he can only take sounds as his objects, and so he is restricted to bird calls, thunderstorms, and the few other sounds that bear a natural resemblance to the sounds of music. Small wonder, then, that Harris should characterize musical imitation as "*at best . . . but an imperfect thing.*"[15] Small wonder, too, that we should find Harris' theory itself at best but an imperfect account of the relation of music to its objects.

◇ 3 ◇   That Harris' account *is* but an imperfect thing can, I think, be readily concluded by considering some fairly obvious examples. Imagine, to begin with, how unsatisfactory it would be to restrict drawing, for instance, to the depiction of "natural resemblance." We are all familiar with the following way of depicting physical motion pictorially (Figure 1).

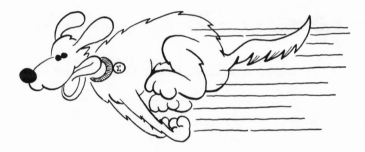

But this is, of course, not convention-free, nor does it in any obvious way "look like" a dog in motion. When a dog runs, he does not leave a string of lines visible behind. We accept that as a convention for the representation of motion; and, indeed, we have become so used to it that, I am sure, we are hardly aware how little like a running dog this drawing really is. Nor need we beat the bushes to turn up musical examples in abundance of a similar kind.[16]

A favorite musical technique, particularly in the Baroque but not by any means exclusive to that period, is the canon, or simply musical imitation as a metaphor for "following" or "leading." Thus, for example, Bach uses canonic imitation between the singer, first and second violin, and basso continuo, in Cantata 12, to illustrate the *imitatio Christi* (Example 1). Or, again, Handel illustrates Moses bringing the children of Israel out of Egyptian captivity with choral writing in close fugal imitation (Example 2).

Now even if one voice following another in canon or fugue really sounded like the Jews physically following Moses out of Egypt—a bi-

EXAMPLE 1
Bach, Cantata 12, *Weinen, Klagen, Sorgen, Zagen*

EXAMPLE 2
Handel, *Israel in Egypt,* Part I

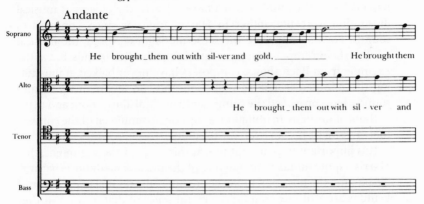

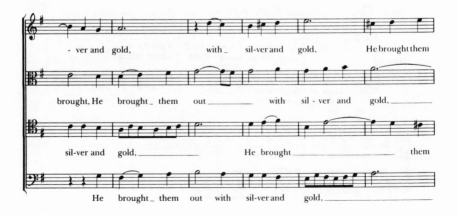

zarre enough claim—it clearly cannot sound like the imitation of Christ, because, of course, that no more has a sound than Thursday has a color or the number two a taste. Clearly, the objects of musical illustration were not, either in Harris' time, or since, confined to sounds. For not only were the sense modalities crossed, the musical medium being employed to illustrate sights as well as sounds, but as the example from Bach shows, composers have never balked at illustrating the non-perceivable as well. Concepts, no less than sights and sounds, have provoked the composer to musical illustration; and to try to think of music as an imitation, a copy or a counterfeit of the conceptual or visible is just an exercise in futility.

It is important to point out too, at this stage of the argument, that Harris is quite mistaken in thinking of the musical medium as natural. To be sure, the materials of music are not conventional in the sense of being bearers of meaning (in the literal sense of that term). But they are by no means free of convention in another sense: they are in large part preformed artifacts. Composers do not start from scratch with some kind of palette of natural sound. They work with melodies, melodic fragments, preformed patches of harmonic fabric, well-worn, secondhand bits and pieces of contrapuntal building blocks: in short, the materials of music are not natural sounds, but music already. And this conventional musical material plays a palpable role in musical illustration, as another example from Bach will clearly show.

In the chorale prelude, "Dies sind die heiligen zehn Gebot" ("These are the holy ten commandments,"), Bach illustrates the number ten by repeating the first phrase of the chorale (that is, "These are the holy ten commandments") ten times, in diminution, as counterpoint to the cantus firmus (Example 3).

Example 3
Bach, Chorale Prelude BWV 635, *Die sind die heiligen zehn Gebot*

That the ten commandments underlie, are the foundation of, the Lutheran faith is symbolized by the ten repetitions of the opening phrase
of the chorale lying under the cantus firmus and supporting it. That
there are ten commandments is, of course, indicated by ten repetitions
of the phrase. But that it is the *ten commandments* being illustrated here,
and not ten other things, was made unmistakably clear to Bach's audience, who knew these hymn tunes by heart, through the use of that
particular preexistent melody associated in the minds of the congregation with that particular text. Nor is this a technique peculiar to Bach,
or to Lutheran church music in general. It has been used again and
again by composers for illustrative purposes, an instance particularly
well-known to symphony concert-goers being Berlioz' use of the Gregorian "Dies irae" in the Witches' Sabbath of the *Symphonie fantastique.*
(I quote the place where the Gregorian melody is combined with the
witches' dance.) (Example 4).

That preexistent musical materials play a prominent role in musical
illustration cannot be denied; and had Harris been more familiar with
the music of his own times he would have been driven to realize this.
Just how prominent that role is we will consider later on. It suffices for
the purposes of the present chapter to have established that Harris'
naturalistic thesis is quite false; that illustrative music is by no means
restricted to what natural resemblance there might be between musical
sounds, say, the timbre of the tympani or flute, and sounds in nature,
like thunder or the warbling of our feathered friends.

One more critical point might usefully be made, I think, before we
put such imitative theories as Harris' behind us. Harris remarks in one
place that our enjoyment of imitation consists in being able to recognize the object in the imitation: "in *Imitations* . . . the principal Delight is
in recognizing the Thing intended . . ."—perhaps an echo of the well-
known passage in the *Poetics* where Aristotle says:

> All men, likewise, naturally receive pleasure from imitation. This is
> evident from what we experience in viewing the works of imitative
> art; for in them, we contemplate with pleasure, and with *more* plea-
> sure, the more exactly they are imitated, such objects as, if real, we
> could not see without pain. . . .[17]

In another chapter, I will have something further to say about the
character of the pleasure we take in musical illustration. At this stage
all I want to point out is that the character of the pleasure we take in
imitation (properly so-called) does not jibe, in one obvious respect,
with the character of the pleasure we take in illustrative music.

Harris, I suppose, is partly correct in observing that we take pleasure

EXAMPLE 4

Berlioz, *Symphonie fantastique, Songe d'une nuit du sabbat*

Dies Irae et Ronde du Sabbat ensemble
Un peu retenu

in recognizing what it is that a musical illustration is an illustration of. There is more to it, I think, than that. But what first strikes the reader of this passage is that "imitation" is quite the wrong word to describe even what Harris himself has in mind, for we hardly take pleasure in seeing what an imitation or counterfeit is an imitation or counterfeit of, in the sense Harris intends. Rather, our pleasure is in *not* seeing it: or, better, in not seeing how the imitation or counterfeit differs from the original. Because once we see *that*, the imitation or counterfeit ceases to please, although we can, after the fact, take a connoisseur's pleasure in seeing how, and how well, the counterfeit was accomplished. In short, it is the point of an imitation or counterfeit to deceive. But that is not by any means the point of a musical illustration. Indeed, the pleasure there lies in not being fooled, but in savoring both the disparity between medium and object, and, at the same time, the likeness achieved. In imitation, medium and object tend to coalesce. That is why a cultured pearl is a far more successful substitute than a plastic one: it is made of the same "stuff." However, in musical illustration, if medium and object coalesce, we cease to have *music*.

Here, perhaps, it will be objected that I am pressing upon Harris the literal meaning of imitation which he never really intended. Surely, the objection will go, all he really meant by imitation was just what we might prefer to call illustration, depiction, representation, or something else of the kind. To a certain extent this is true, and had Harris simply used imitation as a term of art, divorced completely from its literal meaning, all might have been well. But, as usually happens in such cases, Harris plays both sides of the street, sometimes, when it suits him, using imitation more the way we might use less inappropriate terms; often, however, trading on the literal meaning of imitation, as where he restricts the objects of musical illustration to just those things that sound can imitate in the literal sense of the word. For this reason, if for no other, it would be best to leave the notion of imitation behind us, and cast about for other ways of understanding illustrative music. Sound imitations are the province of moose calls, bird whistles and Indian scouts. The composer's tasks lie elsewhere.

◊ 4 ◊   Where, then, do we go from here? Hints have already been dropped in the occasional use of the term "representation." But to begin to answer this question in earnest, and to round off the present chapter, let us return to the passage from the *Poetics* with which we began, this time in a more recent translation, that of W. Hamilton Fyfe (1927):

Epic poetry, then, and the poetry of tragic drama, and, moreover, comedy and dithyrambic poetry, and most flute-playing and harp-playing, these, speaking generally, may all be said to be "representations of life." But they differ one from another in three ways: either in using means generically different or in representing different objects or in representing objects not in the same way but in a different manner.[18]

The remarkable change is, of course, the rendering of μί/μησις now as "representation" rather than "imitation," a change that must surely have been motivated not entirely by philological considerations but by philosophical ones as well. Reading between the lines of the translator's footnote to this passage, in which the word μί/μησις first appears, may help to reveal just what those philosophical considerations might have been.

The explanation of *mimesis,* as Aristotle uses the word, demands a treatise; all that a footnote can say is this:—Life "presents" to the artist the phenomena of sense, which the artist "re-presents" in his own medium, giving coherence, designing a pattern. That this is true not only of drama and fiction but also of instrumental music ("most flute-playing and harp-playing") was more obvious to a Greek than to us, since Greek instrumental music was more definitely imitative. The technical display of the virtuoso Plato describes as "a beastly noise."[19]

The artist then does not give us a copy or a counterfeit, in a word, an "imitation" of life. Rather, he *re-presents* it in his own medium, *giving it coherence, designing a pattern.* Were an imitator or a counterfeiter to give us an object more coherent and better designed than his model, he would have failed in his task. A perfect pearl would be an imperfect copy, since no real pearls are perfect. Whatever, then, can be said for the improvement in translation—and I repeat, I have neither the expertise nor the desire to comment on that[20]—a great deal can be said for the improvement in philosophical doctrine that results from rendering μί/μησις "representation" rather than "imitation." For the way *we* would describe what Aristotle is talking about here would surely be in terms of representation—a word free of all suggestion of copies, counterfeits, or substitutes for reality. Handel does not imitate the exodus; he represents it. Bach does not imitate the imitation of Christ, or the ten commandments, nor Berlioz the day of wrath; they represent them. The liberating force of moving from the concept of imitation to that of representation is clear. For as there is no constraint on representations to resemble, in any direct or literal way, the objects of representation, there is no constraint on them to prevent their crossing sense modalities, or even having as their objects that which cannot be perceived by the senses at all.

An interesting lesson, in this regard, can be learned from a lapse of our translator into the language of "imitation." He tells us that ". . . Greek instrumental music was more definitely imitative [than ours]"; and quotes Plato to the effect that "The technical display of the virtuoso . . . [is]'a beastly noise.' " If we understand Plato correctly here, we can perhaps imagine what these instrumental performances must have been: more like what we would call mimicry than like Schnabel's performance of a Beethoven sonata. Of course we know next to nothing about how Greek music really sounded. But if Plato's "beastly noise" was, among other things, a mimicry of animal sounds, it was, to that extent anyway, not what we would call music, and more appropriately described, as the translator does here, in terms of imitation, not representation.[21] But whenever it is "art" (properly so-called) that is being talked about, it is clear that representation is the word we want. And that, no doubt, was the motivating philosophical force behind the rendering of μν/μησιζ as "representation" rather than "imitation," whatever the philological considerations may have been. And a persuasive force it is, I think.

In inquiring, then, into the nature of what I have rather innocuously been calling musical illustration we had best steer clear of the traditional eighteenth-century theories of imitation, with all of their undesirable implications. Musical representation is our quarry. We must now begin the task of hunting it down.

CHAPTER II

The Cuckoo and the Thin Red Line

◊ 1 ◊ The answers to two general questions will, I trust, emerge from this study. These questions are: Is music a representational art? And (since there are, I shall argue shortly, representations that are not pictures): Is music a pictorial art? They will require a good deal of refinement before they are tractable. The first refinement, a fairly obvious one, can be made straightaway. No one today would wish to argue that music is entirely a representational or pictorial art (or the two together), and it is doubtful that anyone ever made so extravagant a claim. Nor, I think, would anyone wish to argue today that music is primarily a representational or pictorial art (or the two together), although such claims have been made in the past. All I shall be asking is: Are there *any* examples of music—either single compositions or parts thereof—that can properly be called pictorial or representational?

The history of Western music, in modern times, is littered with the debris of disputes and discussions on the subject of musical representations and pictures. The reason is not difficult to see. It is safe to say that Western culture has been obsessed with the concept of knowledge. With a few rare exceptions, no one (the composer included), has ever gladly relinquished the right to be looked upon as knowledge seeker and giver. But how can one make knowledge claims unless one can "represent" what is the case? Behind the musical preoccupation with representation is, I would urge, the stormy love affair of the West with knowing. Be that as it may, as the other arts have, according to Walter Pater, aspired to the aesthetic purity of music, music has at the same time aspired to the "propositional" status of the other arts; and representation or pictorialization has been the peg on which that aspiration has been hung.

Now a number of different kinds of questions have, in the past, been raised by composers and critics about the representational and pictorial aspects of music. There have been times when musical reformers have urged that music be representational or pictorial because, in their view, that is a good thing for music to be, and the music of their times has not, in their view, been pictorial or representational, or has not been to a great enough degree. (So Liszt, in his defense of Berlioz' program music, urges that "we consider the introduction of the program into the concert hall to be just as inevitable as the declamatory style is to the opera.")[1] Conversely, there have been times when it has been argued that music has indulged in too much representation or pictorialization and should turn (or return) from such shenanigans to a purer form of the art. ("One can hear clocks strike, ducks quack, frogs croak, and soon one will be able to hear a flea sneeze and the grass growing," Johann Adam Hiller grumpily remarks in 1754, with apparent reference to the musical practices of the late Baroque.)[2] In both kinds of case, it should be noted, the reformers have acknowledged that music can be and even has been pictorial or representational (although not all, perhaps, have been altogether clear on this point); and the issue they have raised has been a normative one: *should* music continue to be pictorial or representational; or should it become more so? I point this out because I wish to avoid normative questions altogether, and do not wish my views to be mistaken for recommendations or endorsements for any kind of music or musical technique. I will claim that there are clear cases in modern Western music (from about 1600 to the present) both of representational and pictorial music (properly so-called); but I take no stand at all on the question of whether this is a good or a bad thing, whether music should become more or less pictorial or representational, or any other question of that kind. I shall, however, try to make intelligible how music can be and has been representational and pictorial, and answer some ancillary questions and objections along the way.

Finally, it has been claimed (more rarely) that music cannot be pictorial or representational (or both together). In the eighteenth and nineteenth centuries such claims were made with frequency, and with passion, by various composers and critics; and quite recently, the purist view has arisen again, this time in the philosophical literature rather than the musical, supported by new and interesting arguments. After I have laid out my own view on the possibility of musical illustration, I will try to put to rest both the old arguments and the new, that purport to prove the contrary.

◊ 2 ◊   I began this chapter by suggesting a distinction between pictorial and representational music, based on a general distinction between pictures and representations. A good deal of what I have to say in this study hinges on that distinction. So before I get to the specific case of music, I had better, as gingerly as I can, make good my claim to it—gingerly, because it touches on some very sensitive issues in contemporary philosophy of art; and I hope to get away without treading on anyone's tender philosophical toes. I believe the distinction can be made out on a commonsense, intuitive level that will be adequate for present purposes but will not necessitate taking a stand on the basic issues that divide aestheticians these days, in their analyses of the pictorial and the representational.

From now on, then, except where considerations of style or context make it awkward or superfluous, I will refer to representations that are not pictures simply as "representations," even though pictures, of course, are representations as well. I am not, in taking this course, recanting from my conclusion in Chapter I, that my quarry is musical representation. But it is useful, as will become apparent shortly, to distinguish between two basic kinds of musical representation, and I have chosen the terms "picture" and "representation" to mark out this distinction. To a certain extent, these can be taken to be terms of art, although they do, I think, reflect some fuzzy sort of distinction at least vaguely adumbrated in ordinary language. In addition, having appropriated "representation" for a particular purpose, I will require another term to refer to the general phenomenon of musical pictures and musical representations taken together—that is, the class to which they both belong and whose total membership they comprise. For this broad class of musical pictures and musical representations taken together I will continue to use the term "musical illustration," which I introduced without comment in the preceding chapter.

It is my contention that all pictures are representations but not all representations are pictures (in the presystematic sense of "representation" and "picture"). Let me begin to make this out by instancing a case in point: something I take to be a representation and not a picture. In a delightfully kitsch film called *The Four Feathers* (after a novel of the same name by A. E. W. Mason), a great old bore of a retired English general gives a highly exaggerated account of his role in the battle of Balaclava. "Here were the Russians," his account begins: "Guns! Guns! Guns!" (Fruits and nuts are set in a row.) "Here were the British," he continues: "the thin red line." (He dips his finger in claret and draws a line on the table cloth.) The fruits and nuts represent the Russians, the ribbon of wine the British positions; and the whole arrangement, of course, represents the battle of Balaclava. But is it a *picture* of the battle? If ordinary language and intuition are any guide at all, then the answer, I think, must be no. There is something about a picture of ϕ, as opposed to a representation of it, that is likely to elicit such exclamations as "How like φ that really is" or "Yes, that is φ down to the last detail." In a given culture, and, to a large if as yet undetermined extent, cross-culturally, pictures tend to be immediately recognized for what they are, whereas mere representations (as I am now using that term) require an accompanying instruction. (Or, to put it another way, we tend to call "pictures" those representations, in the presystematic use of the term, that are recognized immediately, without instruction.) We require the general's commentary to know that the fruits, nuts, and thin red line represent the battle of Balaclava, or anything else, for that matter. It requires no such aid for us to recognize that Raphael's *Madonna della Sedia* is a picture of a woman with a baby, although it would, of course, for us to recognize it as the Virgin Mary and the Infant Jesus.

This, needless to say, is an entirely rough-and-ready distinction, scarcely meant to be hard-edged. I am not claiming that nothing can properly be called a picture of φ unless we can all recognize, without verbal instruction, that it is a picture of φ. Nor am I under any illusion about the difficulty of stating clearly how the group so cavalierly referred to just now as "all," might be determined. For, as is now well-known (and perhaps a bit overworked), traditionally trained Chinese graphic artists, for example, unfamiliar with Western pictorial conventions, have failed at first in recognizing the "smudges" on pen-and-wash drawings as shadows, and have, indeed, seen them as blots and blemishes. What I am suggesting, however, is that there *is* such a rough-and-ready distinction between pictures and representations in ordinary language, and that whatever its significance (or lack of it) might be elsewhere, it will be useful in solving some problems that have arisen, and continue to arise, in regard to music. So I want to pursue the distinction a bit further. But let me make perfectly clear, before I do, that it is no part of my argument to insist that the distinction drawn between pictures and representations must be presystematic. For whatever I have to say can be said just as well, with proper adjustments, if "representation" and "picture" are taken in this study to be purely terms of art, with no connection whatever to ordinary language: "pictures" being representations recognized within a given group without verbal aids, "representations" recognizable only with them.

A fairly obvious response to the distinction I am drawing between the representation of the battle of Balaclava and the picture of the Madonna is that, in the latter case, we are being presented with a realistic illustration of the subject and in the former, with a schematic representation, or an abstract one. Further, it might be claimed that the picture of the Madonna is realistic by virtue of presenting us with visual cues very like the cues we would be presented with if we were faced with the real thing, whereas the representation is not realistic just because it does not present us with such visual cues. The claim that realism is a function of some kind of phenomenal resemblance, presents some difficulties, now well-known. In reaction to such difficulties, many of which he himself has been instrumental in bringing to our notice, Nelson Goodman has claimed that the distinction between what is realistic and what is not cannot be made on the basis of any supposed resemblance between the visual cues of what is realistic and the visual cues of the object of representation. "Realism," Goodman writes, "is a matter not of any constant or absolute relationship between the system of representation employed in the picture and the standard system."[3] Thus, "Realism is relative, determined by the system of representation standard for a given culture or person at a given time."[4] Further:

> Representational customs, which govern realism, also tend to generate resemblance. That a picture looks like nature often means only that it looks the way nature is usually painted. . . . Resemblance and deceptiveness, far from being constant and independent sources and criteria of representational practice are in some degree products of it.[5]

Now for the purposes of my own discussion there is no need to take sides in the argument between the traditional resemblance account of realism and Goodman's conventionalistic one. For I am entitled both to the distinction in ordinary language between a realistic representation and a not so realistic one, and to that between a representation that is "very like" its object and one that is not. Of course, on the traditional account, realism is generated by resemblance, whereas on Goodman's, resemblance is parasitic on realism. But there is nothing in Goodman's account, at least so far as I can see, to prevent one from maintaining that ordinarily, pictures are realistic representations and what I have been calling simply "representations" are not. Pictures are readily recognized without verbal aids to be what they are, whereas representations are not. Pictures are, in a presystematic sense, "very like" what they are pictures of, representations are not; and just as long as it is remembered that the concepts of realism and resemblance being insisted on here are at the level of ordinary discourse, there is no danger of falling afoul of Goodman's analysis: he must no more deny the validity of such distinctions, presystematically, than he must deny, because of his nominalism, that objects possess properties. Where he and the "resemblance" theorist disagree is with regard to the *analysis* of these presystematic notions; and what I have to say about musical pictures and representations is invariant with that analysis, at least in its traditional and Goodmanian manifestations.

I should perhaps add, by way of a cautionary note, that I do not mean to place too much weight on the explanatory force of "resemblance." All I am saying is that there is, I believe, a connection in ordinary usage between what I am calling "pictures," and the resemblance of pictures to their subjects. But, as Kendall Walton has pointed out, there are cases of close resemblance (in the presystematic sense) that are not, for one reason or another, noticed without prodding, and, conversely, cases of very slight resemblance (in the presystematic sense) that are noticed right away. The contention here is simply that, *for the most part,* we tend to call those illustrations that are readily recognizable without verbal aids, "pictures," and, *for the most part,* tend to see such unaided recognizability as evidence of (or perhaps the same thing as) resemblance or realism.

I should emphasize, further, that I attribute no very heavy significance to this distinction except in the present context. It serves, as we shall see, to correct some misconceptions about illustrational music. Beyond this very specific musical use, I make no claim whatever to its having philosophical interest or value.

With these disclaimers and caveats on the table, I will assume that I have established my right to the distinction between pictures and representations outlined above. I can turn now to my main concern, its application in musical cases. I will begin somewhat tangentially.

◊ 3 ◊   It is customary to describe the sounds that most wild creatures make as "cries," short, I am sure, for "inarticulate cries." But although Solomon, in the Song of Songs, referred somewhat fancifully to "the *voice* of the turtle," there is nothing fanciful or out of the ordinary in his reference to "the singing of birds." Nor does the suggestion that the turtle has a "voice" imply that it also has a "song." Indeed, the only creature besides the human animal that is commonly, without any hint of metaphor or poetic hyperbole, described as a singer, is the bird. Charles Hartshorne is quite convinced that birds literally *are* singers, and their vocal utterances literally songs.[6] Without wishing to beg this rather odd question, I shall nevertheless assume that this is not the case: that the "songs" of birds are natural sounds. But that does not alter the plain fact that the phenomenal aspect presented by the "songs" of birds is very like music. Not exactly like it, as anyone can testify who has tried to notate bird songs in the well-tempered scale and metrical system of Western music. They are always between the cracks, and never quite fit.

Be that as it may, there is certainly nothing in nature so akin to music as the sounds of the avian brood, and this, doubtless, has made bird calls the most common objects of musical illustration. Among them, I venture to say that the most frequently attempted is the song of the cuckoo, which comes close to sounding a descending major or minor third (depending, I suppose, either on the cuckoo or the composer), in a fairly discrete metre. The following example is a familiar one, with a nightingale and quail thrown in for good measure (Example 5).

EXAMPLE 5
Beethoven, Sixth Symphony, Op. 68, Second Movement

Such musical illustrations come closest, perhaps, to the eighteenth-century paradigm of musical imitation. Nevertheless, they are a far cry from a bona fide imitation, as rendered by a bird-whistle, or a person adept at reproducing bird calls. The clarinet is a musical instrument, not a mechanical device for mimicking animal noises. It is played by a performing artist who shapes a phrase and molds a tone. This is making music, not "doing imitations." The difference will be immediately apparent to those, like me, who were involved in childhood performances of Leopold Mozart's Toy Symphony (wrongly attributed in my day to Joseph Haydn), where a cuckoo call, slightly "out of tune," played

on a toy bird-whistle expressly designed for the purpose of reproducing the cuckoo's "song," is worked into the musical fabric. But where
the music stops and the mechanical reproduction starts, is crystal clear,
and immediately audible; and that, of course, is what makes the effect.
Were the bird call to be replaced by a clarinet playing the descending
minor third as a musical line, the effect that Leopold Mozart wanted to
achieve would be lost. For what was meant to be almost music, a bird
impersonation, would have become real music, an artistic illustration
of the cuckoo's "song", and the joke would have been lost.

However, this is not to say that there is no useful distinction to be
drawn between Beethoven's cuckoo, quoted above, and another, more
elaborate sort of musical representation, also with a bird song as its object. Consider, now, a bird of a different feather, Handel's "Sweet Bird,
that shunn'st the noise of Folly," from *L'Allegro ed il Penseroso*. This
rather long-winded bird must be quoted at some length. (Example 6).

EXAMPLE 6
Handel, *L'Allegro ed il Penseroso*

There can be no doubt that we have here, as in the example from the *Pastoral*, a musical illustration of a bird song. It is of course more elaborate; and although that in itself is not quite enough to mark out the difference, it is part of the story. Beethoven, you might say, stayed close to his model. Handel, on the other hand, if he had any specific model at all—the first four notes *are* the cuckoo's descending major and minor third although obscured by the fact that the trill would start on the upper note—simply used it as a stimulus to his musical imagination. More likely than not, Handel had no specific model in mind but, rather, an idealized notion, informed by the musical conventions and tastes of his day, of how a well-behaved warbler should be represented, within the confines of the *da capo* aria. Given, then, the elaborateness of Handel's representation, as opposed to Beethoven's, and its imaginative departure from any specific model it might have had, a most important further difference emerges: in the case of Beethoven's depiction of the cuckoo, any person acquainted with the song of the bird would immediately recognize the illustration for what it is; but without the text, it seems quite unlikely that there would be anything close to universal agreement about what Handel's melodic line is representing, or whether indeed it is representing anything. (More than likely, Handel's intent would be taken to be the displaying of some particular flautist's virtuosity.) Thus we have here, in these very simple and familiar examples of musical illustration—the most common, in fact, in the repertoire—just that distinction we made previously between "pictures" and "representations," based on the (admittedly vague) criterion of unaided as opposed to aided recognition.

◊ 4 ◊ Two things about the question of musical illustration seem to me to be obvious. The first is that music, in the modern era, displays abundant examples both of musical pictures and musical representations; second, that a good deal of unnecessary controversy has been generated by musicians, philosophers and critics, simply by their failure to make this trivial distinction between the two. In the next chapter, I shall be concerned with multiplying examples, both of musical pictures and musical representations, to the end first, of providing food for future thought and second, displaying a kind of "typology" of musical illustration to facilitate the argument to come. But the reader is forewarned that I do not consider this catalogue either complete, or necessarily constructed on the only possible principles of individuation.

CHAPTER III

A Typology of Musical Illustrations

◇ 1 ◇   The potential for pictorialization in Western music is, as all but zealots have always readily admitted, very limited indeed. Its musical significance may be slight, but it must be acknowledged that composers, including very great ones, have gone to a great deal of trouble to make musical pictures; and for that reason alone the subject deserves serious consideration.

What is a musical picture? Certainly I have no intention of producing a set of necessary and sufficient conditions. I suggest merely that if an arrangement of pigments on a canvas can constitute a realistic depiction of a woman, an arrangement of sounds, notated in a musical score, realized upon musical instruments, can sound like a bird song, or a thunderstorm, like the sound of an iron foundry, or a steam locomotive of the Pacific class. If, within our culture at the present time, the vast majority of individuals with minimal sensitivity can recognize without verbal (or other) aids that the *Madonna della Sedia* is a picture of a woman, they can recognize too that there are bird songs in Beethoven's Sixth Symphony without knowing the title of the piece.

This might suggest perhaps, that graphic pictures (properly so-called) are limited to the "looks like" relation, and musical pictures to the "sounds like" one. I make no such claim. I will, however, confine myself, in discussing musical pictures here, to instances that can unproblematically be described in terms of the "sounds like" relation, although I am not completely convinced that one cannot make musical pictures of things other than sounds (or graphic ones of things other than sights). Needless to say, the concept of musical representation, as we shall see, far transcends the world of sound alone; for as Goodman correctly observes, "the forms and feelings of music are by no means all confined to sound . . ."; music may "have effects transcending its own medium."[1]

There is, I think, no need to multiply beyond endurance examples of the various bird songs, thunderstorms and babbling brooks that populate the nature music of the past three hundred years. Nevertheless, it will be rewarding to widen our range of examples at least beyond the cuckoo and its race, for there may be a bit more here than meets the ear.

There is this to be said straightaway. The range of musical pictures is exceedingly narrow, if by musical picture is meant what I have meant by it, namely, a musical illustration that can be recognized as such—whose subject will be immediately and universally identified—without any verbal (or other) aids. Under that severe constraint, little else comes to mind but warbling. Little else—but, interestingly enough, not nothing else; for one can find rather startling examples from the recent but now almost forgotten era of social realism in Soviet music, the most famous (or perhaps notorious) being Alexander Mossolov's *The Iron Foundry* (1928). No quotation from the score can give much of an idea of it. Boris Schwarz's description must suffice: "The piece is a picturization of industrial noises, musically rather primitive, yet very effective in its motoric rhythm and churning drive."[2]

Nothing of this music remains in the symphonic repertoire today. But the composition which, Schwarz thinks, was the "prototype of such 'mechanistic' pieces,"[3] namely, Arthur Honegger's *Pacific 231*, is still occasionally heard. Although the extraordinary illustrative effect of Honegger's *Mouvement Symphonique* can be perceived only by hearing it entire, as it relies on accumulation of sound and acceleration of rhythm, some small notion can be conveyed by quoting from four successive stages in the steam locomotive's journey: at rest in the station, "letting off steam" (measures 1–4); just beginning to move (measures 12–18); at a fast clip on the way, in a tranquil moment (measures 80–84); and, finally, coming to rest at its destination (measures 209–217) (Example 7).

Two things about Honegger's *Pacific 231* thrust themselves upon the listener or reader of the score: first, how strikingly effective the illustration of the steam engine is; and second, how musical the means to the illustrative end. For *Pacific 231* does remain *music,* in spite of its pictorial character. It attains a kind of quiet lyricism in its middle sections and, remarkably, does not require anything in the way of exotic percussion instruments or extra-musical noisemakers. Indeed, the illustration is achieved with scarcely more than the typical post-Wagnerian orchestra; and it is a tribute to Honegger's astounding aural imagination that he is able to realize, in conventional Western notation and with conventional instruments, such a wide variety of "mechanical" sounds.

Interesting points are raised by these examples. If we take the *Madonna della Sedia,* say, as a paradigmatic "picture," one thing about it that almost no musical illustration can match is what we might call its bold-faced "representationality." There is no ordinary circumstance

Example 7
Honegger, *Pacific 231*
Measures 1-4

Measures 12-18

Measures 80-84

Measures 209-217

one can imagine in which it would not immediately be seen, by a "normal" viewer, as a woman and child. Certainly it requires no title to reveal this, nor need we be informed that it is a picture to see at once that it is, and what it is a picture of.

But this can hardly be claimed for very many musical illustrations. Part of the reason, of course, is that music is not normally representational at all; it is not experienced in a context where representation is *expected;* and what we perceive, as we all now know, is very intimately related to what we expect. That, however, cannot be the whole, or even a very large part of the explanation of the Madonna's very palpable representationality, and I have no intention of trying to provide the whole explanation here. What I do want to point out is that many (or most?) musical pictures, as I use the term, require certain *minimal information* beyond what is required by the normal perceiver to perceive the *Madonna della Sedia* as a woman with a baby. This minimal information is simply that an illustration is intended; or, if one prefers to leave intentions out of it (which I do not), that one is being presented with an illustration.

Thus, as I am using the phrase "musical picture," musical pictures can be divided into two kinds: those, like the cuckoo in the *Pastoral,* or (I believe) *Pacific 231,* where the illustration would be recognized as such without text, title, or even the minimal information that one is listening to an illustration; and those like *The Iron Foundry,* perhaps, or the thunderstorm in the *Pastoral,* where one needs to *know* that one is listening to illustrative music in order to identify the object of the illustration, but would need no information other than that (always assuming, of course, that the listener is above a certain level of musical sophistication, and sophistication in general).

It is worthy of note here that the visual arts are not without examples requiring, like some of my examples of musical pictures, the minimal information that one is in the presence of a representation. The reason we do not notice this in painterly cases, say, is that they are almost always presented in a context in which their representational (or nonrepresentational) character is immediately apparent. One seldom finds representational painting cheek by jowl with abstract, or nonobjective works; paintings are more often shown in groups, organized around a period or an artist: one sees a room of Rembrandts, or a room of Impressionists, seldom a Manet next to a Jackson Pollock. But imagine this magnificent Turner (in the Tate Gallery, London), shown not in series with other late Turners, but, rather, in a group of nonrepresentational paintings, no title or artist given (Figure 2).

Would this be recognized as the sun setting over a lake? Would it not rather be taken for a nonrepresentational painting? The latter, I very strongly suspect. Whereas in the environment in which it is customarily viewed (where representation is expected), even were the title and artist not provided, the minimal information that this was a representation, which the context gives, would be enough to assure that it would be recognized at least as a painting of a sunrise or sunset, if not of a lake. (I imagine the same trick could be played with some of Monet's lily pads.)

One further point apropos this division of musical pictures. It would, needless to say, be useful to have some empirical evidence as to which musical pictures (if any) can be heard as such even without the minimal information that they are musical illustrations. But unfortunately, on reflection, it appears that any artificial experiment one might devise would turn out to be self-defeating. If, for instance, I were to play *Pacific 231* to a group of listeners, and then were to ask them to write down what they thought it illustrated, I would have thereby conveyed to them the very information that I expressly wished to withhold, namely, that they were listening to illustrative music. If, on the other hand, I attempted to give some neutral instruction such as, "Write down whatever comes into your head," one of two different things might happen, both, I think, equally frustrating of the sought-after result. I might convey to my "subjects" the misinformation that they were *not* listening to illustrative music; or, failing that, I would likely give them the distinct impression that even were it illustrative music they were hearing, that aspect of it was not what I wanted them to attend to or report. In either case, I would, I suspect, block their natural responses, encouraging them to "freely associate" and give fanciful replies, even when their initial perceptions might well have been "steam engine."

I do not, then, claim for the musical examples I have given of musical pictures that can, and those that cannot, be recognized as such without what I have called the "minimal information," anything more rigorous than my own musical intuitions and impressions. I cannot even claim to be sure that the former is not an empty set (although I am certain the latter is not). That musical pictures are not very numerous or, musically, very significant, has already been granted. It is when we go beyond the "minimal information" into the domain of musical representations, that we encounter numerous kinds of examples, of true musical significance; and to the more complicated typology of these musical representations we must now turn our attention.

◊ 2 ◊   The first examples of musical representation (as opposed to musical picture) that I want to discuss are those closest to the musical pictures we have just been examining. Although I have not insisted that all musical pictures exhibit the "sounds like" phenomenon, I have strongly suggested that this might well be the case, and have confined myself to examples of that kind. The examples of musical representation I will now present, are also of the "sounds like" kind, but they are different in this respect. Whereas the examples of musical pictures just adduced, require merely the minimal information "This is illustrative music," to be successfully heard, the ones to come require more than the minimal information: they require a descriptive text or title.

Now it might, perhaps, be thought inconsistent to say that a musical passage "sounds like" some nonmusical sound, while at the same time insisting that a descriptive text or title is required to recognize the resemblance. For, someone might plausibly argue, if something really sounded like something else, then we would all recognize the resemblance without verbal aids; and the very fact that a descriptive text or title is required to recognize a musical representation is at least prima facie evidence of there being no "sounds like" relation involved at all. There is, I think, no merit in the argument. But it does help to lay bare what is going on in the examples of musical representation I am considering now, and in those that are to come, so it would be worthwhile to pursue it for a moment.

Consider the opening unison passage of the "Sonata" that serves as the overture to Bach's Cantata 31 (Example 8).

EXAMPLE 8
Bach, Cantata 31, *Der Himmel lacht, die Erde jubilieret*

No one, I think, recognizes the resemblance of this musical figure to the sound of laughter unless aware that the opening lines of the first chorus are: "Der Himmel lacht, die Erde jubilieret." ("The heavens laugh, the earth rejoices.") Once the text is known, however, the resemblance becomes apparent: one recognizes the sound of laughter in the sound of the music. But without the additional information provided by the text, we would not get the point; we would not hear the percussive repeated notes as the sound of laughter here, any more than we do when a similar figure occurs, for instance, in Handel's *Fireworks Music*, with no representational intent whatever except, as the title, *La Rejouissance*, suggests, a mood of rejoicing (Example 9).

EXAMPLE 9
Handel, *Music for the Royal Fireworks*

The text helps us to see what the composer is getting at, in this case the representation of laughter through the "sounds like" relation. It is very much a matter of catching on.

Another example will help to reinforce the point. In *Israel in Egypt*, Handel represents the buzzing of flies with a rapid thirty-second-note figure in the violins (Example 10). A similar violin figuration occurs in the first movement of the Fourth Brandenburg Concerto (Example 11). But whereas no one would be tempted to say that the passage in the Fourth Brandenburg sounds like the buzzing of flies, the resemblance in Handel's chorus is marked; and it is the presence of the text, of course, that makes the difference, that makes the resemblance perceived and the representation possible.

Nor is this phenomenon reserved for musical representations. It occurs in graphic ones as well. A coil, in a circuit diagram, is represented thus (Figure 3):

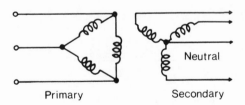

Primary   Secondary

The representation does indeed look (a little) like a coil. But of course it looks like a great many other things too: a bedspring, a snake, and so forth. It is only because we have a key, a "dictionary," that we are able to perceive the relevant resemblance. Similarly, the repeated figure in

EXAMPLE 10
Handel, *Israel in Egypt,* Part I

EXAMPLE 11
Bach, Brandenburg Concerto No. 4, First Movement

Bach's Sonata sounds as much like the beating of a drum, for example, as it does like laughter; and such figures have, indeed, been used to represent that very thing. What disambiguates such figures is the descriptive text or title: that is the key. However, that should not obscure the fact that we are, nonetheless, dealing with representations of the "sounds like" variety. Sometimes it requires a little help to hear the semblance in the sound; there is nothing paradoxical in that.

◊ 3 ◊   The next step in our typology of musical illustrations takes us beyond the "sounds like" relation. But I must emphasize that here, as in all of the other steps we have taken and will take, the boundaries are vague, and borderline cases abound; for as we shall shortly see, it is not always clear from an example of musical representation, whether we are dealing with the "sounds like" relation or not. Let us begin with an ambiguous case and then move on to a clear-cut one. In this way we will be able to stake out this new territory more circumspectly.

The flowing or rushing of water has been a frequent object of musical representation. There is no period in the history of modern music where examples cannot be found, but anticipating the charge that my

examples of musical illustration have been, thus far, heavily slanted towards the Baroque, let me adduce two instances from the Romantic
era (Example 12).

As in the examples just adduced, there can be no question of recognizing what is being represented here, or even that anything at all is
being represented, without extra-musical assistance. But with the text
and context given we do indeed quite readily get the point. We see exactly what those rushing, flowing, rippling passages are meant to represent. We see what is going on, what the composer has intended to do.
Have we, though, by the same means as in the previous examples, been
gotten to hear some resemblance between the sounds of these musical
figures and the sound that water makes? Are we, in a word, still dealing
with the "sounds like" phenomenon? It is hard to say. Certainly these
passages do not sound very *much* like water, either rushing, or flowing,

EXAMPLE 12
Mendelssohn, *Elijah,* Part I

or rippling. But then, I suppose, it might be just as plausibly argued that the Sonata in Cantata 31 does not sound very *much* like laughter. Yet it sounds enough like laughter for us to hear the resemblance, whereas in Mendelssohn's and Schubert's representations of water we have something like a borderline case.

But if we do not recognize that the music sounds like water when we have got the point, when we have been made aware of the representation, what do we recognize? We clearly recognize some analogy between the musical sounds and the natural ones. Just as the water ripples and flows, rushes and roars, so does the music. However, in describing the music as rushing and flowing, we are not necessarily committed to the claim that rushing and flowing music "sounds like" rushing and flowing water, except in the trivial sense that both are described in similar terms. We find such words as "rushing" and "flowing" suitable for characterizing the phenomenal surface of musical

Schubert, *Die Schöne Müllerin,* II. *Wohin?*

sound, as we do for water in motion. That is all. In short, when we begin to go beyond the "sounds like" relation, even where the musical representation is of sound, what the music and its object really have in common may seem in many cases simply to be a *common description* (which is why, in a previous chapter, I remarked, contra Harris, that music cannot literally imitate motion, although it is a common misapprehension that it can). This will become more obvious as we move on to the next category of musical representations, in which sound is *not* the object of representation. For here, where sound is not the object, there can be no "sounds like" relation at all, except in the most attenuated sense.

◇ 4 ◇ When André Pirro[4] and Albert Schweitzer[5] rediscovered J. S. Bach's almost obsessive attempts to reflect his text in his music, even in the chorale preludes where the music was meant to be performed without the text, they revealed, I think, the aesthetic practice not only of a single composer or period, but of modern music as a whole. Schweitzer thought of it as "tone painting": "Beethoven and Wagner poetise in music," he wrote; "Bach paints."[6] In light of the distinction between pictures and representations belabored above, I would prefer to call most of it "tone representation"; for little if any of it fulfills the (admittedly vague) criteria ordinarily associated with "pictures" (as I am using the term), and which the notion of "tone painting" suggests. In most cases, there is no possibility of recognition without the aid of the text that has elicited the representation, and in a great many, the "sounds like" relation is not involved at all; far more abstract and remote analogies are intended.

It should be emphasized that once past the most obvious cases of the "sounds like" kind, the possibility of musical representation depends, as we shall soon see, upon describing sound in ways that at times cross the sense modalities. For when the "sounds like" relation is absent, what music and its object share seems often nothing but a common description; and where the object is not sound, that common description must at the same time be a description of what can be seen, or thought, or touched, or tasted, and what can only be *heard*. A philosophical understanding of such cross-modal descriptions would greatly enhance any attempt to explicate the phenomenon of musical representation, and, indeed, if some kind of justification were needed, would be essential to it. This is an important and complicated enough topic to be dealt with separately, and will be the subject of the next chapter. For the nonce, it must simply be assumed that describing sounds, say, as "bright" or "flowing"—terms more normally associated with objects of sight—is appropriate and unproblematic.

A fairly obvious example will serve to introduce this rather large and elaborate class of musical representations (Example 13).

Handel has represented the duration of God's patience with (literally) "long notes"—the dotted half-note being the longest single note value in the time signature he has chosen, that is to say, three-quarter time. He has added to their length by tying them over the bar, sometimes extending the duration to a value of six beats; and he has explicitly drawn the listener's attention to the length of these notes by putting them in direct juxtaposition to notes of a considerably shorter value: quarter-notes, on which the introductory section is built. The alternate sections of short notes and long notes make it abundantly clear, at a proper tempo, that the note values have lengthened and the musical pace slowed at the appearance of the appropriate text.

As in many other such examples that might be cited, the common description turns out to be, on the musical side, a literal description of the score, quite at home both in the conservatory and in literary circles. Thus, what we have here is a kind of musical pun or play on words;

EXAMPLE 13
Handel, *Belshazzar*, Part I

and such wordplay, I want to emphasize, forms the basis for a great
many musical representations. In this particular instance, the analogy
on which the pun is based is clear and unproblematic. At a given
tempo, dotted half-notes tied over the bar last longer than quarter-
notes—they take up more actual time—as does the patience of God
outlast the folly of men, waiting for repentance and slow to turn to anger.

Such simple analogies as that between real time and musical time do
not by any means exhaust the possibilities of the kind of musical representation we are discussing. The possibilities indeed are as numerous
as are the common ways of describing music and the world, and an
exhaustive list of them would be long beyond imagination. But consid-

ering the extent and importance of these kinds of musical representations, a further example or two might not be otiose or out of place.

The word "harmony" (in its various incarnations) has been used to describe some aspect or other of music since antiquity—long before it became the name for the specific feature of Western music that is contrasted with "counterpoint" and "melody," and that is thought of as comprising a teachable "discipline" and "craft." It is, of course, a word used to describe relations and situations in the nonmusical world as well. It is a nice question whether the musical uses of the term are parasitic on the nonmusical ones, or vice versa; but it is certain that the nonmusical uses of "harmony" have made harmony in modern Western music, with all that it includes, fertile ground for musical representation. Whatever in the world can be described as harmonious or inhar-

monious can of course be reflected in the harmonic aspect of music, by virtue, as I have argued, of the common description. It is not surprising, therefore, that just at the time when the notion of musical harmony was solidifying into the concept we know today—which is to say, in the late Baroque and early Classical periods—such analogies between musical harmony and harmony (or lack thereof) in the nonmusical world were frequently exploited by composers of vocal music.

Dryden's first St. Cecilia's Day Ode begins:'

> From harmony, from heavenly harmony
> This universal frame began.

In the first chorus Handel takes full advantage of the word "harmony," beginning, for emphasis, a capella, with a simple hymnlike chordal progression, unmistakably harmonic, that caresses the first syllable and lingers over it, thus putting into bold relief the parallel between harmony and "harmony" (Example 14).

EXAMPLE 14
Handel, *Ode for St. Cecilia's Day*

Anyone who has heard the splendid effect that this utterly simple, almost naive representation of harmony makes will know what Beethoven had in mind when he said: "Go and learn [from Handel] to produce such great effects by such modest means!"[7]

But just as musical harmony can represent the harmony of the world, it can also, when tampered with within certain limits, represent the disharmony of the world as well. Haydn had a particularly disharmonious marriage, so he must have taken some perverse pleasure in setting (for four voices and piano accompaniment) "Harmony in Marriage" (poem by J. N. Götz), a comic text whose meaning is the very opposite of its title. Haydn begins by "playing it straight." The opening phrase, "O Wunderbare Harmonie," is a simple four-part setting, note against note, with obviously "harmonic" (as opposed to contrapuntal) writing (Example 15). But as the irony of the poem emerges, as it becomes apparent that disharmony rather than harmony is what is meant by *"Wunderbare* Harmonie," Haydn represents this in two ways: by breaking up the four-square harmonic structure into a more polyphonic style, with the voices entering in imitation (that is, the writing is no longer "harmonic" but "contrapuntal"); and by going from simple, diatonic harmonies to three rather sophisticated harmonic alterations, each more outré than the one before, tame perhaps to post-Wagnerian ears, but no doubt quite daring to late eighteenth-century ones. I quote the second instance (Example 16).

EXAMPLE 15
Haydn, *Die Harmonie in der Ehe*

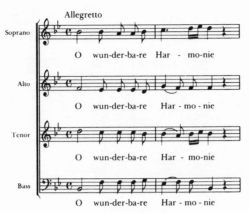

The musical pun on "Wunderbare" is, I think, twofold. Haydn congratulates himself on this "wonderful" bit of partwriting and harmony: it is "Wunderbare" indeed. But "Wunderbare" is ironic as well: the "wonderful" harmony (they are quarreling all the time) is disharmony, in fact; and to the extent that good classical taste will allow, Haydn has represented disharmony in his music—not, of course, by breaking the "syntactic" rules of correct harmonic or contrapuntal writing, but by setting up a paradigm of harmony in the first phrase, diatonic and simple in the extreme, and then giving the *impression* of disharmony by violating this paradigm with the more daring harmonic writing quoted below.

Mozart too knew this technique well and used it in his depiction of Osmin's rage in *Die Entführung aus dem Serail*. Osmin loses his temper, loses control, and the music seems to lose control as well, by going harmonically "out of bounds." But like Haydn, Mozart was too much the classicist to let his music literally go out of bounds. And in a revealing letter to his father (26 September, 1781), he has fully articulated the aesthetic constraints under which he worked in composing this representation of personal "disharmony."

[A]s Osmin's rage gradually increases, there comes (just when the aria seems to be at an end) the allegro assai, which is in a totally different measure and in a different key; this is bound to be very effective. For just as a man in such a towering rage oversteps all the bounds of order, moderation and propriety and completely forgets himself, so must the music too forget itself. But as passions,

Example 16

whether violent or not, must never be expressed in such a way as to excite disgust, and as music, even in the most terrible situations, must never offend the ear, but must please the hearer, or in other words must never cease to be *music,* I have gone from F (the key in which the aria is written), not into a remote key, but into a related one, not, however, into its nearest relative D minor, but into the more remote A minor.[8]

◊ 5 ◊   Among the musical representations that go beyond the "sounds like" relation, two further subclasses should be distinguished in addition to the class of central cases already discussed (and to which we will return shortly). They are what I will call "representations by conventional association" and "internal representations."

By the former I mean those representations that function through some extra-musical association the music has acquired, often through a text, but sometimes simply through use. These can be very naive, as where the Marines' Hymn is woven into the sound track of a motion picture to represent the Marine Corps; or Rule Britannia, to represent the British navy. Or they may be of great subtlety and sophistication, as where Bach introduces the chorale melodies, without text, for representational purposes, relying for his effect, of course, on his congregation's intimate knowledge of the melodies and their texts. A fairly straightforward instance of this has been adduced in a previous chapter. To show how complex these representations can be in Bach's hands requires another example (Example 17).

EXAMPLE 17
Bach, Cantata 12, *Weinen, Klagen, Sorgen, Zagen*

Pirro describes what is going on here this way:

> A chorale mingles with the tenor aria. While the soloist advises the Christian to remain faithful despite ordeals, promising him prosperity after the storm, the bass [that is, the instrumental bass] continues to sing the motif which portrays the course of the wind, while the melody [trumpet] plays the melody of the hymn, *Jesu, meine Freude,* one strophe of which proclaims confidence in Jesus who watches over His own and protects them against the stormy blast.[9]

The verse Pirro alludes to is, in the translation of Henry S. Drinker,[10]

> When in life the storm and strife,
> High with hellish horrors heap me,
> Jesus safe will keep me.

The demands Bach makes on his listeners are remarkable. Not only do they have to recognize the chorale: they have to remember a verse much further on than the strophe that gives the chorale its title. (To make the point more graphically: How many of us know the *second* verse of America the Beautiful?) How vivid such representations are will be, of course, a function of listeners' familiarity with the melodies and texts of the Lutheran faith. For most of us this must be a matter of book learning; to some of Bach's contemporaries it was very much alive, and made these representations "by association" immediately present—not pedantic in the least.

The second subclass of representations, namely, "internal representations," comprises those that are not "inherently" representational but exist merely by virtue of a convention internal to the musical work. Perhaps the most familiar instances of this are the Wagnerian leitmotifs. These may of course display other illustrative features in ways I have already enumerated. But they "represent" the characters and dramatic themes of the *Ring* simply by a kind of musical stipulation on the part of the composer, very much in the way the mathematician stipulates that some symbol is to stand for some given quantity. Sometimes, of course, the composer may actually stipulate verbally what these representations are. Often, however, we infer it from the musical context, as in Humperdinck's *Hänsel und Gretel,* where the witch's theme, for example, becomes her representation simply by occurring in one form or another whenever she is mentioned, thought of, or appears. The theme is, to be sure, expressive of the moods appropriate to the wicked and supernatural (Example 18).

EXAMPLE 18
Humperdinck, *Hansel und Gretel,* Act I

But it *represents* by virtue of Humperdinck's score telling us, essentially, "Let *this* represent the witch."

Now it may well be wondered, at this point, whether we have not really gone beyond the notion of representation entirely, at least with some of these examples, or bent it unrecognizably out of shape. Perhaps it might be more correct to describe some of them as cases of *reference* or *allusion* rather than *representation.*[11] The point is well taken. But as such examples are more or less peripheral to the major concerns of this study, there will be no need to elaborate on them any further. Those who prefer "refer" or "allude" to "represent" with regard to some of what I have been calling "representations by conventional association" and "internal representations," will find little that is to come will hang on that refinement.

◊ 6 ◊   Let us return, briefly, to the central cases of musical representation not of the "sounds like" variety. A final example—our customary borderline case—will work our passage to the next (and final) category of musical illustrations. It is one of the most ubiquitous examples in the repertoire: the representation of motion or direction upwards or downwards by an ascending or descending melodic line. There is no period in musical history, from the Renaissance to the present, where ascent and descent have not almost without exception elicited the appropriate musical rise or fall. Consider, by way of illustration, the following four settings of "descendit de coelis," from the *Credo* of the Mass (Example 19).

In response to these examples it might well be objected that what we are dealing with here are notational artifacts, descriptions appropriate merely to the visual appearance of musical scores as we happen to realize them physically. We don't *hear* the music go up and down, we *see* the notes go up and down the printed page. (How can sounds *literally* go up and down? it will be urged: that is merely a spatial metaphor.) In other words, what is being suggested is that these musical puns on rising and falling (and perhaps others as well) are the result not of how

Example 19
Palestrina, *Missa Papae Marcelli*

Bach, Mass in B-minor

Haydn, *Theresienmesse*

Beethoven, Mass in C, Op. 86

music sounds but of how musical notation looks: they are the result not of how we describe *music* but merely how we describe *notation,* which has no more to do with how music sounds than the way we write "cat" has to do with how Tabby looks.

That there are examples of "music for the eyes" cannot be doubted; and that, indeed, is the next (and final) category in this progression from musical pictures through musical representations. That the rise and fall of the musical line is music only for the eyes is debatable, however. My own intuition is that it is not; that we hear music rise and fall as well as see musical notes do so.[12] I say this because "high" and "low" in music have been with us so long, have become so much a part of our listening experience, have become so ingrained in our descriptions not just of musical notation but of the phenomenology of our musical perception, that we literally hear the rise and fall of musical lines as surely as we hear the particular quality of a diminished chord or the distinctive timbre of the English horn. Perhaps I can support this contention with an example. The following phrase from Mendelssohn's *Elijah*— where the prophet prays to God to let his flaming fires *descend* from heaven—has always sounded wrong to me, almost as if Mendelssohn had committed a "grammatical" error (Example 20).

EXAMPLE 20
Mendelssohn, *Elijah,* Part I

Let them now des-cend! _

The setting of the words "Let them now descend" on a *distinctively* rising line seems to go against the sense of the text in a way that makes the music *sound* quite inappropriate. Perhaps Mendelssohn was, rather, intending to represent in his music not the descent of God's ministers but the ascent of Elijah's prayer. Nevertheless, the word "descend," and the ascending musical line stand out in such bold relief that this alternative representation, if indeed it were intended, is quite defeated. And what results is not in my musical experience an offense to the eye, but to the musical ear. Others may not share my experience in this regard; and that is why I am willing (although reluctantly) to construe the rise and fall of the melodic line as a borderline case between representation in sound of things other than sounds, and representation merely in notation, which is to say, representational music for the eyes. But now let us cross the border, and discuss briefly some bona fide cases of the latter kind of representation—representation that passes beyond the subject (literally construed) of the typology of musical illustrations, since notation is not music.

Georg Philipp Telemann, that indefatigable composer of *Gebrauch-musik,* wrote a trifle called *Gulliver Suite:* a duet for two violins. It contains, among other drolleries, a *Lilluptsche Chaconne* and *Brobdingnagis-che Gigue.* One can well imagine how such a thing might have been brought off in late Baroque style. But what Telemann has done is to make a notational joke that only the performers can see and *no one* can hear (Example 21).

EXAMPLE 21
Telemann, *Gulliver Suite (Der getreue Musikmeister,* Vol. VI)

The joke, of course, is that the Lilliputian's Chaconne is composed in very tiny note values (down to "hundred-and-twenty-eighth-notes"), and the Brobdingnagian Gigue in enormously large ones (twenty-four to the measure), to suit their respective sizes. But none of this can be heard; the peculiar notation makes no real difference to the sound of the music. It is impossible to choose a tempo at which the relative note values would be heard. For if we chose a reasonable tempo for the Lilliputian's Chaconne, then if this tempo were kept for the Gigue (that is, ♪=♪), the pace would be so impossibly slow that it is doubtful we would have anything like music at all, let alone a gigue. If, on the other hand, we chose a reasonable tempo for the Gigue, and preserved the same tempo for the Chaconne (that is, ○=○), it would be too fast to play. Clearly Telemann did not intend this bit of musical representation to be heard. It is a private joke between the composer and the performers. We cannot hear the Lilliputian Chaconne's small notes and the Brobdingnagian Gigue's large ones, the way we can hear the long, sustained notes in Handel's chorus as representing God's enduring patience. To represent big and little in *music* rather than in notation (which is perfectly possible to do), Telemann would have had to choose some other means. We have, here, genuine representation for the eyes alone.

In some musical periods, as a matter of fact, such representation in notation was taken quite seriously. Bach, for example, indulged in it in far from humorous contexts. Whether such representation for the eyes should be construed as *musical* representation is a nice question. I have not so construed it here, and am content to leave it as a limiting case, the outer boundary of my typology of musical illustrations. Like all boundaries, however, it is within what it bounds as well as without. The passage across must be a continuum.

◊ 7 ◊   Enough ground has been covered, and enough detours made, I think, to warrant a brief survey of what I have called, perhaps a bit presumptuously, a "typology of musical illustrations"— presumptuously because that title might suggest a rigor and completeness to which I cannot pretend. The typology falls into two main sections, comprising musical pictures and musical representations. Musical pictures themselves are of two kinds: those that are recognized as such without any nonmusical aids whatever, and those that require for their recognition what I characterized as the *minimal information,* which is to say, the information that one is hearing an illustration. The boundary between these two categories of musical pictures, like all of the other boundaries in this typology, is a vague one, and doubtful cases abound.

Musical representation I divided in three: representations of the "sounds like" kind; representations not confined to sounds; and, finally—the limiting case—representations in notation only, that is to say, representations for the eyes.

Finally, I distinguished two further subcategories of representations not of the "sounds like" variety: those were the categories of "representation by conventional association," that is to say, representations achieved by extra-musical connections; and "internal representations," representations in virtue of a tacit or explicit stipulation made in the work itself. And I maintained that at least some examples of these (though not all) might perhaps be "representations" in only an attenuated sense of that word: that "references" or "allusions" might be the preferred description.

The purpose of this typology, with its profusion of musical examples, is threefold. First, I hope that the sheer proliferation of examples will convince an initially skeptical reader of the significance and extent of musical illustrations in Western music, whether or not they have a full right to that name. Second, I want to provide myself, for what is to follow, with concrete instances to which I can refer. Third, I want to be able to rely on some basic distinctions among musical illustrations, for the purpose of facility in discussion but also, and more importantly, to dispel the confusion that has resulted from thinking of musical illustrations all of a piece and hence all prone to the same difficulties.

But philosophical difficulties cannot be dispelled by distinctions alone, and philosophical difficulties in abundance stand in the way of a satisfactory understanding of musical representation in the West: indeed even cast doubt, in some people's minds, on its very existence. To these difficulties we must now turn our attention.

CHAPTER IV

Music Depicting and Music Described

◊ 1 ◊   I suggested in the previous chapter an intimate connection between how music *depicts,* and how music is *described.* I suggested too, that how we describe music may, in certain instances, raise problems of a philosophical kind. J. O. Urmson has already undertaken a preliminary investigation of these matters in his insightful paper, "Representation in Music."[1] This is where it would be wise for us to begin.

I must, at the outset, dispose of a terminological piece of business. Urmson uses the term "representation" very much in the way I have been using the term "illustration," and not, needless to say, in the specific way I have used "representation" in this work. Whenever possible and wherever relevant, I shall continue to use the terms "picture," "representation," and "illustration" in the ways I have been using them in the preceding chapters. But, of course, when the term "representation" and its cognates occur in direct quotations from Urmson's paper, these uses should not be confused with the rather special use I have established in this book.

Urmson begins his paper with a discussion of musical illustrations of sounds. There is much here with which I am in complete agreement, but as it is not relevant to my present concerns, there is no need to discuss it further. It is where music passes from the illustration of sound to other objects of representation that the particular problems we are presently exercised over begin to arise. At this point, then, we will pick up Urmson's account.

Urmson's account of musical representation is based, in part, on the notion of resemblance. His idea is that in order for A to be a representation of B, A must be *intended* to resemble B in some respect, and "some minimal degree of resemblance should be achieved," it being understood that this is a necessary but not sufficient condition for representation.[2] However, where B is not sound, the following problem is seen by Urmson to arise:

> I suggested that the parallel movement of the thirds in *Nun Wandre Maria* [by Hugo Wolf] represented the parallel movement of Mary and Joseph as they walked together to Bethlehem, clearly implying

that this could be counted as a case of resemblance. But it may well be doubted whether this is, in a straightforward sense, a case of resemblance, for the expression "parallel movement" is by no means clearly univocal. Can a musical part move, in the same sense as a person moves, and can two musical parts move in parallel as two persons can move in the same direction side by side?

In other words, musical representations not of the "sounds like" kind rely on the assumption, according to Urmson, that musical sounds can resemble things other than sounds. This seems at least questionable, for even though to describe music we use terms other than those applicable primarily to sounds, it is not at all clear that such terms are being used univocally in the musical and nonmusical cases.

> There is a wide range of characteristics . . . that we unhesitatingly ascribe both to passages of music and to other things, of which parallel movement is but one. . . . But if parallel motion, and the other features in this class, are not genuine cases of resemblance, or are cases of resemblance only in some extended and philosophically puzzling sense, then our hypothesis is either refuted, or is shown to be philosophically void.[3]

In a moment I will discuss the variety of terms that, Urmson quite rightly observes, are used to describe at once both musical sounds and nonmusical non-sounds. But first we must notice—as Urmson does not fail to do—that what we are dealing with here is a phenomenon neither purely musical nor confined primarily to the arts, nor (which is not the same thing) even exclusively aesthetic. For the matter under discussion—that is to say, the description of musical sound in terms of nonmusical non-sound—is merely a special case of the general tendency to employ descriptions that cross the sense modalities. As Urmson puts the point, "we are not faced with a problem which is exclusively or even primarily, one of aesthetics," since "it seems that many terms . . . occur frequently, in both aesthetic and also quite utilitarian contexts, with application to series of sounds and also to colours, smells, tastes and many more complex phenomena."[4] We are dealing, then, with a general linguistic fact, well-known in the field, and as we shall see, not perhaps well-understood yet, but at least beginning to be.

What kinds of terms, then, are we concerned with? It appears to me that they fall, interestingly enough, into (at least) three clearly defined groups. There are, to begin with, those adjectives that refer to some simple perceptual property perceived by a sense other than the sense of hearing. For example, "bright," "sour," "soft," "sharp," are primarily appropriate to the senses of, respectively, sight, taste, and touch, but are correctly applied to the objects of the sense of hearing, as in the bright sound of the trumpet, the sour notes of Jack Benny's violin playing, the soft sound of the flute in its low register, the sharp report of a pistol shot. Second, there are the adjectives we use to describe the expressive properties of music—sad, cheerful, melancholy, tender—that are, in their primary uses, appropriate to the emotional states of sentient beings. Finally, there are what might be denominated "structural adjectives," which we use to describe the complex, structural properties of music. Many of these have actually become terms of the musical art, but have uses originally nonmusical, or nonaural, or both. Thus we speak of long, or sustained notes, jagged rhythms, parallel motion, imitation, one line following another, rising and falling figures, harmony, and so on, all of which have been used, since time out of mind, to describe the structural features of Western music, but which must surely have originated in uses other than musical ones, and in regard, primarily, to objects other than sounds.

We can look to the science of linguistics for some valuable insights into the first of these categories: that is, the category of adjectives that refer to simple properties perceived by one of the senses originally, and that have subsequently migrated across perceptual modalities. A brief glance is all we can reasonably hope to give at this very complicated, and technical line of inquiry. But it will, I think, be helpful in the present regard.

◊ 2 ◊   According to Joseph M. Williams, "we have little more of a theory of semantic change today than . . . in 1880";[5] and it is, of course, semantic change that we are talking about in alluding to the transfer of reference across perceptual boundaries. Interestingly enough for present purposes, however, Williams himself has offered a possible generalization about the change in what he calls "synaesthetic adjectives"—the very ones we are concerned with in our first category—which it will be well worth our while to examine.

"One of the most common types of metaphoric transfer in all languages," Williams writes, "is synaesthesia—the transfer of a lexeme from one sensory area to another: *dull colors, brilliant sounds, sharp tastes, sour music*, etc."[6] It is, again, of considerable significance to our present concerns, that at least in one circumscribed area, that of nineteenth-century poetry, "the semantic field of tactile experience provided the largest number of lexemes transferred to other sensory modalities; *the semantic field of acoustic words received the greatest number of items*."[7]

The significance of this fact for the study of musical representation
is clear. We will inevitably be faced, in our descriptions of music, with a
preponderance of sensory adjectives that have migrated from sense
modalities other than that of hearing; but to begin with, that should
not in itself worry us unduly. For it has nothing to do, apparently, with
the peculiar nature of music qua music, music qua art, or music qua
aesthetic object. It is simply true of the English language (and other
languages as well, it would seem) that *the semantic field of acoustic words
receives the greatest number of items.* Why this is so is open to speculation.
One is tempted to the obvious conclusion that the semantic field of
acoustic words is a heavy borrower from the other sense modalities because it is poor in adjectives of its own—the rich don't have to live on
credit. If we want to push speculation further, to ask why we should be
poor in indigenous acoustic adjectives, the answer of tradition with
perhaps some new support in evolutionary biology would be that the
sense of hearing is not our epistemically favored one. In addition,
tradition tells us that the sense of touch is in an epistemically favored position, which might help to explain why *the semantic field of tactile experience provides the largest number of lexemes transferred to other sensory modalities.* Perhaps the pre-Socratics are bad witnesses to call on any
question, but two dark sayings of Herakleitos are enticingly relevant in
this regard: "Eyes and ears are bad witnesses to men if they have souls
that understand not their language" (Bywater, fragment [4]); and
"The eyes are more exact witnesses than the ears" (Bywater, fragment
[15]).[8] So if both eyes and ears are bad witnesses (although the eyes
have it over the ears), and if we exclude the sense of taste, what is left as
the odds-on favorite except, of course, the sense of touch? This is certainly the conclusion Berkeley reached, in *An Essay Towards a New Theory of Vision,* where he tried to "derive" the visual perception of distance, solidity and shape from the more primary sense of touch.[9] Be all
this as it may, it would appear to be something like an incontestable
linguistic fact that our vocabulary of sensory sound-adjectives is heavily indebted to the other sense modalities, and particularly, either directly or by the laying on of hands, to the sense of touch. What further
we can make of this besides the obvious—that there is nothing especially musical, artistic, or aesthetic about it—requires some further
consideration of Williams' "law" of semantic change for synaesthetic
adjectives.

What Williams calls his "major generalization" is as follows: "if a lexeme metaphorically transfers from its earliest sensory meaning to another sensory modality, it will transfer according to the [following]
schedule. . . ." (Figure 4).[10]

Thus touch words will transfer to taste words (sharp taste), or color words (dull color), or sound words (soft sound); taste words to sound words (sweet sound), or smell words (sour smell); color words to sound words (bright sound) and vice versa (loud color); dimension words to sound words (deep sound), or color words (deep blue); and smell words to nothing at all, there being "no primary olfactory words in English (that is, none historically originating in the area that have shifted to other senses)."[11]

It is, Williams concludes, a highly confirmed, reliable generalization that: "Sensory words in English have systematically transferred from the physiologically least differentiating, most evolutionary primitive sensory modalities to the most differentiating, most advanced, but not vice versa," and adds, "there is no intrinsic reason why this order should be observed."[12] But what is important to note, for present purposes, is the method by which this generalization has been confirmed. "It is [a generalization] of rather general scope, covering all English adjectives—well over 100, borrowed as well as native, from their first citations (as evidenced by the Oxford English Dictionary and the Middle English Dictionary) to the present—which refer to any primary sensory experience: touch . . ., taste . . ., smell . . ., visually perceived dimension . . ., color . . ., or sound. . . ."[13] It is that familiar philosophical tool, the *Oxford English Dictionary,* and its ilk, then, that provided the data from which the generalization was "induced," and by which future "predictions" can be confirmed. It is the historical lexicographer who tells the "scientific" linguist what sensory words are now in the language, what sense modalities they are now correctly applied to, when it became correct to apply them in this way, when it was not correct, and what the only (and therefore original) sense modality might once have been under which they were correctly applied.

This being the case, we must not be misled by Williams' language when he calls the change across sense modalities a "metaphorical transfer." Whether or not that is a correct description of the *process,* it is not a correct description of the *product* (nor does Williams suggest that it is). The process that transferred "bright," say, from the sense modality of sight to that of hearing may have passed through a stage where "bright" was metaphorically applied to sounds; but the evidence that this transference did indeed take place, that is to say, the evidence of the *Oxford English Dictionary*, is the evidence that, ipso facto, tells us that "bright" is now correctly, literally applied to sounds. Were this not the case, that use of the word would not be sanctioned by that unimpeachable book.

I emphasize this, to begin with, to prevent synaesthetic transfer of the kind Williams is concerned with, from being confused with some perhaps more familiar kinds of synaesthesia, as well as other related phenomena, which might naturally come to mind. The first, which *is* a kind of synaesthesia, is the peculiar association that certain individuals may make between sense modalities that are not generally shared by the community of language users. For example, some people are known to connect certain colors with certain sounds, to the extent that they claim actually to hear the sound of the trumpet, say, as red, or the key of C minor as purple but definitely not green, and so on. Such bizarre cases, interesting though they may be in their own right, are not relevant to present concerns. What we are interested in, in studying musical representation as a public, negotiable commodity, are descriptions of music that are founded upon established English usage. To be sure, synaesthetic transfer of the kind Williams is concerned with is, in part, a function of the perceptual and psychological make-up of homo sapiens, and had we—more of us, anyway—perceived the well-tempered system of keys in technicolor, that would doubtless be reflected in our language. But we don't—and it isn't. So such oddities need not concern us here.

The second notion that I would like to disassociate myself from in this discussion of synaesthetic transfer, is what Wittgenstein called, in the *Philosophical Investigations*, the "secondary sense" of a word;[14] not, I hasten to add, because this notion is totally irrelevant to the issue, but because Wittgensteinians are not themselves agreed about what the master meant by it, and because a preponderance of cases are included that do not fall under the head of synaesthetic transfer, although some are included that do. Three particular kinds of example occur in Wittgenstein. Some seem to be almost on the order of what Gilbert Ryle called, in *The Concept of Mind*, "category mistakes," that is to say, the representation of things "as if they belonged to one logical type or category (or range of types or categories), when they actually belong to another."[15] Thus, in the *Philosophical Investigations*, Wittgenstein suggests, as one kind of example of secondary senses: "Given the two ideas 'fat' and 'lean,' would you be rather inclined to say that Wednesday was fat and Tuesday lean, or the other way around?"[16] But some of his examples suggest instead the kind of bizarre synaesthesia as opposed to genuine synaesthetic transfer just alluded to as in "If I say 'For me the vowel *e* is yellow.'. . ."[17] And, finally, in the *Brown Book*, Wittgenstein, although not using the phrase "secondary sense," discusses what is obviously the same phenomenon, using both of the examples cited just now from the *Philosophical Investigations*, but also the example of "a *deep* sound,"[18] which, unlike the others, is a central case of the semantic change of sensory adjectives, and, therefore, falls within the range of examples relevant to our concerns. (That this kind of example did not find its way into the more mature discussion in the *Philosophical Investigations* may perhaps suggest that Wittgenstein later decided it was not a bona fide case of secondary sense—which coincides with my intuition of the matter.)

By "secondary sense" Wittgenstein insisted that he did not mean either "different sense" or "nonliteral (metaphorical) sense"; rather he wanted to say of words in their secondary sense, "They have a different use."[19] Nevertheless, if secondary sense suggests anything like a peripheral use, or one remote from central and canonical cases (as at times it seems to), it is, for that reason, a phrase ill-suited to describe adjectives that have undergone synaesthetic transfer, although it may, like Williams' phrase "metaphorical transfer," correctly describe an intermediate stage in that process. I emphasize again that we are dealing with terms in their normal and literal sense, and musical descriptions couched in those very terms. This is not to deny that descriptions of music, like descriptions of anything else, employ the full linguistic arsenal, including metaphorical and other extensions of ordinary language. But that, it must be remembered, is not the point at issue here.

But enough now has been said about these linguistic matters. It is time to return to Urmson and the subject of musical representation, for we are now ready, I think, to apply what we have learned to musical cases and, perhaps, to dissolve some of the difficulties that Urmson has so insightfully raised.

◊ 3 ◊   Of what magnitude is the contribution made by synaesthetically transferred sensory adjectives to musical representation? I will venture to say, without argument, that it is not so large as may be thought at first. The contribution lies more in the direction of musical *expressiveness*, which is quite another thing. (More of that in another place.) I will also venture to say that only a very few musical representations rely entirely on such sensory adjectives, for reasons that will become more apparent when we come to discuss our third category of descriptive terms, those I called "structural adjectives." Be that as it may, they *do* play a part; and one *can* even find cases in which a musical representation devolves entirely on a single synaesthetically transferred sensory adjective. I shall adduce such a case here for purposes of illustration and discussion.

At the opening of the *Creation,* after the representation of chaos *(Die Vorstellung des Chaos),* Haydn muddles about in the key of C minor, in subdued tones and low registers, with the chorus and bass soloist accompanied only by muted strings. The sound is dark throughout, and reaches its nadir on the words: "And God said: Let there be light, and there was . . .," sung by the chorus a capella, in unison. But when the word "light" occurs again, in "and there was *light,"* the full orchestra, woodwind, brass, strings unmuted, comes on like Gangbusters, on the "brightest" imaginable C-major chord (Example 22).

The representation is as obvious and simple as the effect is magnificent. The brightness of the First Light is represented by nothing other than the brightness of the C-major chord. That "bright" can correctly, and univocally, be predicated of light *and* of sound is a necessary condition for the success of Haydn's representation; and succeed it does.

But to this the following objection might be made, suggested by one of the difficulties raised by Urmson. How, it might be asked, can light and sound have the common property of brightness, being the objects of two different sense modalities, that is, sight and hearing respectively? And if they cannot share that property, how can they resemble one another in that respect? How can the latter represent the former? Granted that it may be correct English usage to call both light and sound bright, yet if they do not share the property in fact, and cannot really resemble one another in respect of it, then "bright" cannot be being used univocally here: in effect, the sense of "bright" in "bright sound" must be an attenuated, extended, or metaphorical one.

Assume, for the nonce, that resemblance is a necessary (but clearly not sufficient) condition for representation. What argument might we offer in answer to the objection that a C-major chord and light cannot resemble one another in respect of brightness? Let us work backwards from the conclusion that brightness cannot be being predicated univocally. First, I offer as evidence that it *is* being predicated univocally the fact that the *Oxford English Dictionary* indicates it. Second, I offer as evidence that the C-major chord and light resemble one another in respect of brightness, the fact that they are both correctly and univocally

chöpfung, Part I

described as bright. Third, I suggest that they possess the common property of brightness for the very same reason: that is, "bright" applies correctly, and univocally, to both.

But surely, it will be objected, this just begs the question. Granted the *Oxford English Dictionary* tells us that it is sometimes correct to describe both sounds and light as bright. It does not tell us whether these correct descriptions are univocal, however. You must, so the objector will continue, point to something in the light and the sound, besides, of course, the disputed property of brightness, by virtue of which you call them both "bright."

Here, however, the objector (and my reader, perhaps) must be reminded of just what *kind* of property we are discussing. I started off by saying that we are concerned with simple perceptual properties, and to them the adjectives in question refer. So let us remind ourselves what a simple perceptual property (or quality) is like.

> Such properties are directly perceived by the senses. . . . [T]hey are . . . "unanalysable"—that is to say, they cannot be verbally defined, either in terms of simpler qualities or in terms of any set of operations, without mentioning the property itself. I can tell a red tie from a green one at sight, and I can teach any normal person to do the same; but I cannot explain how I do it either by reference to other properties of the tie or in terms of any procedure, without using the words "red" or "green" or other words for the same concepts.[20]

The brightness of musical sounds and of light is just such a simple perceptual property. That is why we cannot point to anything *else* in the music, or in the light, to support our claim that both possess brightness (that is, that both are "bright,") other than the property of brightness itself, any more than we can point to something in the tie other than its redness to support our claim that it is red. This, of course, does not mean that we can reply in kind to *any* application of a simple-property adjective across sense modalities. That is where established English usage and the *Oxford English Dictionary* come in. To call a taste or smell "red" would simply be either to make a mistake in English usage, or to use "red" in an attenuated, metaphorical, or secondary sense. For, as a matter of linguistic fact, "color words may shift only to sound . . .,"[21] and, therefore, no such use of "red" would be sanctioned by the *Oxford English Dictionary*, or any other authority on correct English usage.

We might, of course, be *mistaken* in calling a sound bright, just as we might be in calling a tie red—if the sound were in fact dark, or the tie green. But in neither case would we be making a mistake in English usage. And in neither case would a skeptic be justified in asking us to support our ascription by pointing to anything else in the sound or in the tie beyond the brightness or the color, respectively; for such a demand would be irrational, given the nature of the properties in question. Thus, because of the nature of the properties, namely, that they are simple ones, we are fully justified in offering the argument we have put forward, to wit, that the C major chord (in Haydn's representation of light) resembles light in respect of brightness: the brightness is a common property of each—and both, because brightness can univocally be predicated of sound and light (on authority of the *Oxford English Dictionary*), and can correctly be so predicated (on authority of our eyes and ears). To ask for more justification of univocity than that—in particular, to ask what *other* features besides brightness warrant our claiming that both light and music are (univocally) bright—is to ask for the logically impossible by misconstruing the "logic" of simple-property terms.

The upshot of all this is, I think, that the mechanism of musical representation, although it depends to *some* extent on using sensory adjectives for simple perceptual qualities across the sense modalities, is in no way rendered problematic or defective on that account. For one thing, such synaesthetic transfer is now beginning to be well-understood by linguists; for another, it is, as we have already seen, a phenomenon not restricted to music, or to art, or to the aesthetic. If it *were* problematic, language tout court would totter, not just musical language. Finally, there is, I have claimed, adequate evidence, and there are persuasive arguments for concluding that we can apply synaesthetically transferred nonaural adjectives univocally and correctly to sound, and that we can do so without fear of falling into idiosyncratic, bizarre, or secondary uses of these terms. This much has been shown, and is adequate for the purpose of understanding this aspect of musical representation. It is time now to leave synaesthetic adjectives and go on to the second kind of nonaural terms distinguished above, that is, the *expressive* ones.

◇ 4 ◇   The description of music in emotive terms is quite as widespread, if not more so, than its description synaesthetically. Like synaesthetic description, it is by no means exclusive either to music, or to art, or to the aesthetic (unless one either has a "theory" or begs the question to the effect that expressive qualities are of necessity aesthetic ones). We ascribe expressive qualities to arts other than music, and we ascribe them to nature. Moreover, we ascribe them to nature (but seldom to art) in nonaesthetic as well as aesthetic contexts. (The nature lover, in a fit of aesthetic rapture, may comment on the sombre or melancholy quality of a scene; but a psychiatrist might make the same comment, in a calculating, utilitarian way, in judging it an unfit habitation for a depressive patient.)

Expressive qualities, of course, present problems of a special kind that are well-known, and well-explored by philosophers of art of various persuasions. I have presented my own views with regard to them at some length elsewhere,[22] and I can but refer the reader there for a proper accounting of them. It must suffice for present purposes to say that, on my view, sad or melancholy music is not a *representation* of sadness or melancholy (whatever that would be), although at times (but not always) it is sad or melancholy in virtue of representing something else.

It is a fact, however, that the expressiveness of music plays a part in musical representation; and a fact that historically, musical expressiveness and musical representation have at times been confused with one another, or been consciously substituted for one another, and in general have interacted theoretically in complex and puzzling ways. This I have made the subject of a separate chapter. For the time being we can set musical expressiveness aside as not directly relevant to the problem of musical description as it relates directly to that of musical representation. That leaves the third category of descriptive predicates, what I have called "structural adjectives," to be dealt with. It demands to be examined with some care.

◇ 5 ◇   I introduced the discussion of synaesthetically transferred, simple-property adjectives by suggesting, without argument, that they played a rather small, if nonetheless important part in musical representation. Structural adjectives take, as we shall see, a correspondingly larger role. In explaining the reason for the latter, the missing argument for the former will at least be partially provided.

Clearly, the representation of a complex object, or phenomenon, if the representation is to be in any kind of detail, requires a complex representational matrix for the purpose. I could, of course, represent the battle of Balaclava with a single, undifferentiated object—perhaps with a pin on a map—thus sacrificing such details as the British and the Russians. And the general represents the British with a thin red line, unable, therefore, to distinguish, say, among the cavalry, infantry and artillery. What is needed, then, for representation in any kind of detail, of a structure or system of elements, is *another* structure or system of elements that can more or less be isomorphic with it. For this reason it is musical *structure* that most often plays the leading part in musical representation, for it is usually an object or phenomenon with a complex structure of its own that is the subject of the musical representation. For this reason, too, it can now be seen why the simple perceptual properties of sound must play a secondary representational role. Of themselves they do not possess the structure—the differentiation of parts—necessary for the representation of complex objects or phenomena. If they did, they would not, of course, be simple properties but complex ones. This obviously does not mean that simple perceptual properties cannot be formed into structures for representational purposes. Indeed, Haydn actually makes use of the contrast between two simple perceptual properties, darkness and brightness, to represent the brightness of the First Light: the brightness of the C-major chord is highlighted and enriched by contrast with the darkness of the C-minor tonality that precedes it. Nor does it mean that complex musical structures cannot make use of, among other things, simple perceptual qualities, for representational purposes. But the fact remains that the structural properties of musical sound—properties that, by virtue of their structure, are complex rather than simple—bear the heaviest burden of musical representation, just because the complex rather than the simple, the structured rather than the discrete, is most often the representational object.

Let us, then, cast a backward glance over some of the examples of musical representation that have been adduced, to see what part structures and, more particularly, structural adjectives play. Recall the following examples of musical representation. Bach represents the Christian following Jesus with a canon in which the voices "follow" one another; or, put another way, the imitation of Christ is represented by canonic "imitation" (p. 10, above). Handel represents the enduring patience of Jehovah with "long" notes (pp. 45–47). Handel and Haydn represent harmony with "harmonic" writing (pp. 48–49). Palestrina, Bach, Haydn, and Beethoven represent Jesus' descent from heaven (in the Incarnation) with "descending" musical lines (pp. 54–56). Finally, to appropriate Urmson's example, Wolf represents the parallel movement of Joseph and Mary as they walked together to Bethlehem with "parallel motion" in the accompaniment.

Now the "nuts and bolts" of these examples can be thought of somewhat along the following lines. A musical map or model (if you will) is established, which reflects in its structure some of the parts or elements of an object, phenomenon, or state of affairs, and some of the relations in which these parts or elements stand. Thus, as the faithful follow the precepts, teachings and life of Jesus, the lines of Bach's aria follow one another in strict canonic imitation. The "parts" of the aria—that is to say, the lines of music in the polyphonic texture—correspond roughly to the Christian and Jesus, and stand in relation to one another as Jesus to his followers. Again, the long, sustained notes in Handel's chorus in *Belshazzar* stand for the long, enduring patience of God, and as the length of God's patience is held (at least tacitly) in the relation of "longer than" to the persistence of men, so the lengths of the notes on which the word "long" is sung stand in the relation of "longer than" to the surrounding note-values. Handel represents the harmonia mundi with "harmony"; and the isomorphism of the two is obvious enough to require no further comment. Haydn's representation is more complex, in that both harmony and disharmony are represented; and although the same isomorphism relates harmony to harmony, the structure of Haydn's representation presents further complication (as well, therefore, as further opportunity for isomorphism of representation to object). For the elements of diatonic harmony, in their structure, are isomorphic with the elements of a harmonious marriage, as are the elements of chromatic harmony isomorphic with an inharmonious one. Moreover, the relation between the harmonious and "disharmonious" (that is, the contrapuntal and chromatic) sections of Haydn's composition are as the relation between a harmonious and an inharmonious marriage.

More obvious, perhaps, than all of these is the structural isomorphism that obtains between physical descent and the descent of a musical line (as exemplified by Palestrina's, Bach's, Haydn's, and Beethoven's settings of "descendit de coelis"). Here there is, one might say, a one-to-one relation between the intervals, either in notation, or as sounded pitches, and the successive stages of a physical descent (as one might imagine it to be). A similar musical "map" plots the successive movements of Mary and Joseph in Wolf's song: the musical lines moving in tandem, note against note, one going in the direction of the other, as Mary dogs Joseph's footsteps. Whether one thinks simply of marks on paper, or sounded pitches, the elements exhibit a structure that reflects the "structure" of the Holy Family's progress to Bethlehem.

It has been necessary to go over these examples in this rather mind-deadening detail to bring out an important point, namely, that in all cases in which structural adjectives apply to musical representations, there is an isomorphism between representation and object, *regardless of whether or not the adjectives are used univocally* when applied both to the music and to the object of musical representation. It makes no difference at all, in this regard, whether "follow" and "imitation" are used univocally when applied to musical lines and people, no difference whether "long" is used univocally when referring to musical notes and the duration of a psychological state, nor whether "harmony" is used univocally when applied to music and to marriage. The parallel thirds in Wolf's song are isomorphic with the parallel motion of Joseph and Mary whether or not "parallel" and "motion" are used in literally the same senses in the respective cases. All that is necessary to preserve isomorphism is that relationships in one domain have relational counterparts in another. There is no need for the relationship to be the "same" (literally) or that the model "resemble" what it models in any obvious or ordinary sense of that word. What must be preserved is analogy of *structure*. A map need not resemble what it maps. A model need not reflect the relations of "above" and "below" between physical objects with elements that are literally above and below one another. All it need do is reflect those relations between physical objects with relations between representational elements that preserve the relevant aspects of the structure. (Thus there is no reason whatever that a representational system cannot model the relations of "above" and "below" with the relations of "to the left of" and "to the right of," just so long as it is consistently worked out.)

What I am suggesting, then, is that whenever there is isomorphism of structure, the bare bones of representation exist. This is not to say that isomorphism is a sufficient condition for representation, any more than resemblance is. For isomorphism is, like resemblance, a nonintentional concept; whereas intention to represent is, as I shall argue in a later chapter, a necessary condition for representation. Furthermore, isomorphism, like resemblance, is a reflexive relation: that is to say, if A is isomorphic with B, B is isomorphic with A. Yet, of course, that a representation is isomorphic with its object, although it would imply that the object is isomorphic with the representation, would not imply that the object is a representation of the representation. (The descending figure in Beethoven's setting of "descendit de coelis" is isomorphic with the imagined physical descent of Jesus from heaven in the Incarnation. The descent of Jesus is therefore isomorphic with Beethoven's descending figure. But it does not, of course, represent it.) Nor, it is important to note, is isomorphism, at least as I construe it, a necessary condition for representation, for it requires complexity— that is, some degree of structure. Haydn's bright C major chord represents light simply by virtue of their both possessing the simple property of brightness. They may be isomorphic in the limited sense that something in the chord, that is, its brightness, corresponds to something in the First Light, namely, *its* brightness; but beyond that simple correspondence, there is no structure in the one to model structure in the other (nor is there structure in the other to model).

What I want to draw out of this discussion now, is the conclusion that even *if* structural adjectives were *not* applied univocally to music and to the world, it would not follow that music so described could not resemble the world in respects relevant for representation. So even if resemblance *were* a necessary condition of representation (as Urmson thinks), the correct description of music in terms of what I have been calling "structural adjectives" implies that that condition is fulfilled. Even if Bach's aria does not literally resemble the imitation, or following, of Christ in respect of imitation or following, it does resemble it in respect of a common structure in which there is a one-to-one correspondence of relevant elements. And the same can be said for all of the examples of musical representation just discussed: Handel's representation of God's patience, Handel's and Haydn's representations of harmony, Palestrina's, Bach's, Haydn's, and Beethoven's representations of descent, Wolf's representation of parallel motion. In all of these instances, even if the musical representations do not literally resemble the objects of imitation in the respects which the structural adjectives describe, they do resemble them in respect of structure, with the appropriate elements standing in the appropriate relationships in each. That in itself is enough to assure that there is the necessary mechanism for this kind of representation, regardless of whether or not what I have called structural adjectives are determined to be univocally applied in their musical and nonmusical uses. Univocity is required of synaesthetically transferred, simple-property adjectives, but not of the structural ones.

But, it might be objected, isomorphism alone cannot bear the whole weight of representation in the examples discussed. For if that were all there was to it, then any piece of music could represent anything, since one can always find elements in any piece of music to match elements in whatever in nature is complex enough to have them. That, however, is to forget the fact that we are talking about cases in which the music and the object represented also have a common *description*. Our problem is, can there be representation even if, as is not the case, the descriptive predicates are not used univocally? What I am arguing is that there can, just so long as there is structure in the music that the descriptive predicates refer to, mirrored by structure in the object illustrated that the same predicates pick out. Harmony in music can represent harmony in marriage, even if "harmony" is not being used univocally in the two cases, just because harmony in music is a "consonant," well-adapted relation of parts, and harmony in marriage is a "consonant," well-adapted relation of a husband's and wife's behavior, desires, and personality traits. Parallel thirds can represent parallel motion just because there is an isomorphism of structure, but also because linguistic convention, if nothing else, decrees that the descriptive predicate "parallel," whether or not it is used univocally, is appropriate to both. And the same goes for "rising" figures, "following" lines, "long" notes, and the rest. It is this that I referred to early on as the (perhaps) punning quality of musical representations: the same quality that would allow me, by pun or hieroglyph, to "spell out" the old adage "Grin and bear it" with the help of a drawing of Ursus Americanus.

It is fair to conclude, then, that there is enough in the combination of isomorphism and commonality of description, sans univocity, to make musical representations of the kind I was talking about a going concern. Isomorphism alone, of course, is not enough; but it is, where the predicates in question are not the names of simple perceptual qualities, a fruitful ingredient. Structural adjectives, then, do not require univocity to vouchsafe musical representation. Nevertheless, the question of whether they possess it is both interesting and relevant, and I shall conclude this chapter with a discussion of that question.

◇ 6 ◇   It is not altogether clear how one shows that a word is used with literal sameness of meaning in such contexts as musical sound and, say, natural phenomena, psychological states, or social institutions, if there is any initial doubt. It is not easy to decide, or obvious *how* to decide, when a term is being used in its literal sense, and when in an extended or metaphorical one; nor is it obvious when an extended sense becomes a nonliteral one. (To complicate matters further, there are those who think that the question of whether a word has the same meaning in different contexts is nonsensical.) I shall, therefore, be feeling my way here, playing it by ear, as it were, and will not advance what I consider firmly established conclusions. But as the establishing of univocity of applications with regard to structural adjectives is not, as we have seen, strictly necessary for the mechanism of musical representation, I am not particularly disturbed, nor should the reader be, by the tentative quality of my remarks.

It would appear that structural adjectives fall into two basic groups, with an abundance of borderline cases left over. They are, quite simply, those terms that are used, informally, to describe music as well as other things, and those that have a quite specific, technical sense in music, but that, like the nontechnical terms, also have uses elsewhere. (There is also, of course, a whole range of technical terms in music, such as dominant seventh, inessential passing tone, and so on, that have no nonmusical uses at all; but these are of no concern to us here.) With regard to those terms that concern us, I shall venture the not very daring hypothesis that nontechnical terms are univocal between musical and nonmusical contexts and technical terms are not. (Borderline cases are, needless to say, also borderline cases of univocity.) I shall discuss an example of each, with this hypothesis as the guiding principle.

It seems to me (to instance a case in point) that a fairly obvious and convincing argument can be made for the univocity of "long" between "long note" and either a long period of time or a long distance in the nonmusical realm. Of course, "long" in both its musical and nonmusical uses is a relative term. A half-note may be long in one musical composition and short in another, just as a second is a short period of time in the life of a man but a long period of time in particle physics, and twenty-six miles a long foot-race but a short astronomical distance. And at least when "long" is used in reference to time, there seems no doubt about its being used univocally of music and of the world. For musical duration is real time; a whole-note lasts a discrete period of real time, at any given tempo and time signature, and lasts longer than a quarter-note at that tempo and in that time signature. Even if, as some have claimed (quite wrongly, I think), musical time is, in some deeply metaphysical or phenomenological sense, of a different order from real time, it is not thereby necessarily claimed that musical time is not measured in duration, is not susceptible of such determinations as "longer than," "shorter than," "before," "after," and so forth. In other words, it is not necessarily being claimed that musical time is not *time*, or that the above predicates are not applied univocally to it and to nonmusical time. (What *is* being claimed, I need hardly say, is not altogether clear.)[23]

A more interesting question, with, perhaps, a somewhat less obvious answer, is whether "long" is applied univocally in "a long time" and "a long distance." As I suggested above, I do not know how one could go

about *proving* anything one way or the other, but the following considerations seem to me fairly convincing. Time and distance, one would
imagine, have always been measured in terms of one another. Time—
whether kept by the sun, the flow of water or sand, the burning of a
candle, the movement of a clockwork or the vibration of an atom—has
always been measured in terms of distance: something getting from
somewhere to somewhere else. To quote a philosopher with an obses-
sion in this regard, "duration is always expressed in terms of extension;
the terms which designate time are borrowed from the language of
space. When we evoke time, it is space that answers our call."[24] Conversely, distance is frequently, commonly, and quite characteristically
measured in terms of time, as when the distance from one place to another is given (in ordinary discourse) in terms of *how long* it takes to get
there in some given way (for example, "It's just a five-minute walk
from here"), and, of course, where astronomical distance is measured
in terms of "light years." (I will say nothing about the interpenetration
of time and space in modern physics.) This *proves* nothing, I suppose;
but in the absence of any argument to the contrary, it strongly suggests
that "short," "long," and their synonyms are not used in any attenuated
way or secondary sense either when referring to time or distance.
What sense could, after all, be the extended or secondary one, since, if
I am right, there never has been a time when "long" and "short" have
not been applicable to both.

Perhaps, though, there is an argument waiting in the wings to show
that interchangeable or not, "long" (and "short") cannot mean literally
the same thing when applied to time and to distance. After all, it might
be insisted, they are referring to two entirely different categories of
"thing" in each instance, and therefore cannot be being applied univocally. But this is either a manifest begging of the question, or simply a
non sequitur. Surely it is not a category mistake to call a duration or
length "long" or "short," as it would be to call a color long or an idea
short. In the event, it turns out to be unclear just what counts as a category mistake (if anything), and what does not. Nor is it the case that
because a term may be applicable to diverse kinds of thing, it must be
ambiguous, witness the well-known example of "good," which, of
course, ranges over a wide variety of kinds. There are good eggs and
good men, but no reason to believe that "good" is not used univocally,
cannot be literally true of both (or, for that matter, that there must be
some esoteric or nonnatural property that good eggs and good men
have in common, to assure the univocity of "good"). This is not to say,
of course, that the criteria for being a good egg are the same as those

for being a good man. Difference in criteria of application, however, does not imply difference in meaning.

Urmson thinks it counts decisively against "long" and "short" being used univocally between time and distance that: "If precisely the same feature were attributed to space and time when we speak of their being long [or short] there would surely be an indisputable answer to such questions as whether fifty-miles or six months was longer, or what distance was exactly the same length as six months."[25] But this, I think, places much too severe a constraint on univocity, for on this view "good" could not be being used univocally between good egg and good wine, since there is no clear answer to such questions as whether a good egg is better than a good wine, or how good an egg has to be to be as good as a 1945 Lafite Rothschild. The decisive factor for Urmson in determining whether a term is being used univocally or not, would seem to be whether "precisely the same feature" is present in all the cases. But that again seems to me to be an overly severe constraint on the concept. Indeed, it seems to have been just such a constraint as this that led G. E. Moore and others to assert that "good" must name some "nonnatural" quality, one of the working assumptions being, I suppose, that "good" is used univocally in many disparate contexts and, therefore, since there is no "naturalistic" feature common to them all, a "nonnaturalistic" one must be present. A more balanced view, I believe, is that not all adjectives are of the kind where precisely the same common feature must be present in all cases in which the adjective is used univocally, "good" and "long" (or "short") being typical cases.

For reasons similar to those adduced above to show that "long" and "short" are univocal between musical and nonmusical cases, I am reasonably satisfied that structural adjectives of the nontechnical variety are literally true of music and not used in any extended or figurative way, borderline cases always allowed for. Let us turn now to the technical ones where, according to the hypothesis under which we are working, this is not the case, and see, first, whether the hypothesis stands up, and, second, if it does, what implications this has for musical representation.

◊ 7 ◊   The *Harvard Dictionary of Music* defines imitation as "The restatement in close succession of a melody (subject, motive) in different parts of a contrapuntal texture."[26] In imitation, musicians say, one part or "voice" (whether the composition is instrumental or vocal) "follows" another, and although this use of the verb "to follow" is not legitimized by the *Harvard Dictionary of Music* (or any of the other well-known musical dictionaries I have consulted), it has become such an integral part of the musician's vocabulary that it can, I think, be considered a technical term in its own right.

"Imitate" and "follow" are closely related musical terms, often interchangeable. It is easy to see their relations to the terms as they are normally used in nonmusical discourse. When the theme in one voice of a contrapuntal texture exactly "imitates" another, it is a replica of it: or, to be technical, it is a token of the same type. Usually, in a contrapuntal piece such as a canon or fugue, the voices imitate one another in succession: that is to say, as performed, one voice "enters" the composition at time t, and the next, in imitation, "follows" at $t+1$. It seems as if the second voice is a living thing, playing follow-the-leader with the first, doing what the first has done right after it has done it (or at a respectful distance). Such, then, are the obvious strands that connect "imitate" and "follow" as they are used in music and in the "real world," and they enable us at least to surmise how these terms came to be used in music in these ways. But as Urmson correctly observes, "a genetic account of how a word comes to have a use is not to be confused with an account of its use."[27] What, then, is the most reasonable conclusion with regard to these terms, as they are used in music, and in the nonmusical universe of discourse?

A case might be pressed for synonymity, but my own feeling is that "imitate" and "follow" in their musical contexts are technical extensions of the terms as used in ordinary discourse. To imitate is, in its root sense, consciously to ape; and, of course, a melody cannot consciously ape another. Musical description is indeed redolent with animistic overtones, but no one, I presume, is willing to attribute intention and will to a melodic line. "Follow" may perhaps be closer to its literal, nonmusical uses when applied in musical contexts; for musical performances are temporal events, and the voices of a fugue commence (literally) one after another in performance. But whether, when we are referring to a musical score and the musical work which it notates but is not identical with, we are using "follow" literally, I very much doubt. In addition, musicians tend to give "follow" the same active connotation as "imitate," suggesting that a musical line is, as if consciously, following in the footsteps of its predecessor. If, then, "follow" does not fall clearly within the class of the extended and nonliteral in its musical uses, it is, at best, a borderline case.

What, then, are the implications of this for musical representation? As we have seen, that structural adjectives may not be being applied univocally between musical and nonmusical cases in no way obviates the fact that they are, when applied to music, and to the nonmusical world, picking out segments of corresponding structure that are held in common. And this isomorphism of structure provides ample mechanism for successful representation. That the voices in Bach's aria do not literally follow one another should not be allowed to obscure the fact that voices "following" one another in a contrapuntal texture constitute a structure isomorphic with, mirroring the elements and their relations in a real case of following, or an allegorical case (as the Christian "following" Jesus). That "canonic imitation" is not literal imitation likewise in no way implies that canonic imitation does not model real imitation, or the metaphorical imitation of Christ. But, interestingly enough, the lack of literalness of structural adjectives of the technical kind actually gives an *added* dimension to the representations in which they play a part.

I have in mind here, what I referred to in Chapter III as the punning character of some musical representations. We can now see that musical representation takes on the character of musical pun just in those cases in which structural adjectives of the technical kind are the operative ones. One is reminded, in this regard, of the role puns play in dream representation, according to Freud. A German lady, Freud tells us, dreams of Italy, although she has never been *to Italy* (gen Italien in German); *to Italy* is claimed by Freud to be the dream representation of genitals (Genitalien in German).[28] Or again, he tells us a girl's dream:

> she was walking through the fields and cutting off rich ears ["Ähren"] of barley and wheat. A friend of her youth came towards her, but she tried to avoid meeting him. The analysis showed that the dream was concerned with a kiss—an "honourable kiss" [Kuss in Ehren, pronounced the same as "Ähren," literally, "kiss in honour"].[29]

In a similar if less convoluted manner, I would suggest, there is a kind of punning quality in the use of musical imitation to represent the nonmusical kind; or in the use of parallel musical motion to represent parallel physical motion; or in the representation of the ten commandments as the foundation of the Lutheran faith by putting the first phrase of the chorale "These are the holy ten commandments" in the bass (base) of the composition. For "imitation," and "parallel motion," and "bass" in musical usage are technical terms, terms of art, and although we can discern the strands that connect them to the literal meanings of the words (as we cannot, of course, in the kinds of puns Freud is concerned with), they nevertheless no longer possess these literal meanings in their musical contexts. Musical lines do not literally imitate one another. Music does not literally move, so, a fortiori, does not literally exhibit parallel motion, and the musical bass of a composition is its lowest "voice," not necessarily its literal base (whatever that would be).

We can conclude, then, that far from impoverishing musical representation, structural adjectives of the technical kind and the structure they describe, add an additional element, the element of pun, to the representational matrix. I do not want to overemphasize this, or exaggerate the connection between musical puns and Freud's interpretations of dreams, for the major operator in structural adjectives, both of the technical and nontechnical kind, is structural isomorphism, neither synonymity nor pun. But the element of pun is there; and in some cases even prominent. We had best leave it at that.

◇ 8 ◇   It might be well, in concluding the present chapter, and making transition to the next, to remind ourselves what reflections gave rise to this discussion of musical description, and what conclusions can be drawn from it. In moving from musical representations of the "sounds like" kind, to those that cross perceptual modalities to represent phenomena other than sound, it will be recalled that we moved beyond cases in which there was any obvious similarity between sound and what it represented. It is obvious what the buzzing of flies and the "buzzing" of violins have in common, but not at all obvious what the common property (if any) is of long notes and enduring patience, or harmony in music and harmony in marriage. It seemed that perhaps all such musical representations had in common with their representational objects was a common *description,* and if the operative adjectives in those descriptions were not being applied univocally between musical and nonmusical cases, there would not even be that.

It was concluded, however, that both simple, perceptual quality adjectives, of the synaesthetically transferred kind, and structural adjectives of the nontechnical kind, are being applied univocally in musical and nonmusical uses. Further, it was concluded that if a synaesthetically transferred sensory term is being applied univocally and correctly to a piece of music, and to what it represents, they must have not only the description in common, but also the simple perceptual property that the synaesthetically transferred adjective names. Finally, it was concluded that both technical and nontechnical adjectives of the structural kind, when applied correctly to music and to the objects of musical representation, imply isomorphism—commonality of structure—even when, as in the case of technical adjectives, they are not applied univocally. Thus, if resemblance is, as Urmson and others claim, a necessary ingredient in representation, music is not deficient in that regard, even when it represents phenomena other than sound. It can resemble its objects both in respect of structure and in respect of simple perceptual properties, even where those structures and properties belong to objects of different sense modalities.

Thus far, then, we have failed to turn up any glaring, fatal disanaology between musical representations and representations of the less contested varieties. But there are other characteristics of bona fide representations yet to be canvassed, and to one of these, the representational *medium,* I want now to turn my attention.

CHAPTER V

Music as Medium

◊ 1 ◊   I take it that we all have some kind of intuitive, presystematic idea about what an artistic medium, or medium of representation might be. The fact is that in arts like painting and sculpture, what
the medium of representation is is to a large degree obvious and unproblematical. There is something palpably physical there that the artist must work, and that must yield to raw physical manipulation. The
painter spreads with brush or palette knife a thick, viscous substance
on a piece of stretched, grainy fabric, or lightly applies a thin watery
liquid to papers of various kinds. The sculptor digs hands into a soft,
moist, pliable material, or hammers and chisels at substances offering
varying degrees of physical resistance. The medium is oil on canvas, or
water color; clay, or stone, or wood (or even, as in collage, bits and
pieces of "reality"). There is, in other words, something quite physical
and easily identifiable as the medium of representation in all those arts
that can logically fall under the concepts "original," "copy," "forgery":
those arts that Nelson Goodman (and others after him) have called
"autographic."

By contrast, the "allographic" arts, that is, the arts possessing notations, and (sometimes) publicly manifested in performances are
harder to decipher. It is by no means so obvious what the medium of
music, or literature, or dance is. One is tempted to say sound, language, and human bodies respectively (dancing bears excepted), but
even a little philosophical pressure will bend these notions out of
shape. The relationship that the composer has to sound is far different, one would think, from the direct physical involvement that the
sculptor has with clay and marble, or the painter with oils and pastels.
Since the development of a sophisticated musical notation, the high
musical art of the West has had a more complicated relation to its
medium—and a more complicated, or at least more elusive,
medium—than it had in a time when it existed only as improvisation,
and was preserved (if at all) only in memory. For if one imagines the
performer/composer producing at once a composition and a performance, where the art of composing and the art of performing are one art
rather than two, the relation of the composer to his or her medium

seems much more direct—much more like the relation between the sculptor and the clay, or the painter and the paint—than does the relation of composer to medium mediated by a notation, and given to the public by a performer or performers. When a composer/performer in a nonnotational tradition, plies his or her trade, the relation of artist to medium is very physical indeed. Drawing horsehair over the dried entrails of sheep, or blowing on a vibrating piece of wood attached to a pipe, is itself an earthy enterprise that smacks more of the forge than the poet's garret. And when that is the process whereby the musical medium is molded and formed, the contact between composer and sound is hardly less physically immediate than that between sculptor and marble, or painter and paint. Anyone, I think, who has mastered a musical instrument to the extent of being physically "intimate" with it will understand what I am saying here more readily, perhaps, than the nonmusician can.[1]

But once an elaborate musical notation is available the waters are muddied. It is said that Bach was overzealous in demanding release from his princely employment in Weimar, in 1716, with the result that he was placed under arrest. According to Karl Geiringer, "from November 6 to December 2 Sebastian remained in jail, making the best use of his enforced leisure by working on his *Orgelbüchlein.* . . ."[2] Whether or not this story is true is beside the point, but that it *could* be true is of the utmost importance. Only the existence of a notation made it possible for Bach to compose organ music of this complexity in the complete absence of an instrument on which to play—that and the musical mentality capable of becoming so fluent in such a notation that the composer could hold in his imagination sound structures of the complexity of Bach's and record them with pen and ink. So powerful is this notation, and so much a surrogate for that which it notates—that is, the work of music itself—that there is a strong temptation to reify the notation and mistake it for the music, forgetting, perhaps, that scores, like words, are wise men's counters and the money of fools. Be that as it may, once a notation pops in between the composer and his medium, the medium is no longer the transparent thing that it was (and remains) in the world of improvisational music. It becomes, rather, a problematic concept to be scrutinized with the philosopher's eye.

The most elaborately worked out philosophical account of the medium of musical representation that I know of comes from an unexpected source, Adam Smith, whose "analysis of vocal and instrumental music clearly ranks among the most significant theoretical essays on the relationship of music to the other arts in eighteenth-century Britain.["3] Like all such Enlightenment efforts in this regard, it is couched in the inevitable, and unacceptable terms of imitation. But Smith himself has taken at least some preliminary steps towards purging the objectionable connotations of the concept of imitation from his essay on what he calls the *imitative* arts, although the word and many of its undesirable consequences remain. And suitably laundered, it is the best place, I believe, to begin to understand the medium of musical representation, and the pleasure we take in it.

◊ 2 ◊   Shortly before he died in 1790, Adam Smith is supposed to have destroyed a large number of manuscripts which he thought unfit for posthumous publication. He left behind, for his literary executors to dispose of as they saw fit, others which, apparently, he deemed more worthy. These were printed in 1795, under the title *Essays on Philosophical Subjects,* together with "An Account of the Life and Writings of Adam Smith, LL.D.," by Dugald Stewart, reprinted from *Transactions of the Royal Society of Edinburgh.* It is with one of these posthumous essays, "Of the Nature of that Imitation which takes place in the Imitative Arts," that we shall be concerned.

Smith's essay on the imitative arts starts with a consideration of what he obviously thought of as the paradigms of artistic imitation: painting and sculpture. "The most perfect imitation of an object of any kind," he begins, "must in all cases, it is evident, be another object of the same kind, made as exactly as possible after the same model."[4] It is not altogether clear what Smith might have meant by "kind" here. But as the example that immediately follows this assertion is that of one carpet being an imitation of another, one might venture to suggest that he intended "kind" to be taken simply in the vague sense of "kind of thing" or "kind of object": rug or table or chair. Thus, the best imitation of a carpet would be another carpet (same kind) exactly like the first ("exactly as possible after the same model"): the kind being the universal, the model an individual answering to it. Now when we fashion a copy or imitation of one kind of thing in the form of another of the same kind, there is no particular merit accruing to it simply by virtue of its being an exact imitation. Indeed, when the kind in question is the kind we call "work of art," there is demerit, for "the exact resemblance of two productions of art, seems to be always considered as some diminution of the merit of at least one of them; as it seems to prove, that one of them, at least, is a copy either of the other, or of some other original."[5]

But here a puzzling fact obtrudes, for when the imitation is an object

of a different kind—more particularly, when the imitation is a work of
art and its model any *other* kind than that—there does seem to be merit
in the exactness of the imitation simply qua imitation. "But though a
production of art seldom derives any merit from its resemblance to another object of the same kind, it frequently derives a great deal from its
resemblance to an object of a different. . . ."[6] The puzzle is this. Why
does an object derive no merit at all, or even demerit, from its being an
imitation of another object of the same kind, whereas works of the "imitative arts" do derive merit from being imitations of things other than
works of art? It cannot be imitation simpliciter that bestows merit; for
if that were the case, then all imitations, not merely artistic ones, would
derive merit from being imitations. But if the merit of artistic imitations qua imitations does not derive from the imitation, from whence
does it come?

Good Newtonian and Humean that he is, Smith frames no hypothe-
ses on this regard, and never attempts to answer the question. Rather,
he takes it as a brute fact, and attempts instead to lay out the parameters and variables. It is a fact of life, Smith believes, that the imitative
arts derive merit from being as exact imitations as possible of things
other than works of imitative art: this we know from our senses, and the
question he raises (to carry through the Newtonian and Humean
theme) essentially is: What "laws" or regularities can be discovered in
this fact? On what variables does the merit of artistic imitation depend?
How does *it* vary with *them*?

In brief, Smith's major thesis is that the merit of an artistic imitation
is a complex function of the exactness of the imitation and the disparity of the objects; or, to put it more precisely, the merit of an artistic
imitation is in direct proportion to the closeness of the imitation but in
inverse proportion to the resemblance of the objects, merit being measured, apparently (and not surprisingly, given his basically Humean
value theory), by the amount of pleasure the artistic imitation qua imitation provides.

> In painting, a plain surface of one kind is made to resemble, not
> only a plain surface of another, but all the three dimensions of a
> solid substance. In Statuary and Sculpture, a solid substance of one
> kind, is made to resemble a solid substance of another. The dispar-
> ity between the object imitating, and the object imitated, is much
> greater in the one art than in the other; and the pleasure arising
> from the imitation seems to be greater in proportion as this dispar-
> ity is greater.[7]

Smith's idea, then, is that the materials—that is to say, the medium—of an artistic imitation may be naturally more like, or less like the object of the imitation; and the less alike the object and the imitative medium, the more pleasure any given degree of success in imitation will provide. Thus we can, it would appear, set up (at least as a Gedanken-experiment) a kind of hedonic calculus of artistic imitation, such that if X and Y are both artistic imitations of object Q, at the same level of imitative success, then if X is done in a medium less "like" O than is Y's medium, it will give proportionally more pleasure than Y, and hence be a greater success as a work of art, although not as an imitation qua imitation. As the above quotation makes clear, Smith has in mind here, in particular, the contrast between a two-dimensional and a three-dimensional medium: the two-dimensional medium of painting and drawing being less "like" the three-dimensional objects of imitation than is the three-dimensional medium of sculpture, thereby putting it perhaps in a disadvantageous position relative to exactness of imitation, but in a distinctly advantageous one with regard to the payoff on even moderate representational success.

I need hardly say that Smith's notion of natural resemblances and disanalogies of medium to objects of imitation is somewhat simplistic and problematical, and, of course, although Smith sometimes substitutes "represent" and "representation" for "imitate" and "imitation," he is not enough aware of the inadequacy of the latter pair. When I come to adapting what he does say of value to my own uses (and I would not be spending my time with Smith's essay if I did not think there were considerable value in it), those matters will be carefully taken up, and any inadequacies made good. In the meantime, I will elaborate Smith's doctrine with these loose ends untied.

Numerous corollaries seem to follow from Smith's major thesis, as outlined above, although Smith does not draw the logical connections himself, preferring, rather, to state them as additional facts about the arts of painting and sculpture. Perhaps, had he prepared this essay for the press, more of these connections would have been spelled out in detail. Nevertheless, I do not think I am mistaken in seeing them as implications of Smith's major thesis, rather than as isolated observations: there is an implicit structure of argument here. A couple of these implications are worth laying out to help limn in Smith's position. As I do this, I will draw those connections that I can, in the conviction that Smith meant them to be drawn, one way or another.

One rather important fact that Smith observes about painting and sculpture is that there is, so he thinks, a wider latitude in possible objects of imitation permissible in the case of painting. In particular, the ugly and disagreeable are proper objects of painterly imitation but not of sculptural.

> In Painting, the imitation frequently pleases, though the original object be indifferent, or even offensive. In Statuary and Sculpture it is otherwise. The imitation seldom pleases, unless the original object be in a very high degree either great or beautiful, or interesting.[8]

Clearly, this a priori limit on the sculptural simply reflects a long-standing artistic fashion, still current in Smith's day, and not some transcendental form of aesthetic thought. Nevertheless, it can be seen to follow, or at least be explained after the fact, on the basis of Smith's main premise. For if we think (as Smith did) of the pleasure in artistic imitation as being a summation of forces—one being the pleasure we take in the excellence of the imitation, another the pleasure we take in the beauty or agreeableness of the object imitated, a third the pleasure taken in the unlikeness of medium to object—then when the object of imitation puts nothing into the equation, or, as in the case of the ugly and disagreeable, a negative quantity, this can be made up, in the hedonic calculus, by an increase in the excellence of the imitation; but where that has reached its limit, as in the case of a master, it can be made up only by an increase in the dissimilarity of medium to object. Hence, on Smith's view, painting has it over sculpture, since the medium of painting, being two-dimensional, is more unlike its three-dimensional objects than is the three-dimensional medium of statuary. This, I suspect, is something like the line of reasoning Smith must have had in mind, but left unspoken, in observing what was commonplace in his time, that the objects of painting could be low (witness the Dutch school of the seventeenth century), but those of sculpture must be exalted, since painting could make up for the disagreeableness of the subject by the dissimilarity of the medium, whereas sculpture could not, and had to rely more on beauty of model. For this reason, too, he reached the familiar conclusion of such comparative arguments in his day that: "There would seem, therefore, to be more merit in the one species of imitation [that is, painting] than in the other."[9]

Another distinguishing mark favoring painting over sculpture is the presence of color in the former. Sculpture is traditionally uncolored, and displeasing (on Smith's view) otherwise. (I presume that Smith and his contemporaries did not yet know that Greek statues were colored.) This too follows from the major thesis of Smith's essay;

but unlike the previous corollary, Smith does not fail here to make the implication clear. His argument is an intriguing one which, as we shall see, has significance beyond the specific point in question. What Smith is maintaining, essentially, throughout the essay, is that artistic imitation—representation, as we would call it and Smith occasionally does—is a delicate balance of excessive failure and excessive success: that is, between imitation that is not convincing at all, and imitation that is too convincing, thus becoming illusion. Sculpture, because its three-dimensional medium is very like the three-dimensional objects that it represents, is constantly in danger of coming too close to its original; and lack of color (since its objects of course are colored) keeps it from falling over the edge into a kind of trompe l'oeil or waxworks. Painting, however, since its two-dimensional medium is very unlike its three-dimensional objects, can absorb the extra realism that color affords without falling into illusion.

> It is not the want of colouring which hinders many things from pleasing in Statuary, which please in Painting; it is the want of the degree of disparity between the imitating and the imitated object, which is necessary, in order to render interesting the imitation of an object which is itself not interesting. Colouring, when added to Statuary, so far from increasing, destroys almost entirely the pleasure we receive from the imitation; because it takes away the great source of that pleasure, the disparity between the imitating and the imitated object.[10]

If we recall the three variables in our hedonic calculus of imitation, the point can be put another way. Pleasure in artistic imitation, it will be remembered, is directly proportional to the success of the imitation and the beauty or agreeableness of the object imitated, inversely proportional to the likeness of medium to object of imitation, with illusion as the upper limit on imitative success. When we color a statue, we do indeed increase the success of the imitation, which is a positive quantity in the equation; but we already begin, in sculpture, with the scales heavily tipped towards illusion, because of the similarity of medium to object of imitation. The introduction of color upsets the balance and, being too much of a good thing, results in "trompe l'oeil," or "deception," as Smith describes it.

There is no need, for our purposes, to discuss the other disparities between painting and sculpture that Smith enumerates, interesting though they all are, for our major concern is, of course, with his observations on music, those on the other arts merely necessary preliminaries. But there is a general conclusion that emerges from these observations on painting and sculpture already alluded to, and that is important for us to draw. It is this:

> The proper pleasure which we derive from those two imitative arts, so far from being the effect of deception, is altogether incompatible with it. That pleasure is founded altogether upon our wonder at seeing an object of one kind *represent* so well an object of a very different kind, and upon our admiration of the art which surmounts so happily that disparity which Nature had established between them.[11]

Smith correctly observes that illusion, or "deception," is quite inimical to artistic imitation; that our appreciation of it depends upon the imitation being recognizable, but depends too on its never being convincing to the extent of trepanning us. Once awareness of the artistic medium is lost—that is to say, once we take the imitation for the object imitated—the imitation ceases, on Smith's view, to be *artistic* imitation; for "our wonder at seeing an object of one kind represent so well an object of a very different kind" is lost once we cease to be aware of the "kind" doing the representing: that is, once we cease to be aware that there is a medium of representation and cease to perceive what that medium is (at least as a "phenomenological" object). And what is most interesting and philosophically important in the passage quoted above, is that in making this valid and perceptive point, Smith, unconsciously perhaps, substitutes "represent" for "imitate." This was just the point that was made in the first chapter, in response to the eighteenth-century theories of music as imitation. What Smith is really on the verge of realizing is that the concept of imitation is itself the wrong one for him to be using, just because imitation properly and well-brought-off implies illusion, deception, and loss of awareness of medium, all the things which Smith quite rightly decries in what he calls, most of the time, "artistic imitation," and what he should have called, and occasionally does call, "artistic representation." Had Smith realized why, at this crucial point, he felt obliged to speak of representation rather than imitation, he would have been able to express himself in this way. Artistic "imitation" is not imitation at all but representation, with all that that latter term does *not* imply: illusion, deception, and forgetfulness of the artistic medium of representation. I shall return to this point, which is an important one, in the closing sections of the present chapter; with the foregoing considerations in mind, we must now turn our attention to Smith's treatment of musical imitation.

◇ 3 ◇   Adam Smith held a theory about the origin of music, common in his own day, and in the century before. It is that music had its origin in speech. "The human voice," he wrote, "as it is always the best, so it would naturally be the first and earliest of all musical instruments: in singing, or in the first attempts towards singing, it would naturally employ sounds as similar as possible to those which it had been accustomed to; that is; it would employ words of some kind or other, pronouncing them only in time and measure, and generally with a more melodious tone than had been usual in common conversation."[12] From such theories of music's origin, it was customary to draw conclusions, usually unwarranted, about the nature of the musical art. Smith does not fail us in this; and in his case it is the imitative character of music, as well as the objects of musical imitation, that apparently (but not explicitly) are dictated by music's vocal-speech origins.

It is Smith's claim, to go straight to the point, that ". . .'Music, married to immortal Verse,' as Milton says, or even to words of any kind which have a distinct sense or meaning, is necessarily and essentially imitative."[13] Vocal music, for this clearly is what Smith has exclusively in mind here, imitates two separate but related things: human speech and human passion.[14] That being the case, purely instrumental music, without voice or text, can scarcely imitate at all on Smith's view, since it would be next to impossible for musical instruments alone, he believes, convincingly to simulate the human voice, and the human speaking voice is, he believes, for all intents and purposes, the *only* object of musical imitation. "The imitative powers of Instrumental are much inferior to those of Vocal Music; its melodious but unmeaning and inarticulated sounds cannot, like the articulations of the human voice, relate distinctly the circumstances of any particular story, or describe the different situations which those circumstances produced; or even express clearly, and so as to be understood by every hearer, the various sentiments and passions which the parties concerned felt from these situations: even its imitation of other sounds, the objects which it can certainly best imitate, is commonly so indistinct, that alone, and without any explication, it might not readily suggest to us what was the imitated object."[15]

That there really are, properly speaking, *two* objects of musical imitation, the human voice *and* human passions, rather than just one, is not altogether clear. For although Smith frequently talks about vocal music imitating the passions (instrumental music *arouses* them), what he seems to mean by that is merely that vocal music imitates the human voice as it would sound under the influence of, and expressing, one passion or another: "instrumental Music does not imitate, as vocal Music, as Painting, or as Dancing would imitate, a gay, a sedate, or a melancholy person. . . . [I]nstrumental music sooths us into each of these dispositions. . . ."[16] So what it all comes down to is that vocal music imitates the human speaking voice, and imitates the "passions" only in the sense of imitating the way the human voice sounds under their influence, when expressing them. In either case, it is the human speaking voice that seems for Smith the sole object of musical imitation, frequent remarks about music "imitating" the "passions" to the contrary notwithstanding, since imitating the passions in music is just a special case of imitating the human speaking voice.

At this point in the argument, Smith anticipates the charge that vocal music is hardly capable of producing any considerable resemblance to the human speaking voice, its supposed object of imitation. However, his previous remarks on painting and sculpture have laid the groundwork for a reply. "But it should be remembered, that to make a thing of one kind resemble another thing of a very different kind, is the very circumstance which, in all the Imitative Arts constitutes the merits of imitation; and that to shape, as it were to bend, the measure and melody of Music, so as to imitate the tone and the language of counsel and conversation, the accent and the style of emotion and passion, is to make a thing of one kind resemble another thing of a very different kind."[17] The point is an important one, vital to my argument to come, so I will take the liberty of quoting Smith in this regard at somewhat greater length. He continues:

> The tone and the movements of Music, though naturally very different from those of conversation and passion, may, however, be so managed as to seem to resemble them. On account of the great disparity between the imitating and the imitated object, the mind in this, as in the other cases [that is, painting and sculpture], cannot only be contented, but delighted, and even charmed and transported, with such an imperfect resemblance as can be had. Such imitative Music, therefore, when sung to words which explain and determine its meaning, may frequently appear to be a very perfect imitation.[18]

Now the bare observation that musical imitation, like the painterly and sculptural kind, thrives not just on the exactness of the imitation achieved, but on the dissimilarity between medium and object of imitation, is helpful so far as it goes. But Smith misses a golden opportunity here to strengthen and widen the prospects of musical representation, by failing to make clear the full implications of his own system. Had he been able to prepare his essay for the press, I cannot believe he would have allowed this omission to stand, and in rounding out Smith's account of musical imitation, I will take the liberty of repairing this defect, in the conviction that Smith would have done the same.

It will be recalled that the pleasure we take in painting and sculpture, on Smith's view, is a compound sum of the pleasure we take in the beauty or agreeableness of the object imitated, the success of the imitation, and the disparity of medium to object: the pleasure being directly proportional to each. Smith further points out that the disparity between medium and object of imitation, in painting and sculpture, is (at least in large part) a function of *dimensionality,* there being a descending order of similarity from the three-dimensional medium of sculpture to the two-dimensional medium of painting (where the objects of imitation are assumed to be three-dimensional). Surely, though, it is logical to extend this series to the nondimensional medium of music, that is to say, sound. Thus, what Smith ought to have said, beyond what he did say, in reply to the charge that musical imitation must be defective, since musical sound is so incapable of being at all like the objects of its imitation, is that being lowest in the series that begins with the three-dimensional medium of sculpture and ends in the nondimensional medium of sound, musical imitation makes up for its imitational deficit with the extraordinary disanalogy of its representational medium to the objects of its imitation. Had Smith made this move, implied by his own carefully worked out theory, he would then have seen, further, that there was no need for him to restrict both vocal and instrumental music to the imitation of *sound.* What he should have seen, and perhaps would have in preparing his essay for the press, is that he was not making full use of his principle of medium-disparity in music in so restricting it; insisting that sound, being dimensionless, can only imitate sound would be tantamount to insisting that painting, say, being two-dimensional, can only imitate two-dimensional objects. On the contrary, just because of the dissimilarity of its two-dimensional medium to its three-dimensional objects, a little bit of painterly resemblance goes a long way, according to Smith. What he failed to see is that the same argument could be applied to music; just because of the dissimilarity of its nondimensional medium to three-dimensional objects, even less musical resemblance would go even further. Smith's theory was far richer in possibilities for musical imitation than he himself apparently realized at the time of its formulation. I intend to make full use of that richness in what follows.

◊ 4 ◊   Adam Smith's theory is an ingenious one, and well worth the trouble of mulling over if only because of that, but I have not dredged it up from relative obscurity just to exhibit it as an historical curiosity, for it seems to me that it is not merely clever and well worked out, given the conceptual constraints under which Smith languished. I think there is something in it that is basically correct and useful in helping us to understand whatever fascination musical representation may hold for the listener. In order, however, to reap these benefits, I must, to a certain extent, meddle with Smith's theory; and it would be well for the reader to be warned that from now on I do not pretend to be interpreting Smith, but, rather, to be partially rebuilding his structure to suit contemporary needs.

Let me begin by saying, straightaway, that I will substitute my own terms, "picture," "representation," and "illustration," for Smith's "imitation" throughout, and at this point in the argument, there is, I think, no need to explain or justify that alteration, or to define my terms. I will also, naturally, be presenting my version of Smith's theory not just as a theory of vocal music, but of music tout court. With these preliminaries out of the way, we can begin in earnest.

I take it that a lot of eyebrows will be raised by Smith's rather naive-sounding assumption that there is a kind of natural likeness or unlikeness to be discerned between certain media of representation or picturing, and the objects illustrated. I am not convinced that that is so far from the truth, but in order to avoid unnecessary controversy, and also to reveal some further points of interest and importance, I shall try to express what Smith is getting at in a slightly less objectionable way.

Let me suggest, in this regard, that various artistic media might be described as more or less "recalcitrant" for various representational purposes, and that this has a bearing on—is a contributing factor to—our appreciation of the representation or picture. To illustrate what I have in mind here, what could be more recalcitrant material than marble in which to model pillows and upholstery? It is, surely, this seeming intractability of the material medium that contributes substantially to the effect of the representation, for example, in Antonio Canova's well-known rendering in marble of Napoleon's sister, Pauline Borghese, as a reclining Venus (Figure 5).

I say *seeming* intractability to underscore the point that it doesn't matter whether or not marble really is harder to represent pillows with than, say, clay (although I imagine it is), for the recalcitrance I am talking about need only be in the eyes of the beholder. It is, in part, our imaginatively perceiving the hardness of marble and the softness and pliability of upholstery, that enables us to savor the tour de force, the virtuosity of Canova's rendering. We must be aware of the material of representation as much as of the representation itself to appreciate the full artistic effect.

What I am suggesting, then, is that we substitute the notion of recalcitrance for natural resemblance in Smith's account to the following good purpose. It covers, to begin with, more relevant cases than the notion of natural resemblance can, even if the latter were a valid notion. Further, it avoids a concept that is now philosophically suspect in some persons' eyes. For recalcitrance is not necessarily a function of lack of resemblance, although in some instances it may be. Nor does it, as I have said, imply any *real* physical difficulty, although, again, that may indeed be present. It matters not whether it would have been easier for Canova to represent upholstery in clay than in marble. Perhaps it was easier for him in marble, and easier for someone else in clay. But it is how the aesthetic perceiver "identifies" with marble and clay, as a function of his or her real or imagined experiences of those materials, that determines what perhaps should be termed the *aesthetic* recalcitrance of marble as a medium for the representation of pillows and upholstery, and human flesh, for that matter.

If we now reconsider the general outlines of Smith's theory with this in mind, we get the following. Painting, sculpture and music each have, vis-à-vis any particular object of representation, some kind of "recalcitrance quotient." And in general, perhaps, though not in each particular case—another emendation of Smith's theory—the recalcitrance quotient increases, vis-à-vis three-dimensional objects of representation, from the three-dimensional medium of sculpture, to the two-dimensional medium of painting, to the nondimensional medium of music. I emphasize that this is an approximation because, on my view, there are three-dimensional objects for the representation of which some three-dimensional artistic medium might be more aesthetically recalcitrant than some two-dimensional medium. Thus I think marble is a more aesthetically recalcitrant medium for the representation of upholstery and flesh, say, then oil paint, although the former is a three-dimensional medium and the latter a two-dimensional one.

If we take the two parameters of artistic representation that have to do with the medium, on Smith's view, that is, the success of the representation (in any particular medium), and the aesthetic recalcitrance of the medium itself (I am not interested here in the beauty or agreeableness of the object of representation, Smith's third parameter), then we find that the pleasure we take in the representation increases, within certain limits, as the success of the representation and the recalcitrance of the medium.

Here, again, some alterations of Smith's theory will, I think, have to be made to accommodate contemporary philosophical sensibilities. For one thing, pleasure, even if one does not, as the eighteenth-century British tended to do, reify it into a mental object of palpable quantity, seems to suggest a kind of simple reaction to the work of art, on a par with eating ice cream or (when things go wrong) wormwood. Furthermore, Smith's treatment of the three variables, beauty or agreeableness of the object of representation, success of the representation, and recalcitrance of medium, suggests that like the relation, say, of pressure to temperature in a gas, the pleasure sum—that is, the value of the artwork qua representation—is a universal and infallible result. Both of these implications must be rejected. I propose, therefore, to substitute the concept of "appreciation" for that of "pleasure," and to make it clear that the relationship between our appreciation of artistic representation, and the variables of representational success and aesthetic recalcitrance of medium is by no means universal or indefeasible. Let me expand on this.

By the appreciation of a work of art I mean a complex perceptual and mental activity that involves, among other things, seeing, or hearing, or otherwise becoming aware of various aesthetic and artistic properties; conceptualizing, judging, reflecting on what one becomes aware of, in other words, whatever *relevantly* goes on when works of art are experienced by competent spectators, hearers, readers. I place all of this under the head of appreciation with, I believe, the sanction of English usage. And among the things that take place in the process of artistic appreciation, *one* of them often is, clearly, the apprehending of artistic representations. In that apprehension, I suggest, Smith is perfectly correct in distinguishing the appreciation of the success of the representation, and the appreciation of the aesthetic recalcitrance of the representational medium, relative to the representational success. The appreciation of a representation, as opposed to an imitation, demands both apprehension of the success of the representation and simultaneously, the continued consciousness of the medium of representation as medium along with its relative aesthetic recalcitrance, or lack thereof. I am sure Smith is correct too, in his claim that our appreciation of artistic representation is increased *both* by awareness of the success of the representation *and* awareness of the relative aesthetic recalcitrance of the representational medium. But because appreciation (as I construe it) is such a complex of various mental and perceptual activities, the waters are considerably more muddied than Smith would have us believe. In particular, there can be no simple relation as: appreciation increases as a compound ratio of representational success and recalcitrance of representational medium, for there are just too many other relevant factors in even the simplest examples of artistic representation waiting to perturb such a facile generalization. All we can safely say—but say with some confidence, I think—is that representational success and aesthetic recalcitrance of the medium of representation are always relevant to the appreciation of an artistic representation, and sometimes decisive.

◇ 5 ◇   But what of musical illustration, which is, of course, our principal concern? It seems to me that Smith's theory, as emended above, casts considerable light on the musical medium of illustration and, in particular, on our appreciation of the kinds of musical illustration we have discussed in the preceding chapters.

A frequent charge brought against the claims of musical illustration, in Smith's day as in ours, is that the capabilities of music to represent the world are so meagre as to render whatever clumsy success there may be in the endeavour completely barren of musical or aesthetic interest. But we now have both a way of formulating this objection more precisely, and at the same time, of providing something of an answer. The charge, simply put, is that the aesthetic recalcitrance of the sound medium for the illustration of any object or event, is too great to allow the degree of minimal success necessary for artistic appreciation of the illustration, even if it should be recognized as such. The answer is that the propounder of the objection has clearly overlooked the part that that very recalcitrance plays in making musical illustrations of artistic interest. He is hoist with his own petard, for the very aesthetic recalcitrance of medium that limits the success of musical illustrations, as compared to painting and sculpture, makes that limited success larger than life. The appreciation of musical illustration, like so much else in art, is the appreciation of obstacles overcome, difficulties circumvented, success over external or self-imposed constraints.

Further—and predictably, on Smith's view—it is just where the musical medium lacks aesthetic recalcitrance, in the picturing of things like bird songs and bells, that success of illustration is greatest and, of course, artistic interest nearly at the vanishing point. (It is just too easy to imitate a cuckoo's call on a flute.) Conversely, it is precisely when we pass beyond musical pictures of the most direct kind, to musical pictures that require the minimal information, and to musical representations both of sounds and non-sounds, that the medium becomes recalcitrant, illustrative success limited, relying on linguistic props, and musical interest increases exponentially. It is the ingeniousness of the musical picture or representation, its surprising success given the extreme recalcitrance of the medium of sound for the task, that fascinates us in Bach's and Handel's representations of everything from the plagues of Egypt to the doctrines of the Lutheran faith. And it is the sheer impossibility (we imagine) of representing a steam engine in a *musical* form, that makes *Pacific 231* so startling and aesthetically successful a piece of illustrative music. Honegger calls it a *Mouvement Symphonique*, which indeed it is, displaying all of the familiar techniques of motivic development one would expect in a symphonic piece. It is, as we saw, scored not for some exotic collection of noisemakers and percussion instruments, like Varèse's *Ionisation*, for example, but for the conventional large orchestra. It even achieves a distinctive kind of lyrical quality in some of its quiet moments (it *has* quiet moments) quite in contrast to the unrelieved din of Mossolov's *The Iron Foundry*. Symphonic, lyrical, quiet, conventionally orchestrated—what could be more aesthetically recalcitrant for the illustration of a piece of heavy industrial machinery than such a medium? It is, I am suggesting, that very recalcitrance, and the remarkable success within the constraints that that recalcitrant medium imposes, that makes Honegger's illustration artistically interesting, not merely a musical curiosity. Urmson observes that: "Since the sounds of the world around us are in general readily distinguishable from anything that could be called music in the conventional sense, it follows that musical representation will be in general unlike what is represented," and adds, in defense of musical representation, that "such departures from strict fidelity as are dictated by the nature and conventions of the medium do not count as impairing the resemblance."[19] Perhaps it would be better, in light of Smith's theory, as emended, to put this conclusion in a more positive manner. Far from impairing musical representation, the lack of fidelity dictated by the nature and conventions of the musical medium— which is to say, its aesthetic recalcitrance—aesthetically enhances it.

I have been arguing, then, that the medium of musical sound holds interest for us as a medium of illustration not in spite of its aesthetic recalcitrance but, in effect, because of it, and I have tried, with the help of an updated version of Adam Smith's theory of musical imitation, to spell this out in some detail, giving what explanation I could. But it has been assumed, right along, that the notion of sound as the medium of musical representation, is as unproblematical as the notion, say, of marble as a medium of sculpture or oil on canvas as a medium of representational painting. However, at the outset, it was observed that where music is notational—as is all of the music with which this book concerns itself—the musical medium is far from easy to descry. And yet I believe that in spite of the complications that notation and scores bring to the question, it makes perfect sense to describe the medium of musical representation as sound—the same sense, in fact, as it makes to describe Phidias' medium as marble or Seurat's as oil on canvas. But this claim requires argument.

◇ 6 ◇   I begin with a story that may be true. Brahms, it is said, was once invited by a friend to attend a performance of *Don Giovanni* (I think it was), and is supposed to have replied, pointing to the score on his shelf: "Why should I go out, when I can hear just as good a performance at home?"

It is difficult, perhaps, for the uninitiated to imagine exactly what goes on when someone of Brahms's musical stature reads a score. We must believe that Brahms "heard in his head" a full-fledged performance of Mozart's work. There are few musicians in any generation either with the thoroughness of training or the mental equipment to perform this feat, but what Brahms was describing is the favored relationship of musician to score and score to music: all other relationships fall short. So it is to this optimal use of the musical score that we must refer in defining its nature, and its relation to music and the musical intellect. Briefly, a score, which is the most refined and complex form that Western musical notation takes, can be "realized" by the musician who is sufficiently gifted, as a "mental performance."

In this particular sense, I think, a score is markedly different from, say, the printed text of a play, although philosophers have tended recently to lump the two together under the head of "notation." The difference, put quite baldly, is this. When I read *Hamlet* I do not "hear voices"; but when Brahms "read" *Don Giovanni* he "heard music." To refine this somewhat, I am not failing to respond optimally or properly to the printed page when, in reading the text of *Hamlet*, I fail to reproduce in my imagination the sounds of voices in soliloquy and dialogue. Perhaps there are people who do respond to texts in this way; but that would not be the typical response. Reading is not usually or optimally taken to be a process whereby "mental speech" is produced. A musical score, on the other hand, is being "read" properly and optimally just when it is producing in the musical imagination of the "reader" the mental sound of music. Reading a text does not normally entail the production of mental speech. Reading a score *is* intended, at its best, to produce a mental performance.

Of course, in calling the relation of reader to score where the reader can realize a mental performance the "optimal" one, I am not suggesting this as the only proper relationship; but reflection on the history of the musical score as we know it, and on the difference between a score and a set of performance parts, or a tablature, will underline, I think, the very special role that the score has come to play in Western music.

Although polyphonic music before about 1225 was written in, and performed from score, from that time until the seventeenth century, scores, apparently, did not exist at all. And from the beginning of the seventeenth to the end of the eighteenth, they went from "very rare" to "not all that common." It is sometimes said that the major function of

the score is to give the musician instructions for realizing a performance. The fact is that the artifacts that best fit the description "instructions for realizing a performance" are performing parts and tabla-
tures. Indeed, we can obtain the score of a Renaissance motet, for
example, only by deriving it from the part-books, in which form the
music survives. Part-books, distributed among a group of singers, provided them with instructions for realizing a performance; and if each
correctly followed his part, a performance emerged. The modern vocal score was unheard of in the "golden age" of choral singing. The
individual singer could not see what was going on in the other parts
and like the performers in a string quartet or a symphony orchestra,
he could only follow the instruction in his part, trusting that the others
would follow theirs.

A set of parts alone cannot give a picture of the whole, as can a score.
A tablature is, indeed, a kind of score, for, unlike a part, it contains the
whole composition. But it does not contain the music as a visible structure that eye and mind can translate into "mental sounds." It is merely
a recipe—instructions for the fingers—which, if properly followed, will
result in a performance of the work.

What then is the peculiar essence of the score? Scores came on the
scene, I would urge, when music became an object to be studied, and
not merely something ephemeral to be performed, heard, and then
forgotten. To be sure, a score was also a practical necessity when musical compositions became so complex and the band of performers so
large, that a conductor was required to realize a performance ade-
quately. But as late as Haydn's time, conductors frequently had before
them only a figured bass, if they conducted from the keyboard, or a
first violin part, if from the concertmaster's desk. The score is preeminently the musical work carved in marble: it provides the means
whereby a permanent "master piece"—which is what music has now
become—is preserved for perusal by those who are capable of "reading" it. To perform Beethoven's *Eroica* one still needs only a set of
parts. To "read" it one needs a score. Dump a set of parts in a musician's lap and only if he is a Mozart can he comprehend the whole work
from them, and even Mozart had his limits. It is the score that makes a
musical work "readable," and although it has other (important) uses as
well, it is preeminently the means whereby Brahms could "hear" *Don
Giovanni* at home.

There is, interestingly enough, a much discredited theory of language, that of John Locke, which seems to me to be (on one interpretation, anyway) a viable and enlightening account of the relation at its

optimal level of "reader" to musical score. Locke, it will be recalled, in Book III of the *Essay Concerning Human Understanding*, represents speech and written language as a kind of stimulus-instrument whereby the speaker or writer may hope to arouse in his listener or reader those ideas which he is presently experiencing, is now conscious of, and wishes to convey to another. "The use then of Words," Locke says, "is to be sensible marks of *Ideas*; and the *Ideas* they stand for, are their proper and immediate Significations."[20] He continues:

> The use Men have of these Marks, being either to record their own Thoughts for the Assistance of their own Memory; or as it were, to bring out their *Ideas*, and lay them before the view of others . . . . When a Man speaks to another, it is that he may be understood; and the end of Speech [or writing] is, that those Sounds [or written words], as Marks, may make known his *Ideas* to the Hearer [or reader].

Now it is innocuous enough, and trivially true, to state, as Locke does, that the end of speech and writing (or one of the ends, at least) is to make known our ideas to others, just so long as an unexceptionable construction be put on "idea" and "make known"; for surely all would agree that one of the main uses of the spoken and written word is to make our ideas known to others. The fact is, however, that Locke notoriously does not put unexceptionable constructions on either, but, rather, looks upon making known one's ideas as somehow giving rise in the hearer or reader to the same mental events that are directly present to one's consciousness when one speaks or writes. Thus:

> Concerning Words also it is farther to be considered. *First,* That they being immediately the Signs of Mens *Ideas;* and, by that means, the Instruments whereby Men communicate their Conceptions, and express to one another those Thoughts and Imaginations, they have within their own Breasts, *there comes by constant use,* to be such a *Connexion between Sounds, and the* Ideas *they stand for,* that Names heard [or seen], almost as readily excite certain Ideas, as if the Objects themselves, which are apt to produce them, did actually affect the Senses.[21]

As Jonathan Bennett glosses such passages:

> To attach meaning to an utterance, then, is to make it "stand as a mark" for one or more "internal conceptions" or "ideas" in one's own mind, and language's main task is to transfer ideas from one

mind to another. This is the translation view of language: wishing to share with you something in my mind, I translate it into the public medium of articulate sounds; you hear the objective, interpersonal noises that I make, and re-translate them back into something in your mind; and so communication is complete.[22]

I have no intention of rehearsing in detail the many familiar objections to Locke's theory of language, except to point out that one very general difficulty with it turns out, on reflection, to be just what makes it a good account of scores and score-reading. It seems an unnecessary and irrelevant demand on language that the mental events or ideas running through my head when I utter or write "Man bites dog" be stimulated in my hearer or reader for understanding to take place. My "thought content" may (or may not) have consisted in a very vivid image of a short, wild-eyed, red-haired man biting a Saint Bernard on the nose, while my hearer or reader, in understanding correctly what I have spoken or written, may have no mental image at all, or a very different one, say, that of a tall, neatly dressed, dark-haired man biting a Barkless Basenji on the ear. My evidence for having been correctly understood is a proper response, not an accurate introspective report. It is not necessary for my utterance or writing to produce in my hearer or reader a mental image or mental "linguistic performance," for it to have served its communicative purpose. But that is just what a musical score must do in the optimal case. Indeed, a musical paraphrase of Locke's most unfavorable account of his theory of language quoted above—the account which lends itself most readily to what Bennett calls the "translation view of language"—is the most favorable for describing what went on when Brahms "read" *Don Giovanni:*

> Concerning scores, they being immediately the signs of men's musical ideas, and by that means the instruments whereby men communicate their musical conceptions, and express to one another those musical thoughts and imaginations they have within their own minds, there comes by continual use such a connection between certain notational devices and the sounds they stand for, that the notational devices almost as readily excite certain "sounds in the mind" as if the sounds themselves did actually affect the senses.

All properly trained musicians undergo, early on, what is called "ear training and dictation," in which they are required to record in musical notation increasingly long and complex musical passages played by the teacher at the keyboard. This is the beginning of that process designed to make musical notation "by continual use" to have "such a connection" with heard sounds that "the notational devices almost as readily excite certain 'sounds in the mind' as if the sounds themselves did actually affect the senses." Few ever reach the ultimate goal: the ability to "read" a score in lieu of a performance, or record musical thoughts, as Bach did the *Orgelbüchlein,* without the aid of a musical instrument, as readily as one is able to record one's thoughts in written language, without the necessity of reciting aloud first. But the paucity of those who achieve such facility with a musical notation should not be allowed to obscure the fact that *that* is the heart of the matter.

A notation stands to a musical performance and the musical medium in *something* like the way the engraver's copper plate stands to the prints that are pulled from it, although I do not at this point want to carry the analogy to its logical and ontological conclusion. Neither the plate nor the score is an end unto itself. The medium of the engraver is ink on paper, and the medium of the composer is sound. But the engraver must know what to do to the copper plate in order to get his print to come out right, and the composer, likewise, must know what to do within his notational system to enable others to "pull" performances from his score, either mentally, by reading it, or physically, by playing from it or from parts. Thus the copper plate stands between the engraver and his artistic medium, ink on paper, as an instrument that must be mastered in order to work the medium satisfactorily; and since the seventeenth century (before which scores were rare), in Western art music, the score has likewise, stood between the composer and *his* artistic medium, *sound,* as an instrument that must be mastered in order to work that medium. The difference—a not inconsiderable one, but irrelevant at this point—is that musical notation is a symbol system and the engraver's copper plate is not, which is why the composer but not the engraver can make a syntactical mistake (for example, notating D-sharp for E-flat) without impairing the effect that his notational instrument has on his medium.

The upshot of all this is, I hope, to show that although notation makes the relationship between the composer and his medium more indirect and complex, it does not make the concept of the musical medium as sound either suspect, or in any way problematical, any more than the intervention between the engraver and his medium of the copper plate puts it in doubt that his medium is ink and paper. It is indeed the case that the relationship between the engraver and his plate is a physical one while that between the composer and his score is distinctly cerebral. That may have all sorts of psychological, sociological, and practical implications. Perhaps it eventually made the composer an "intellectual," and hence more welcome in the drawing room (although Haydn, for a large part of his creative life, still wore livery and ate in the kitchen). Be all that as it may, the "physical" composer/performer, who works without a notation, has as direct a physical relationship to his or her medium as any worker of wood or engraver of plates. Notation and scores made (and make) that relationship less direct; but the medium remains sound. What must be remarked, simply, is that the kind of musical mind notations and scores require is just that kind of mind that can achieve the intimate relationship to the sound medium, through the notational system, that makes possible Brahms's reading of *Don Giovanni* and Bach's composition of the *Orgelbüchlein* under house arrest.

◇ 7 ◇   The purpose of this chapter has been twofold: to explore some of the parameters of sound as the representational medium of music; and to argue that the existence of notation and score do not cloud the issue to the extent of rendering talk about sound as the medium of music metaphorical, or anything less than literal. The overarching purpose, however, has been to head off any claim to the effect that because there is no identifiable medium of musical representation, music cannot, properly speaking, be representational at all. For the present, I will consider that claim satisfactorily answered, although a contemporary revival of it will be discussed in detail when we come to consider various anti-representational claims of the musical "purists."

It would be a mistake, however, to downplay the implications of notation and score for a satisfactory philosophical account of music in general, and musical representation in particular. For although the fact that music is an "allographic" art does not, as we have seen, undermine of itself the commonsense notion that sound is its representational medium, it does raise other questions, of a serious nature, as to the very possibility of representation in music. Our account cannot be secure without coming to terms with them in at least a provisional, if not conclusive way.

CHAPTER VI

Notation as Representation

◇ 1 ◇   Observers of the contemporary scene in the philosophy of art will not be surprised to find the name of Nelson Goodman occurring in a discussion of the significance of musical notation for an account of representation in music. For it is safe to say that all philosophical discussion of musical notation must begin with Goodman, since he is, so far as I know, not only the first, but the only philosopher of rank to have given musical notation a philosophical—that is to say, a logical—treatment. This alone would have demanded recognition by anyone pretending to write seriously on the possibility of representational music. But further, it was one of the conclusions of Goodman's investigation, as a matter of fact, that musical "representation," strictly speaking, is impossible, if the music one is talking about is notated in the standard way: "if a performance of a work defined by a standard score denotes at all," Goodman writes, "it still does not represent. . . . [M]usic under standard notation," he continues, "if denotative at all, is descriptive." This he calls "a minor curiosity, especially since denotation plays so small a role in music."[1] But though perhaps a "minor curiosity" for a general theory of representation, it is a disastrous one, if true, for a theory of musical representation. So we must either refute or come to terms with it if what has preceded, and what is to follow, are to stand. I intend to do a little bit of both in the present chapter. But before I can do either, we must first master at least the bare bones of Goodman's system, along with its carefully worked out but somewhat off-putting terminological distinctions. To that preliminary task we first must turn. It divides itself into two parts: an account of notation; and an account of representation—from the two of which Goodman's conclusion with regard to the impossibility of musical representation is meant to follow.

◇ 2 ◇   Notational systems, whether musical or not, must, on Goodman's view, satisfy two syntactic and three semantic requirements.

The first syntactic requirement is that of *character-indifference.* "Two marks are character-indifferent if each is an inscription (that is, always belongs to some character) and neither one belongs to any character the other does not."[2] A lower-case "a," a capital "a," and an italic "a" are character-indifferent, each belonging to one character and no other, and all, therefore, interchangeable. The characters in a notational system must, in other words, be *disjoint*. A written mark might *look like* an instance both of the first letter of the alphabet and the fourth, and that is the kind of practical problem that arises in the design of any notational system. But it is a logical requirement of notational systems that no mark *is* an instance of more than one character, regardless of the practical difficulties there might be in determining which character it is an instance of (for example, in deciphering a manuscript). The mark is either an "a" or a "d"—it cannot be both—and this leads to the second syntactical requirement.

The second syntactic requirement of a notational system "is that the characters be *finitely differentiated*, or *articulate*."[3] The opposite of such a system is one that is syntactically *dense:* where there are "infinitely many characters so ordered that between each two there is a third," such that "no mark can be determined to belong to one rather than to many other characters."[4] This does not mean that if we have no specific procedure for deciding whether a mark is or is not an instance of a given character, we do not have a syntactically articulate system. (We do not have such a system for the alphabet.) "Rather, we adopt a policy of admitting no mark as an inscription of a letter unless and until we can decide that the mark belongs to no other letter."[5]

"The first semantic requirement upon notational systems is that they be *unambiguous;* for obviously the basic purpose of a notational system can be served only if the compliance relationship is invariant."[6] The basic purpose of a notation is uniquely to define a class of correct performances. Such a class is a "compliance-class," and members of the class are said to "comply" with the notation. A score is a character in a notational system, and it seems to define all correct performances, all bona fide instances of a musical work. The semantic requirement of being *unambiguous* can be illustrated either by a score—say, the score of Beethoven's *Eroica*—or some individual character in a notation—say, the character for middle C. Both must be unambiguous in that there can be no more than one correct way of complying with each.

Any ambiguous *character* must be excluded, even if its inscriptions are all unambiguous; for since different inscriptions of it will have different compliants, some inscriptions that count as true copies of each other will have different compliance classes. In either case, identity of work will not be preserved in every chain of steps from performance to covering score and from score to compliant performance.[7]

That is to say, the very purpose of a notational system uniquely to determine a compliance class of performances, will have been defeated if ambiguity creeps in.

The second semantic requirement of notational systems is that *"the compliance-classes must be disjoint.* For if two different compliance-classes intersect, some inscription will have two compliants such that one belongs to a compliance-class that the other does not; and a chain from compliant to inscription to compliant will thus lead from a member of one compliance-class to something outside that class."[8] Work or compliance identity will thereby be destroyed.

Finally, a notational system requires semantic *finite differentiation.* That is to say, *"for every two characters K and K' and every object h that does not comply with both, determination either that h does not comply with K or that h does not comply with K' must be theoretically possible."*[9]

◇ 3 ◇   We are now in a position to see what Goodman means by a "score," and what by a musical "work." Goodman writes: "a score, as I conceive it, is a character in a notational language, the compliants of a score are typically performances, and the compliance-class is a work."[10] Let us unpack this.

As I understand it, Goodman is using "score" here in a somewhat wider sense than would a musician. As we shall soon see, however, he also uses it, because of the heavy syntactic and semantic requirements he places on notational systems, in a narrower sense as well. What makes his use of "score" more lenient than the musician's is his willingness to call, say, the first oboe "part" of the *Eroica* a "score," whereas the musician would reserve the word "score" only for the whole, of which the oboe "part" is an extract. A "score," on Goodman's view, is any character or series of characters in a notational system that has a compliant, and since all proper renderings—that is, "performances"—of the first oboe part are compliants and constitute a compliance-class, the part qualifies, in Goodman's system, as a score, as would, I suppose, any fragment of a score with a compliance-class.

Goodman is well-known in philosophical circles for his nominalism, and clearly, it is his nominalistic commitments that inform his notion of what a musical work is, and what relation it bears to its score. Unwilling, I take it, to allow the musical work the status of a type or universal

(construed Platonically), he identifies the musical work—the *Eroica,*
say—with the class of correct performances: that is, the compliance-
class. Spelled out more fully:

> A score, we found, defines a work but is a peculiar and privi-
> leged definition without competitors. A class is uniquely deter-
> mined by a score, as by an ordinary definition; but a score, unlike
> an ordinary definition, is also uniquely determined by each mem-
> ber of that class. Given the notational system and a performance of
> a score, the score is recoverable. Identity of work and of score is
> retained in any series of steps, each of them either from compliant
> performance to score-inscription, or from score-inscription to
> compliant performance, or from score-inscription to true copy.
> This is ensured by the fact, and only by the fact, that the language
> in which the score is written must be notational—must satisfy the
> five stated requirements.[11]

Two important ancillary points follow from this: first, that nothing
qualifies as a performance of a work unless it complies *exactly* with the
score; and, second, that anything not satisfying the five requirements
is not, properly speaking, a part of the score or, in consequence, a requirement of a performance. As a result of the first point, a rendering
of the *Eroica* with one wrong note in the second oboe part is not a "performance" of the *Eroica* at all—is not an instance of the *Eroica,* since it
does not comply (exactly) with the score. As a result of the second
point, the instruction *Allegro con brio,* which Beethoven put at the beginning of the first movement, is not a proper part of the score, since
the language of *verbal* tempo indications is not a notational system, violating the *unambiguity, differentiation,* and *disjointness* criteria.[12] "On the
other hand, metronomic specifications of tempo do . . . qualify as notational and may be taken as belonging to the score as such." The seemingly paradoxical result of this would be that a "performance" of the
first movement of the *Eroica* at ♩=61 would not be a performance of
the *Eroica* at all, since Beethoven marked it ♩=60; whereas a "performance" of the first movement of the Fifth Brandenburg Concerto,
marked by Bach *Allegro,* if it lasted ten hours from beginning to end,
would be a performance of that movement, as the metronome had not
yet been invented, and the designation *Allegro,* not being a proper part
of the score, on Goodman's view, would not be a proper part of the
definition of the work. It is, of course, this second point that caused me
to say, earlier, that Goodman uses "score" in a narrower sense than
does the musician, who would "check the score" to see if Bach had

made a tempo indication for the first movement of the Fifth Brandenburg.

I do not yet offer either of these two "paradoxical" results as criticism
of Goodman, although many find them decisive against his view of the
musical work. I shall, further on, raise the question of their plausibility
(or lack thereof); but the question has deeper implications than simply
whether Goodman is right or wrong on these two specific points, and,
in fact, has to do with just how, in a very basic sense, one goes about
doing philosophy. For the nonce, I leave it merely stated; for our task
right now is to see how, on Goodman's view of music, it follows that
music cannot "represent." We have the bare bones of the musical theory. We must now proceed with the theory of representation.

◇ 4 ◇   I shall not go further into the intricacies of Goodman's theory of representation than is necessary for the purpose of understanding his proscription of musical representation, except to make the
most basic terminological distinctions. On Goodman's view, for something to represent something else, it must "denote" it. "The plain fact is
that a picture, to represent an object, must be a symbol for it, stand for
it, refer to it. . . . Denotation is the core of representation and is independent of resemblance."[13] Thus, a portrait of Sir Winston Churchill
denotes, refers to, Churchill.

This immediately raises an obvious question. How can denotation
be a necessary condition of representation, since in the case of unicorns, there are pictures that represent them, but, no unicorns for the
pictures to denote, as the picture of Churchill denotes the man? Here
Goodman wishes to distinguish between an *x*-picture and a picture of
x. A picture of Churchill may picture him as an English bulldog. It is a
picture of Churchill, and denotes *him;* but it is an English-bulldog-
picture. The picture of the unicorn in the Unicorn Tapestry is a
unicorn-picture; but it is not a picture *of* anything, does not denote at
all.

Saying that a picture represents a soandso is thus highly ambiguous as between saying what the picture denotes and saying what
kind of picture it is. Some confusion can be avoided if in the latter
case we speak rather of a "Pickwick-representing-picture" or a
"unicorn-representing-picture" or a "man-representing-picture,"
or, for short, of a "Pickwick-picture" or "unicorn-picture" or
"man-picture." Obviously a picture cannot, barring equivocation,
both represent Pickwick and represent nothing. But a picture may

be of a certain kind—be a Pickwick-picture or a man-picture—without representing anything.[14]

If, then, denotation is a necessary condition for being a representation at all, it shares that condition with at least one other kind of symbol: the *description*. What distinguishes the two? In brief, descriptions are *articulate,* representations are *dense.* More fully:

> A notational system, we saw, satisfies five requirements. A language, notational or not, satisfies at least the first two: the syntactic requirements of disjointness and differentiation. Ordinary languages usually violate the remaining, semantic, requirements. Nonlinguistic systems differ from languages, depiction from description, the representational from the verbal, paintings from poems, primarily through lack of differentiation—indeed through density (and consequent total absence of articulateness)—in the symbol scheme. . . . A scheme is representational only insofar as it is dense; and a symbol is a representation only if it belongs to a scheme dense throughout or to a dense part of a partially dense scheme.[15]

We can now see why, on Goodman's view, music cannot *represent.* Put quite succinctly, it is because musical notations, and their compliants, are articulate rather than dense. In a dense scheme every gradation is significant. In a series of pictures of men at a given distance: "According to the representational system, any difference in height among these images [of men] constitutes a difference in height of men represented."[16] These images, considered as marks of characters in a symbol system, as Goodman so construes them, in this sense are dense, not articulate; whereas the following examples of musical notation are articulate, not dense (Example 23).

EXAMPLE 23

Marks of the characters are of different sizes in the two instances, but each mark in the first excerpt, though larger than the corresponding one in the second, is a mark of the same character; and any other gradations of size we might want to put in between would be equally irrelevant. So, on Goodman's view, the descending figure to which Beethoven sets the words "descendit de coelis" in the Mass in C, is, like "descendit de coelis" itself, a description rather than a picture of the Incarnation, for "descendit de coelis," like Beethoven's descending figure, is part of an articulate system.

◇ 5 ◇   The implications of Goodman's conclusion for present purposes are not easy to determine in any clear or completely conclusive way. Much of what I have characterized as musical illustration, would, I am certain, survive as musical "description" in Goodman's sense of that word. Some crucially important things would not survive, however; and I will get to those in a moment. But if one were to find Goodman's account of representation palatable, one could, I think, at least be able to bring some of what I have had to say (and will have to say) into conformity with it. Indeed here, as almost nowhere else, ordinary talk and received musical opinion seem, if not to support Goodman, at least not to contradict him, for what I have called musical "pictures," "representations," and "illustrations" are often called indifferently, musical "descriptions." And "descriptive music" as a label for a lot of what I have been talking about is quite canonical.

But as is well-known, a great many of the ways Goodman wishes to talk about music are quite at odds with the ways those that spend a good deal of their lives talking about it are wont to do. Goodman's attitude towards objections, that he runs roughshod over ordinary art-talk, is equally well-known. In response to the claim that it is absurd to say a "performance" with one wrong note is not a "performance" (of the work in question), Goodman's response essentially is *so much the worse for the way we ordinarily talk:*

> the composer or musician is likely to protest indignantly at refusal to accept a performance with a few wrong notes as an instance of a work; and he surely has ordinary usage on his side. But ordinary usage here points the way to disaster for theory. . . .[17]

There surely is no quick answer to Goodman's preference for philosophical theory over linguistic practice, or, for that matter, a quick answer to the opposite preference. Indeed, as I suggested earlier, the two alternatives represent a sharp dichotomy in philosophical method and taste. And I cannot do better in characterizing it than to quote Stuart Hampshire's well-wrought characterization of this same dichotomy, as represented in the moral theories of Aristotle and Spinoza. Hampshire writes:

> Aristotle states clearly that moral theory must be in accord with established opinions and must explain these opinions as specifications of more general principles. . . . Acceptable theory will not undermine moral opinions nor bring about a systematic moral conversion.
>
> By contrast, Spinoza in the Ethics claims to be showing a path to a necessary moral conversion which philosophical and moral theory introduce. . . . admittedly, most of our ordinary moral opinions are reaffirmed after the conversion; but a few of them are wholly repudiated, as depending on a false theory of the mind and on a false metaphysics.[18]

For present purposes I can only take this division of philosophical methods to be irreconcilable. One must adopt one or the other of them as a matter of faith, or intuition, or taste. My own taste (I have neither faith nor intuition) is Aristotelian; and I prefer to talk music with the philosophically vulgar, who are, at the same time, the musically learned. While admiring the austere beauty of Goodman's system, I will, I am afraid, lay dirty, workman's hands on it, and do what I must to bring it into conformity with language in the musical workshop. For this I beg indulgence of the gods of theory (if gods there be).

It might be well to begin by remarking again on some of the aspects of what the musician normally calls a score that Goodman rules out because of his stringent syntactic and semantic conditions on notation. It is customary to consult the score to determine at what tempo a piece is to be performed; but if the tempo is indicated in words and not metronomically, as it would have to have been before 1816, and frequently is even in music composed after the invention of the metronome, it is not a proper part of the "score" on Goodman's construal, and a performance *at any tempo at all* a compliant with the score and, hence, a bona fide instance of the work. Again, if the composer marks his composition *espressivo,* or *dolce,* that is to say, uses language, technical or not, to describe the manner (apart from tempo) in which his piece should go, he is not doing anything to his score, and hence, on Goodman's view, is placing no constraint on what is a bona fide instance of the work.

Now there is no doubt that certain departures from proper tempo or manner of performance do not result in cases that would ordinarily be described as "not an instance of the work at all." If I play the first movement of a Haydn piano sonata *Andante* when it is marked *Allegro,* and ignore all of the other instructions as to manner of performance that Haydn has left us in his score, my performance might be described as inept, or insensitive, or something of the kind; it would be thought a very bad performance, but scarcely a non-performance—certainly a genuine instance of the work. On the other hand, it is possible to ignore such instructions to a degree that destroys the musical integrity of the work and would thus constitute a failure to produce an instance of it. Thus, I suggested earlier, a rendering of a movement that would ordinarily take ten minutes to perform, at a tempo that would make it last ten hours, would be described as an instance of the work by scarcely anyone but the most confirmed convert to the gospel of Goodman.

More to the point, it seems to me that certain of the properties of musical works (as usually construed) that fall *outside* those works on Goodman's construal, contribute palpably to many of the kinds of musical illustration I have been discussing—indeed are, in part, constitutive of them. Tempo, for example, not only contributes to the effectiveness of certain musical illustrations but is absolutely essential to their effect—in my opinion, essential to their being illustrations at all. The buzzing of insects that Handel represents in "He spake the word," in *Israel in Egypt,* cannot possibly work if the tempo is too slow (it is marked *Andante Larghetto* in the Chrysander edition), for it relies upon the thirty-second notes in the violins going fast enough to chatter and hum. In this particular case, the representation is of the "sounds like" variety, and tempo is one of its essential parameters. The same is true of the Sonata that opens Bach's Cantata 31. The representation of laughter can only come off (again, it is of the "sounds like" kind) if a tempo within a certain range is chosen. (The Bachgesellschaft edition has it marked *Allegro.*) Choose, for example, *Largo,* with ♪ = 60, and the relations of note values remain, but all resemblance to the sound of laughter will vanish. One can, of course, obstinately insist that such things are not essential properties of the music; that performances that completely obliterate representational parts of a work are very bad performances, but performances of the work nonetheless. But to so insist would be to fly in the face of all musical intelligence and sensibility. There is, after all, a limit even to the nonsense that can be written about music.

Honegger's *Pacific 231* is an even more startling case in point. For the whole pictorial effect is the result of choosing the proper tempo, and manipulating rhythmic pulse and note value in such a way as to achieve the sounds of an engine in motion. Honegger uses metronome indications throughout, and these, of course, fulfill Goodman's notational requirements, but it is easy to imagine such a piece being given only the traditional linguistic directions as to tempo. In that case tempo would not be a part of the work, sending all pictorial qualities up the spout.

It would be well to dwell for a moment on the implications of these cases. If one believes, as I do, that illustrative properties are genuine properties of musical works, and if it is indeed the case, as I have tried to show, that tempo is often an essential part of such representational properties, then, if one construes an instance of a work as a compliant with the score, one must allow linguistic instructions as to tempo, which do *not* fulfill all of Goodman's notational criteria, as proper parts of scores. My own view of the matter is that if the illustrative character of works like *Pacific 231* must fall by the wayside in construing works and scores as Goodman construes them, then so much the worse for Goodman's construal: it must be brought into conformity, in this regard, with the ordinary concepts and language of musicians.

What of those, though, who are committed followers of Goodman here? They must be content, I think, to see a great deal—although by no means everything—that would be considered illustrative in music go by the boards. Nor is tempo the only troublesome parameter. I cannot see that, on Goodman's view, certain aspects of dynamics could be saved—aspects that are essential to various illustrative effects in music. To understand this we must remind ourselves just what it is about verbal indications of tempo that Goodman finds objectionable. It is, it will be recalled, that they violate the notational conditions of *unambiguity, disjointness,* and *differentiation.*

> Apparently almost any words may be used to indicate pace and mood. Even if unambiguity were miraculously preserved, semantic disjointness would not be. And since a tempo may be prescribed as fast, or as slow, or as between fast and slow, or as between fast and between-fast-and-slow, and so on without limit, semantic differentiation goes by the board, too.[19]

Thus, whereas numerical tempo indications of the metronomic kind are unambiguous, disjoint, and differentiated—there is one discrete, unambiguous, unique compliant, say to ♩=60, not admitting of degrees—verbal descriptions of tempo violate all three. Is *Allegro moderato* faster than *Allegro ma non troppo*? How fast is *Quite briskly*? And, of course, since as Goodman points out, gradations between verbally indicated tempi are continuous rather than discrete, they are in this respect *dense*, and hence not properly notational.

But the very same nonnotational features accrue to verbal indications of dynamics, *piano, forte, pianissimo*, and the like, and to the musical signs that mark the gradual increase and decrease of volume: that is, *crescendo* and *descrescendo*. Were dynamic levels to be indicated in decibels, say, the indications, like metronomic ones for tempo, would be notational in Goodman's sense. However, the prevailing system of rather vague verbal descriptions, open to a range of interpretations and continuous rather than discrete gradations, violates the very same notational conditions as do verbal indications of tempo and "mood." How loud is *forte*? Clearly not as loud for a flute in the low register as for a trumpet's "clarino" notes, and, of course, *cresc.* and *decresc.* are *dense*, allowing of continuous, infinite gradations.

The problem for a theory of musical representation is that dynamics, like tempo, obviously play an essential role in many musical pictures and representations; for example, Mossolov's *The Iron Foundry* is sprinkled with dynamic markings, a goodly number in the loud to very loud range. (If it is a bore, it is a crashing one.) Now on Goodman's view, such markings are not proper parts of the work, and proper compliants with the score—instances, that is, of the work—need not comply with them. A performance of *The Iron Foundry, pianissimo* throughout, would, on Goodman's view, be an instance of the work. It would, I submit, retain virtually none of the pictorial qualities of the work, all of which rely on a dynamic level several orders of magnitude above *pianissimo*. But if, as I believe, the pictorial qualities of *The Iron Foundry* are proper qualities of the work—indeed, one wonders what would be left of it without them—and if, as I also believe, these qualities must be notated in the score for them to be a part of the work, then I must, as a consequence, construe dynamic markings as proper parts of the score, although they violate Goodman's conditions on notation. The same argument applies, with equal force, to such examples of illustrative music as *Pacific 231*, which rely for their effect not just on being played at a given dynamic level, but on the ebb and flow of dynamics in various subtle ways: in the case of Honegger's score, obviously, to illustrate the rising and subsequently falling dynamic level of the engine, as it proceeds from rest, to motion, to violent motion, to rest once again. If these representational qualities are part of the work, it does not seem to me possible to adhere unswervingly to the letter of Goodman's account of musical notation and the musical work.

A possible strategy, at this point, is to claim that those representational qualities resulting from such parameters as tempo, dynamics, and the like—that is to say, the parameters not belonging to the score as Goodman construes it—although they cannot be properties of works, can, at least, be properties of good performances, and thus not lost entirely to us.[20] On this view, although Handel's *Israel in Egypt* (the work) does not contain in it a representation of the buzzing of flies, a performance of the work at the proper tempo does. The problem with this strategy, however, is clear: it simply does undue violence to our musical intuitions, as do so many other implications of Goodman's view. For it is the *work*, we want to say, that possesses these representational qualities, as it does the structural qualities that the Goodmanian score endorses: they are not fleeting qualities of this or that performance, but permanent qualities of the thing itself. Handel put the representation of flies into *Israel in Egypt* (the work) just as surely as he put in the harmony and counterpoint. We may not think that it is one of the more important qualities of the work (although Handel I am sure thought that it was); to say that it is not a proper part of the work, however, but merely of a proper (in that respect) performance of it, surely smacks of a desperate, ad hoc hypothesis to save a foundering theory. And that is too high a price to pay.

There is, to be sure, a kind of musical attitude that finds echo in Goodman's severe constraints on notation, score, and work. A very well-known music critic once said that when listening to Schubert songs he seldom had the slightest idea what the words were and didn't think it of the slightest musical interest to find out. The pitches, relative durations of tones, their structural relations, which are the characteristics of music that notation captures on Goodman's construal of it, lie at the very core of the musician's interest. Were the titles *Hebrides* and *Fingal's Cave* to be lost, but the score of Mendelssohn's overture to survive, the representational qualities of the work would no doubt be lost as well. But what *musical* qualities would we no longer have? None to speak of. What is the representational element in comparison to that which the score (on Goodman's construal) preserves? Isn't the latter *really* the music, to all intents and purposes? Tempo, dynamics, mood, manner all go into making a performance of acceptable *quality,* but the *music,* properly so-called, is there just so long as the structure of sound is preserved. Loss of representation is a "minor curiosity" to Goodman and to the music critic whose name I blush to give, because what really matters to them is Hanslick's "tönend bewegte Formen."

I began by calling this an attitude because an *attitude* it is: that is to say, a normative stand on what is and what is not of primary interest in

Western art music of the past five-hundred years. To a large degree, I
share that attitude. But whatever one may think about the importance,
or lack thereof, of the representational elements in music, one legis-
lates them out of the work on systematic grounds, at the risk of placing
theory so far from practice that the listener may be motivated to ask:
theory of *what?* I would, needless to say, rather have the Goodmanian
score of *Symphonie fantastique* than the program, but if I lacked the program, I would lack a part of Berlioz' work; and in a more obvious way, if
I lacked the pictorial elements of *The Iron Foundry* or *Pacific 231* I would
scarcely have the work at all: a little more of the cat than the smile, but
not much. A score, it seems to me, must reflect that fact, and it must
reflect it, so far as I can see, by containing, as proper parts, what on
Goodman's view are nonnotational elements. A Goodmanian score can
give me, perhaps, the *Art of the Fugue* entire, but hardly *La mer.*

It might be worthy of mention here, in reinforcing this point, that
what Leonard Meyer calls the "secondary parameters" of music,
among which are just those that, on Goodman's view, are not proper
parts of scores or (hence) works—verbally described tempi, dynamics,
and so forth—became in the Romantic era, Meyer argues, more and
more prominent as principles of musical *structure.*[21] In other words, to
tamper with, or ignore them in music of the nineteenth century would
be tantamount to undermining not just good musical performance, or
the representational aspects of works, but the very structural integrity
of the music itself. Thus, if Meyer is right, it is not merely some representational properties of music that are lost if tempo and dynamics are
denied a place in the score, but some genuine structural properties as
well. And this, it seems to me, even the musical purist, to whom representational properties are cheap, will say is too high a price to pay in
musical practice for elegance of musical theory.

◇ 6 ◇   What, then, of our original speculations as to the plausibility
of Goodman's system, with all of its assets in theoretical integrity, and
all of its liabilities in remoteness from ordinary musical discourse and
intuition? Little, I think, turns on whether one wants to call what I have
been talking about "musical description" or "musical representation,"
apart, of course, from the systematic advantages of Goodman's theory,
taken as a whole. A great deal, I think, turns on whether one can or
cannot save that part of what I have been calling musical pictures and
representations that in Goodman's system cannot be a proper part of
score or (hence) work.

Suppose, then, one were to adopt a polyglot notion of score, which included both notational and nonnotational features (on Goodman's construal of notational and nonnotational). This, in effect, is what I myself would do. It would then be a matter of choice either to buy the rest of Goodman's package, or to reject those parts of it that, it was felt, departed too far from common musical practice, or were unacceptable in some other way. For example, one might or might not want to accept Goodman's notion that one wrong note is a sufficient condition for a performance of the *Eroica* not being an instance of the work. It would still be consistent with allowing verbal indications of tempo and dynamics as a proper part of the score of the *Eroica* to take the view following Goodman, that if the second oboe were to omit to play the E-flat in measure 549 of the first movement, one would not have heard the *Eroica,* in spite of the fact that the error would scarcely be perceptible to anyone save the person making it. And, of course, one could have the rest of Goodman's account of the other arts into the bargain.

What one could *not* do is describe those aspects of a musical representation that are notational (in Goodman's sense) as truly *representational.* Thus, neo-Goodmanians whose scores were polyglot would have to distinguish between those parts, say, of *Pacific 231* that are descriptive (which would be just those parts relying on notational elements) and those that are representational (which would be just those relying on *dense,* nonnotational parameters like tempo and dynamics). But this would hardly, I think, be a problem, for in a perfectly ordinary, straightforward way, we make the same kind of distinction between those aspects of a poetic "description" of sound that properly describe it, and the onomatopoetic aspects that more properly imitate, that is to say, represent it. So far as I can see, the distinction would make perfectly good sense in music, and would do nothing to undermine the integrity of the illustrative music in which it would have to be made. The polyglot Goodmanian, then, once he has accepted nonnotational elements into his scores to save the *dense* aspects of musical illustrations, and whatever else essentially musical that depends on them, can have as much more of Goodman's system as he wishes.

For myself, there is much in Goodman's account that, on musical grounds, I cannot accept. In particular, I believe pernicious conclusions of various kinds follow from construing compliance in the strict way Goodman does. The relation between proper instances of a work and its score seems to me to be much more like the relation, say, of actual gases to the ideal gas laws, then like a class to a definition, as Goodman would have it. Such a relation allows for acceptable deviations, and thus avoids the absurdity of construing an *Eroica* with one wrong note as a nonperformance. There is, in other words, elbow room for something analogous to reasonable approximation, or "experimental error."

Perhaps as a result of this—in any case, in addition to it—there is no need to assume that the musical work, as opposed to musical notation, is not a *dense* symbol system. Indeed, it is not clear that all of the logical characteristics of musical notation must transfer to works, any more than the characteristics of the ideal gas all transfer to real gases. One may, in fact, go so far as to grant that musical notation is a symbol system but deny that music is. On Arthur Danto's view, every artwork must make at least a minimal statement; or, put more circumspectly still, even though a work might not be about anything, might have no subject at all, "the question of what its subject is, is not ruled out and rejected out of hand."[22] If this is the case, then music would necessarily be a symbol system, or at least be symbolic, since it is only of symbols, I presume, that it is logically appropriate to ask: What is its subject? What is it about? (Which is not to say, as Danto is careful to point out, that art is a language.[23]) But even were it the case—and I find it hard to believe that it is—that all music makes at least minimal statements, that the question of what a musical composition is about, what its subject is, is always logically in order, it is thought by many non-Goodmanians as well as the true believers, that all representations denote. Denotation is, of course, a symbolic function; and that being the case, one would have to grant that where music is representation, it is symbolism, though not necessarily non-*dense*. Even that, I think, is arguable. But this is not the place—nor, perhaps, am I the person—to argue it. All I wish to bring out here is what *minimal* changes must be made in Goodman's account of notation to accommodate the spirit, if not the letter, of the present account of musical representation. Those changes, as we have seen, involve the acceptance of such *dense* elements as verbal tempo and dynamics indications into the sacred precincts of the musical score. For the rest, what I hope to do is present an account of musical representation as compatible as possible with all real contenders for the correct philosophical analysis of representation in general, with the added proviso that, in my view (unregenerate Aristotelian that I am, in this regard), an account of representation that rules out representation in music is not really a genuine contender.

◊ 7 ◊   One rather predictable reaction to Goodman's strictures against musical representation, on the part of one of his "followers," V. A. Howard, is to locate a good deal of what most of us ordinarily call the descriptive, representational, illustrative, pictorial, or programmatic features of music in its *expressive* part. For being expressive, on Goodman's view, is well within the capabilities of music. Thus, Howard writes: "Many a musical 'program' so-called is purely expressive." And again: "A proper performance of Debussy's *La mer*, for instance, may not so much describe the sea as express qualities of it, many of which belong literally to the sea and metaphorically to the music, for example, shimmering, swirling, heaving, swelling, ebbing, flowing, gurgling."[21]

I call this a "predictable" reaction because, for one reason or another, musical representation has been problematic ever since there has been musical representation at all. And ever since it has been seen to be problematic, a standard move has been to dump the representational in music onto the expressive, since the expressive is seen to be the peculiar province of music, hence, less problematic and more musically respectable. That musical expressiveness plays a role in musical illustration cannot be doubted. That the expressive can account for any given instance of the representational in music is, I think, quite false. That is to say, those examples that have traditionally been taken to be representational, *La mer* included, *are* representational, pace Howard and a great many others. They are undoubtedly expressive too, and their expressiveness is certainly part of their representationality. But the two are, nevertheless, quite distinct musical phenomena.

The reasons, and motivations, for attempting to "translate" the representational in music into the expressive vary from period to period. In the following chapter we shall look at some of these with a view towards gaining a clear picture of why these attempts have been made, and we will conclude with an account of just what the role of musical expressiveness in musical representation really is.

CHAPTER VII

Representation as Expression

◇ 1 ◇ Honegger's *Pacific 231* has forced itself upon our attention frequently throughout this book as perhaps the paradigm of musical illustration: the most musically successful sound picture in the literature. For this reason it was the appropriate choice for my musical epigraph; and it is for this reason too that what Honegger said about his work is so altogether surprising. "I have not attempted the imitation of the sound of an engine in *Pacific 231*, but the expression of a visual impression and physical pleasure in a musical construction," he is quoted as remarking in an interview.[1] It is surprising, of course, because if *any* musical composition succeeds as an easily recognizable imitation of sound in music, it is Honegger's. If he did not intend this remarkable imitation of an engine, we must assume what is almost beyond belief: that the resemblance is purely fortuitous, a lucky (or unlucky) accident.

Why should Honegger have said such an extraordinary thing? That he was so self-deluded as not to have known what he was in fact doing, compositionally, seems as much beyond belief as that the remarkable picture of sound *in* sound was unintended. Yet so strong was his desire not to be taken for an imitator of sounds that he was impelled to say about his work what could not possibly have been true.

It is tempting to think that Honegger, like me, is really rejecting the concept of *imitation* rather than denying that his composition is a picture of sounds that, in fact, sounds remarkably like what it pictures. Or perhaps what Honegger really intended to convey, by hyperbole, is that *Pacific 231* is not *merely* an imitation or illustration of sounds, but an expressive musical composition in its own right, with some of the same *musical* values to be found in all serious symphonic writing. (It surely is no accident, in this regard, that he gave it the subtitle, *Mouvement Symphonique*.) All of this may have a grain of truth in it. The piece is a fine example of symphonic writing, with many lyrical and expressive passages. It is not merely a sound picture, like, say, Mossolov's *The Iron Foundry*. But Honegger, after all, said what he said; and perhaps it would be more fruitful (not to say more honest) to try to understand what exactly he did say, and why he said it, rather than to try to say not what he said but what he *meant* (or what he *meant* to *say*). For what he said is not, by any means, unique in the history of music. The prejudice against musical illustration, and in favor of musical expression—they almost invariably come in each other's company—is deep-seated in composers, and of longstanding in the profession. It behooves us to take this seriously, and to fathom its import.

◇ 2 ◇ How far back in time the argument between illustration and expression can be pushed I do not know, but it is clear that the Renaissance madrigal composers were devoted—their critics might have said addicted—to musical representation. And these so-called "madrigalisms" in which they indulged, along with certain criticisms their efforts elicited from the theorists preparing the way for monody, opera, and the musical Baroque, constitute a clear enough example of the tension between the concepts of musical representation and musical expression to provide us with a reasonable starting point, if not a true historical beginning.

Musicologists would surely agree that one of the most important of such theorists working in the seam between Renaissance and Baroque was Vincenzo Galilei (father of Galileo). He laid the theoretical foundations for the development of monody and opera, and, in the process, made illuminating remarks of a critical nature on Renaissance music in general, and musical representation in particular. The latter are of some interest to us here, and I will quote them at some length. Gallei writes:

[Composers] will say that they are imitating the words when among the conceptions of these there are any meaning "to flee" or "to fly"; these they will declaim with the greatest rapidity and the least grace imaginable. In connection with the words meaning "to disappear," "to swoon," "to die," or actually "to be extinct" they have made the parts break off so abruptly, that instead of inducing the passion corresponding to any of these, they have aroused laughter and at other times contempt in the listeners, who felt they were being ridiculed. Then with words meaning "alone," "two," or "together" they have caused one lone part, or two, or all parts together to sing with unheard-of elegance. . . . And then, as sometimes happens, the conceptions they have had in hand have made mention of the rolling of the drum, or of the sound of the trumpet or any other such instrument, they have sought to represent its sound in their music, without minding at all that they were pronouncing these words in some unheard-of manner. . . . At another time, finding the line:

> He descended into hell, into the
> lap of Pluto,

they have made one part of the composition descend in such a way that the singer has sounded more like someone groaning to frighten children and terrify them than like anyone singing sense. In the opposite way, finding this one:

> This one aspires to the stars,

in declaiming it they have ascended to a height that no one shrieking from excessive pain, internal or external, has ever reached.[2]

What strikes the reader straightaway about Vincenzo Galilei's difficulty with representational music is not that he thinks representation in music to be impossible; rather, that it always seems to him to be a violation of musical good taste in one way or another. Thus, when composers represent "fleeing" or "flying" with running passages, they must be executed "with the greatest rapidity and the least grace imaginable." When they represent the sounds of instruments (in vocal music, of course) they represent them "without minding at all that they were pronouncing these words in some unheard-of manner." When they represent ascent or descent with an ascending or descending line, they either take the voice so low that "the singer has sounded more like someone groaning to frighten children," or take it so high that the singer seems to be "shrieking from excessive pain."

But why, one wonders, need this necessarily be the case? Can't good taste and representation be served at the same time, even if it was not by the composers whom Galilei takes to task? Why must running passages be written so that they have to be taken too fast when they represent flight? Why can't the trumpet's sound be represented with proper declamation? And surely there is no need to take an ascending or descending line beyond the acceptable range of the voice, in representing ascent and descent. The thing can be done in moderation, one would think, and the idea still come across. There must, one suspects, be something deeper here than this, for Galilei is not just saying that composers in his time have been doing representation badly. He is making a stronger claim, presumably: that, in principle, if it is done it *must* be done badly. Where, though, is the argument for that?

A hint is dropped, I think, in the passage just quoted, where Galilei says: "In connection with the words meaning 'to disappear,' 'to swoon,' 'to die,' or actually 'to be extinct' they have made the parts break off so abruptly, that *instead of inducing the passion corresponding to any of these* [my italics] they have aroused laughter and at other times contempt in the listeners. . . ." Two points are worth noting here. First, Galilei is suggesting that there is something altogether appropriate in *arousing emotions* in listeners, as there is something inherently inappropriate in *representing* anything, even when music is capable of so doing: that is to say, arousing emotions is peculiarly musical, part of the special genius of the art, whereas representation is not, but, rather, something alien to it, even where possible. Second, he suggests that there is something the composer can do entirely consonant with the emotive character of music, in lieu of representation, namely, arouse in the listener the emotion (or emotions) corresponding to the things he might wish to represent: in this case, one assumes, the emotions we tend to associate with disappearing, swooning, dying, or being dead (whatever these might be).

◊ 3 ◊   The development of such hints as Galilei's into a doctrine of musical representation by way of musical expression awaited the advent, in the eighteenth century, of what Paul Oskar Kristeller has aptly called "The Modern System of the Arts."[3] When music, literature, and the visual arts had been gathered up into one class of objects—or, perhaps, as this was in process—theories were naturally required to explain (a) what it was about these seemingly disparate activities of writing, painting, sculpting, composing, that made them all of a piece, all of the same genus; and (b) what, nevertheless, distinguished them from one another. The prominent view, of course, was that the fine arts or beaux-arts, the arts of the beautiful, were, as Aristotle and Plato had long ago conjectured, the arts of imitation. That being the case, how was music, first of all, to be considered one of the fine arts at all, since so little of it seemed to be imitative in any obvious sense of that word, cuckoo calls aside? And, second, what was it about *musical* imitation, if there really were such a species of the thing, that distinguished it from painterly imitation, say, or literary representation? What was the peculiarly *musical* genius of musical imitation?

The problem, and its most pervasive solution for the Enlightenment, is best displayed in one of the more influential aesthetic treatises of the time, Batteux's *Les beaux arts reduits à un même principe* (1747). The very title of Batteux's work poses the problem in admirably succinct terms: How to reduce the arts of the beautiful, the fine arts, to a single principle. That principle, of course, was the imitation of la belle nature, according to Batteux. But how reduce music to the imitation of nature, while still retaining what was thought, since ancient times, to be the peculiarly *musical* in it: that is to say, its *emotive* "content"? The answer was clearly dictated by the "même principe." If emotive content was music's "difference," and the imitation of nature its "genus," then its whole nature must be the imitation of the emotions. Thus, for Batteux, "the principal object of music and dance [is] the imitation of the sentiments or passions. . . ."[4]

But what could it mean to "imitate" a sentiment or passion? Whatever might plausibly be described as an imitation of a passion or sentiment (if anything can), it would not seem to be music. What *can* be imitated or represented by music, Batteux (quite correctly, I believe) concluded, are the tones of voice with which our passions and sentiments are expressed.[5] And because music can "imitate" passionate human speech, it has the emotive import of that speech: it has, Batteux insists, "a meaning, a sense" (une signification, un sens).[6] Usually, that meaning or sense was cashed in, in the eighteenth century, in terms of the propensity of music to arouse in the listener the emotions which it was described as possessing: its significance or sense was a dispositional property, gained through the imitation of the "natural language" of passionate speech.

The arousal theory of musical expression was not, as I have argued elsewhere, the only one in the running.[7] But it surely was the most common one; and, more important for our purposes, the one that became, in the eighteenth century (unfortunately, I think), most intimately connected with the theory of musical representation as musical expression. Thus it became common for Enlightenment writers to recommend to the composer that he not try, as the Baroque composers had done, to "paint" or "imitate" things in his music, but, rather, that he try to make music that would arouse in the listener the emotion that would be felt if that object were actually present and perceived. Johann Adam Hiller, for example, in his essay "On the Imitation of Nature in Music," suggests that if music is to represent, say, a ghost or spirit, it must not "attempt to portray the quivering or drifting around of the spirit; it attempts only to portray it fearfully. . . ."[8] Or again, Jean-Jacques Rousseau says of the composer: "He will not directly represent things, but excite in the soul the same movement [that is, emotion] which we feel in seeing them."[9]

It is important to realize fully just how influential this doctrine of representation as expression has been, not only among critics, theorists, and philosophers, but among composers as well; and, it should be added, not just as an understandable reaction in the sixteenth and eighteenth centuries against real or imagined "literalism" in musical representation, but an attractive, one might almost say mesmerizing, alternative to musical representation in which one can have one's musical cake and eat it too, under the assumption that musical representation is at least unmusical and in bad taste, and, perhaps, even impossible. Without multiplying examples beyond endurance, let me simply call the reader's attention to some of the better known and more striking instances of the view in the past one hundred fifty years. There is, to begin with, the obvious and important case of Beethoven's Sixth Symphony, obvious because Beethoven himself apparently embraced the theory of musical representation as musical expression, explicitly if not always in practice (as we shall see); important because he not only expressed his belief in the theory, but gave us a masterpiece to exemplify it. A barren theory we can perhaps afford to ignore; but a theory fecund enough, in the hands of a genius, to produce the *Pastoral*, we ignore at our peril.

The clearest statement of what Beethoven intended in the *Pastoral* is to be found in the following sketchbook notations: "Every kind of painting loses by being carried too far in instrumental music. *Sinfonia pastorella* . . . it is [a record of] sentiments rather than a painting in sounds." And again: "*Pastoral* Symphony not a painting, but an expression of those sentiments evoked in men by their enjoyment of the country, a work in which some emotions of country life are described" (1807–1808).[10] Beethoven, of course, is not one with whom we tend to associate tone painting and program music: he is our paradigm of the "pure" instrumental composer, so it comes as no real surprise to us that in his one "programmatic" symphony he disavows musical illustrationism. More surprising is the fact that Berlioz, whose name is almost synonymous with the musical program and musical representation, apparently made a similar disavowal in regard to what we take to be his quintessential programmatic effort, *Symphonie fantastique*. Thus Edward T. Cone takes Berlioz as intending "not to describe scenes and incidents, but to depict his hero's reactions to them,"[11] and adds: "Berlioz makes this clear in a footnote to one of the early editions of the program, where he firmly rejects, for example, the 'notion of painting *mountains*' in favor of the attempt to express 'the *emotion* aroused in the soul . . . by the sight of these imposing masses.' "[12] Moreover, it is clear, I think, from the vigor with which Cone goes on to persuade us of Berlioz' espousal of musical representation as musical expression that it is Cone's view as well, and that he is somewhat relieved to find Berlioz, the arch-illustrator, really on the side of the angels after all. He concludes:

> Berlioz's position, then, seems to be that an instrumental composition is the communication of an experience, transformed into abstract sound. A program can tell us something about the subject of that experience and the specific circumstances giving rise to it. But the experience the music records is not the event described by the program; it is the reaction of the subject to that event. . . .[13]

Quite in line with this interpretation of musical representation as musical expression, although considerably less subtle, is J. W. N. Sullivan's, in his popular biography of Beethoven. Sullivan writes that what he calls the peculiar character of program music

> does not consist in any correspondences that may exist between auditory and other physical perceptions, but in the analogy between the musical emotions communicated and the emotions aroused by the external situation that forms the programme of the composition. If it be said, for instance, that Debussy's L'Apres-midi d'un Faune makes the impression of "a vegetable world alive in quivering hot sunshine . . . the life of trees, streams and lakes, the play of light upon water and on clouds, the murmur of plants drinking, and feeding in the sunlight," it is not because musical sounds can evoke images of heat and light and vegetables, but because a man in such surroundings may typically experience emotions analogous to those communicated by the music. Programme music, in the strict sense, may be defined as music that communicates musical experiences analogous to extra-musical experiences that may be associated with some definite external situation. It does not, any more than any other music, depict any part of the external world.[14]

Enough examples have been adduced, I think, to make the point that the theory of musical representation as musical expression of some kind has been ubiquitous in the history of Western art music from the Renaissance to the present. What must now be determined is how much truth (if any) there is in the theory and (antecedently) how that theory can best be understood.

◇ 4 ◇   In order to evaluate the theory of musical representation as musical expression we must first become somewhat clearer about what the theory is, and, in particular, how the word "expression" is to be construed.

We saw that the theory, as it emerged in the Enlightenment, generally construed the emotive content of music to be its disposition to arouse emotions in the listener. On such a theory, then, expression is to be understood as arousal, and "the music is ϕ" (where "ϕ" names an emotion or mood) as "the music arouses ϕ in the listener." But it is by no means clear that emotive expression, or depiction, or evocation was so construed by all of those since the eighteenth century who have believed that musical representation is really a matter of musical expression, or depiction, or evocation. Beethoven, to begin with, says that he intends the *Pastoral* to be an "*expression* of those sentiments evoked in men by their enjoyment of the country," and again, "a work in which some emotions of country life are *described*." Nowhere does he tell us (so far as I know) how we are to construe "express" and "describe" in this regard; nor is there any suggestion that he thought the *Pastoral* was to *arouse* the emotions of country life in the listener. Certainly "describe" would be an odd word to choose if arousal were intended, and although "express" would at least be consistent with "arouse," at least as it was used in the Enlightenment (which was, essentially, as a term of art), it would scarcely be synonymous with it in its presystematic use.

Nor does Berlioz, as interpreted by Cone, commit himself to saying that music arouses the emotions which its objects of representation would arouse if perceived. He too uses the noncommital "express"; and Cone himself, neither in his account of Berlioz nor in the representation of his own views, commits himself to construing musical expression as emotive stimulation.

Sullivan, indeed, is committed to a theory of musical expression as emotive arousal, derived, no doubt, from Tolstoy, whose views Sullivan's closely resemble. "Music as an expressive act," Sullivan tells us, "evokes states of consciousness in the hearer which are analogous to states that may be produced by extra-musical means. It is usual to describe these states as 'emotions.'" And again: "The most valuable states or 'emotions' that music arouses are those that spring from the richest and deepest spiritual context."[15] Among the four post-Enlightenment examples, then, of the theory of musical representation as musical expression—Beethoven's, Berlioz', Sullivan's, Cone's—only Sullivan's forces us to construe expression as arousal; the others leave it an open question, and even seem recalcitrant to such an interpretation where words like "describe" are used.

There are, I think, fairly persuasive reasons for not (under ordinary circumstances at least) construing "the music is ϕ" as "the music *arouses* ϕ" (where "ϕ" names an emotion or mood). I have presented some of them elsewhere, as have others; and there would be nothing to gain by rehearsing such arguments at any great length here.[16] It will suffice to point out the following. (a) Emotions are generally aroused by a combination of experiences (for example, falling in love) and beliefs (for example, believing that your lover is unfaithful) that music cannot provide. (b) Emotions characteristically make themselves evident in certain observable ways (for example, behavioral expression and physiological symptom) which listeners do not display (that is, they do not get red in the face and shake their fists when listening to the angry contortions of Beethoven's *Grosse Fuge*). (c) People generally try to avoid, if they can, experiencing such unpleasant emotions as sadness and anguish, whereas they by no means avoid sad and anguished music per se, suggesting that such music is not sad or anguished in virtue of arousing these emotions in listeners. (d) The only clear case of music arousing full-blooded *nonmusical* emotions—that is, by association with personal experiences—is a case quite irrelevant to our emotive characterizations of music qua art work; for although the first chorus of Handel's *Judas Maccabaeus* (for example) always fills me with cheerful feelings of nostalgia, because I performed in it during a particularly happy period of my life, which it invariably recalls to me, it remains a wonderfully mournful and melancholy piece. And so I would describe it to anyone, in spite of my personal associations, private to me, and no part of the music as a public object.

It would seem, then, that if we are to have any hope of formulating an at least initially plausible theory of musical representation as musical expression, we cannot, for the foregoing reasons, construe musical expression as emotive arousal. How then is it to be construed? Again, I must refer the reader elsewhere for my fully elaborated views on this question.[17] Briefly, I would suggest, as others have done, that the operative word in this regard be "expressive" rather than "expression" or "express" (although the words do to a certain extent overlap).[18] Weeping willows and the faces of Saint Bernards are *expressive* of sadness, but they need not make us sad. Nor are they, properly speaking, *expressions* of sadness. For to truly say that someone is *expressing* sadness, he or she would have to be actually experiencing that emotion—that is to say, he or she would have to *be sad*; but weeping willows cannot experience emotions, and Saint Bernards' faces are expressive of sadness whether or not the creatures are sad or happy (or stuffed). We recognize the emotive properties of music, I suggest, in very much the same way we recognize the sadness of the weeping willow or the Saint Bernard's face, as properties of the object rather than as dispositions to arouse emotions in us, or as expressions of vegetable souls, depressed canines, or composers. The emotions, then, are "in" the music, not in us; but in no very mysterious sense (for symphonies no more have souls than do weeping willows). Just as many creatures and insentient objects possess expressive properties, so too does our music. But I cannot go into the details of this possession here, nor need the reader accept my version of them, just as long as he or she is willing to accept, at least as a working hypothesis, the claim that in *many* (I do not even say *all*) of the central cases, music is φ (where "φ" is the name of an emotion or mood) in the way that the weeping willow or the Saint Bernard's face is sad: as *expressive* of the emotion or mood.

We can now formulate the thesis that musical representation is musical expression in a version that does not, at least, fail immediately for irrelevant reasons. We need not, that is to say, understand the musical representation of a mountain as involving the impossible task of making me feel the way I would feel if I saw the mountain: music can only do that by sheerest accident. What music can do, perhaps, is be expressive of the emotions one might feel in contemplating a mountain, or (more important) be expressive of the same emotions that the mountain might be expressive of (since mountains, I presume, like weeping willows, or the faces of Saint Bernards, can, and often do possess expressive properties). The theory of musical representation as musical expression, then, in its optimal form, is the theory of musical representation as musical *expressiveness:* that music represents things by being expressive either of the emotions that those things might arouse in us if we were experiencing them face to face, or by being expressive of the emotions those things are expressive of, or both. It is this version of the theory of musical representation as musical expression that I wish now to examine critically.

◇ 5 ◇   It appears to me that anyone who has followed the argument of the preceding chapters must believe, as I do, that the theory of musical representation as *solely* musical expressiveness is wholly false. Too many examples have been adduced that are clearly sound pictures and representations of various kinds, and not so in virtue of being expressive either of the emotions their objects might arouse, or of what the objects themselves might be expressive of, for the theory of musical representation as musical expressiveness pure and simple, to stand in unqualified form. Can it stand in any form at all? I think that it can, in a fairly obvious version, which perhaps can best be gleaned from looking not at what composers say, but at what they do. Consider, for a moment, some of the illustrative effects Beethoven achieves in the *Pastoral*: in particular, in the second and fourth movements, entitled, respectively, *Szene am Bach* (Scene by a Brook) and *Gewitter, Sturm* (Thunderstorm).

The *Szene am Bach* is one hundred thirty-six measures long (in $\frac{6}{8}$ time); and of these one hundred thirty-six measures, at least one hundred three contain a running sixteenth-note figure, the following being a fairly representative example (Example 24).

EXAMPLE 24
Beethoven, Sixth Symphony, Op. 68
Second Movement

That the movement is called *Szene am Bach*, and that it is permeated by this "flowing" figure is not, needless to say, an accident. It is, of course, the traditional representation of running water that we have already seen in Mendelssohn's setting of "The waters gather, they rush along," and Schubert's representation of the brook in *Die Schöne Müllerin* (Example 12). It "flows" through the entire movement, sometimes in the foreground, sometimes the background—but its presence is always felt.

Nor is this the only purely illustrative music in the movement; for it is in the *Szene am Bach* that we hear the previously quoted cuckoo, nightingale, and quail (Example 5). And well before the entrance of these three characters—they appear only in the coda—we have heard the unmistakable representation of less carefully painted (and unnamed) warblers in the strings (Example 25).

More obvious still is the musical thunderstorm which comprises the fourth movement. The noise is all there, in the most naively pictorial way, with grumbling double basses and rolling tympani. Nor does Beethoven omit the lightning, which cuts jaggedly across the musical texture, in the first violins and violas (Example 26).

Thus, no matter what Beethoven says about the *Pastoral*, there are plenty of musical representations and pictures in it. But what *does* he say, after all? Only that it is not *so much* a pictorial work as an expressive one. And that is the truth, I suppose. There are certainly more expressive features in the *Pastoral* than there are purely illustrative ones. That, perhaps, is all Beethoven was saying, except, of course, for the implicit and implied prescription for listening: "Don't concentrate too much on the illustrative features, or look for them where they do not exist, just because my symphony is called 'Pastoral' and has movements with descriptive titles. If you do, you may miss the far more numerous expressive features that I intended you to hear, and with which I achieve most of my illustrative and musical effects."

In what way, then, can expressiveness contribute to musical illustration? For that clearly, is what I am suggesting takes place in the *Pastoral* (and elsewhere, of course), and what I am certain Beethoven must have been quite well aware of. The illustrative and expressive features of a well-wrought musical composition cannot, after all, be wholly unrelated.

The answer, I think, is more or less obvious. The objects of musical illustrations, as well as the musical illustrations themselves, can possess expressive properties; if one can represent, say, the brightness of the sun, as Haydn does, by giving a bright quality to his music, one can represent it too (or, rather, help to represent it) by giving the music whatever *expressive* properties the sun might possess: in Haydn's case, joy, for one. Brooks, as opposed to rivers, are gay and lively, as well as flowing. Beethoven has represented his brook, in the *Pastoral*, by making his music flow, with the help of the "flowing" sixteenth-note figure that permeates the second movement. He has also represented it—its liveliness and gaiety, that is—by making his music lively and gay, and since thunderstorms are somber, brooding, ominous, as well as noisy,

EXAMPLE 25

Beethoven has made the fourth movement—*Gewitter, Sturm*—not only noisy, but somber, brooding, and ominous as well.

Another example, perhaps, will drive the point home. Mendelssohn titles his familiar overture, Opus 26, *Fingal's Cave* or *The Hebrides*. As a musical seascape (of which there are many examples), it is unsur-

EXAMPLE 26
Beethoven, Sixth Symphony, Op. 68, Fourth Movement

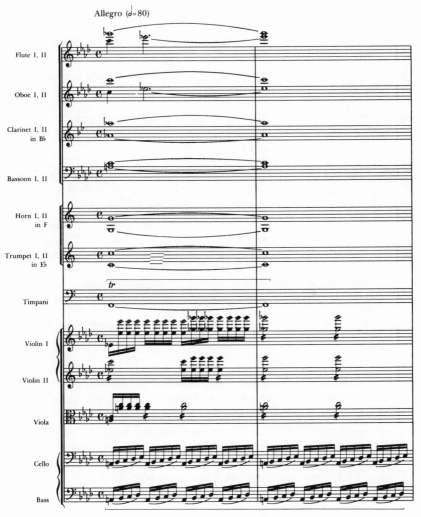

passed, and seldom equalled. It begins with the unmistakably seething ebb and flow of a heavy sea, represented by the persistent repetition of a musical figure obviously designed to give the impression of a periodic wave motion or swell. The motive "ripples" and "heaves," and is both melodically and harmonically constructed to allow for its reiteration on various scale degrees, and in various keys, for the purpose of representing the lapping or breaking of waves on the rocky coast (Example 27).

EXAMPLE 27
Mendelssohn, Overture, Op. 26 *(The Hebrides or Fingal's Cave)*

But what makes this a representation of the Scottish seas and not, perhaps, the sea at Brighton or Coney Island on a sunny day in July? These musical waves *could* break anywhere, were it not, of course, for their expressive quality—dark, brooding, melancholy, like the expressive quality of the Hebrides' seas themselves. It is, thus, by a union of illustrative and expressive features that Mendelssohn achieves his musical seascape. And it is, perhaps, somewhat misleading to distinguish illustrative from expressive features in such contexts as these (or, rather, it should be made plain that they are all illustrative but not all expressive, the expressive being a subclass); for on our construal of the expressive, these features of music are as illustrative as those we have been calling illustrative, being all illustrative by being all properties that are shared, one way or another, by music and by its objects of representation.

But there are, we said, two kinds of expressive features that might figure in the theory of musical illustration as musical expression: the features already discussed, that music and the objects of its representations might share: the gaiety of the brook, the brooding quality of the Hebrides' seas; and the emotions that such objects might arouse in the spectator: the terror a thunderstorm might evoke in a child, or the awe and wonder of the Alps. What role, if any, might these latter features play in musical illustration?

Often, it is clear, the two kinds will tend to coincide: that is to say, the gloom of a dark, densely wooded forest is *also* the emotion it would tend to evoke in the spectator. The gaiety of a brook is *also* the gaiety it might make me feel. Indeed, we sometimes say "X is ϕ" (where "ϕ" names an emotion or mood) when we mean not that X is expressive of ϕ but that X is evocative of ϕ (as in "sad news" or "glad tidings"). Now in cases where the emotion aroused is also the emotion the object is expressive of, composers tend not to distinguish carefully between them (they are, after all, composers, not philosophers), and even if they were so to distinguish them, it would be all one with their compositions. Whether Beethoven, say, intended to make his music expressive of the gaiety of the brook, or the gaiety of the spectator, which the brook might arouse, the music, in either case, was made expressive of gaiety. And whether Beethoven intended it or not, the gaiety of *Szene am Bach* contributes to the representation of the brook. If it was also supposed to be expressive of the gaiety the brook might arouse in a spectator (Beethoven, perhaps), it achieved this at the same stroke.

Sometimes, however, an emotion that an object, scene, or event might tend to arouse in a spectator will not be an emotion that the object, scene, or event is expressive of. In such a case, would making music meant to illustrate the object, scene, or event expressive of that emotion, contribute in any way to the illustration? The answer to this question seems to depend very much on how widely one might want to construe "contribute" or "illustration" or both. My own instinct (and that is all it is) is to construe them widely, simply because illustrations, representations, and pictures come in such an enormous variety, and what contributes to them is so much a matter of the enormous freedom and flexibility of intellect, imagination, and communication. Certainly, in the *direct* way in which an expressive property of an object can (by being made an expressive property of a musical representation) contribute to that representation, dispositional properties of objects (which is, of course, what we are talking about) cannot so contribute when they are made expressive properties of musical illustrations. The resurrection of the dead, which the faithful await (in the *Credo* of the mass) is a joyous occasion more in the dispositional than expressive sense of the word. It will *cause* joy in the spectator or participant. This is the joy that musical settings of the text are almost invariably expressive of. Does this expressive property contribute to the representation of the event? (The musical settings are, with equal frequency, replete with rising musical figures to represent the raising of the dead.) Not in any direct sense. On the other hand, one would find it singularly odd, jarring, even inappropriate to come upon a setting of "et expecto resurrectionem mortuorum" expressive not of joy but of some opposite emotion like grief or melancholy. One would look for an explanation: some point being made, or some musical exigency being served. And if emotive appropriateness is thought of as contributing to the musical representation, then I suppose both kinds of emotive properties of objects—the expressive and the dispositional—contribute to musical illustration when made expressive properties of it. This, then, is the grain of truth in the otherwise false thesis that musical illustration is really musical expression (or expressiveness) tout court.

◊ 6 ◊   What has emerged, then, not very surprisingly, from this examination of the "musical illustration as musical expression" thesis is simply that the thesis is overstated. Clearly, both directly and indirectly—as common expressive property and dispositional property of objects, but expressive property of musical illustrations—expressiveness *contributes* to musical illustration: indeed, in the former case, is a species of it. However, that all musical illustration comes in the end to musical expressiveness of one kind or another is plainly false: too many nonexpressive pictorial and representational techniques have been adduced in the preceding pages for that thesis to stand unchallenged and unmodified.

But it would be ending this chapter on a false note, I think, to simply conclude that the thesis is false as it stands and true as amended. For perhaps it was never meant to be taken for truth at all. It has been enunciated, more often than not, not as a revelation of musical reality but as a passionate statement of musical policy. It is, in other words, more normative or prescriptive than neutrally descriptive: a call to musical reform or revolution. The "illustrationism" of the madrigalists was rejected as unmusical by Galilei, as was the "illustrationism" of the Baroque composers by the preclassical defenders of sentiment and the "natural." Far from being denounced as impossible, such musical pictures and representations were all too possible according to their critics, their possibility proved, as Aristotle would say, by their very palpable actuality, cluttering, as they did, the music of those whose styles were being rejected by another generation.

How music is to be composed—whether it should or should not be pictorial or representational—these are maters, of course, for composers, not philosophers to decide. For Beethoven to have turned his back on a good deal of the "tone painting" of the Baroque (as Haydn, by the way, did not, in the *Creation* and *Seasons*) was, doubtless, a wise stylistic choice on the composer's part, and one that only Beethoven himself could have made. This, needless to say, does not make any more plausible the charge that Bach's illustrationism—the product of perhaps the greatest musical intellect the West has seen—is "unmusical." If Bach is unmusical, then Shakespeare is not a poet, and all things possible. *Unmusical* for Beethoven's style, no doubt; but supremely, sublimely musical for Bach's and Handel's

But such normative questions are not to the present purpose. It suffices for me to have shown that expressiveness is part of musical representation, but not the whole. There I must let the matter, and this chapter, rest.

CHAPTER VIII

Music as "The Beautiful Play of Sensations"

◇ 1 ◇ As the subtitle of this book, *Reflections on Musical Representation,* was meant to suggest, there is a certain spontaneity to my argument. I have followed it where it led, but have made no attempt to assure its completeness. I do not pretend to have explicated every way in which music can represent, or explained thoroughly even the ways of representation I have explored, and I have certainly not anticipated every possible objection. But to the limited extent that I have endeavoured to outline a coherent theory of musical representation, that theory is now before the reader. What remains is peripheral—but not, for that reason, unimportant.

To begin with, there is the question of musical purism, which owes its spirit, though perhaps not its letter, to Kant, and which produced, in the nineteenth century, Hanslick's well-known *The Beautiful in Music,* and Edmund Gurney's lesser known, undeservedly neglected, *The Power of Sound.* Musical purism flourishes still, and no account of musical representation would be taken seriously that did not pay its respects to the purist doctrine.

The title of this chapter is taken, as many will recognize, from Kant's characterization of music, in the *Critique of Judgment,* as an art of "the beautiful play of sensations"[1]—a most inviting phrase for anyone who wishes to construe music as lacking all semantic, representational, and expressive properties: in other words, a phrase tailor-made for the musical purist. But although Kant's so-called formalism was a moving force in the development of musical purism in the nineteenth century, there are very good reasons for not involving ourselves in a discussion of Kant. For one thing, the task of interpreting him is such an imposing one that it would lead us far afield of the present inquiry. For another, Kant had no well-worked-out views on the nature of music, and so a Kantian music aesthetics must be a project of creation and surmise, not strictly one of exegesis. Our considerations must be confined, therefore, to more recent manifestations of the doctrine of musical purism.

◇ 2 ◇   A reasonable place to begin such considerations might seem to be the writings of Hanslick and Gurney, the two musical pundits that recent philosophy has singled out, not implausibly, as the bastions of musical purism in the nineteenth century. But, again, there is, as in the case of Kant, good cause to pass them by.

Both Hanslick and Gurney were far more interested in musical expression than in musical representation: that is to say, far more interested in purging musical theory of its (to them) excessive preoccupation with the role of emotions, either as the content, subject, property, or effect of music, than in any excessive claims in the direction of musical illustration. Indeed, neither Hanslick nor Gurney denied that music has representational powers, and, all things considered, they were probably not very much more chary of musical representation than many another musical writer in no way identified with the purist line. Both were, in fact, to varying degrees, willing to countenance bona fide representational elements in music, whatever their views regarding the relation (or lack thereof) of the representational in music to its beauty or success qua music.

Hanslick, a music critic by trade, did not possess any great talent for rigor or system; and it is nearly impossible, in my opinion, to extract a self-consistent position from his well-known monograph on musical aesthetics, familiar to English language readers as *The Beautiful in Music*.[2] For our purposes, it suffices to note that at least one of Hanslick's positions on representation in music, far from denying its possibility, actually supports it, where the representation does not have as its object the human emotions. He writes in this regard:

> Whenever the question of the representation of objects by musical means *(Tonmalerei)* is under debate we are, with an air of wisdom, assured over and over again that, though music is unable to portray phenomena which are foreign to its province, it nevertheless may picture feelings which they excite. The very reverse is the case. Music can undertake to imitate objective phenomena only, and never the specific feeling they arouse.[3]

But compare this passage with a more characteristically formalist one somewhat later on:

> As music has no prototype in nature, and expresses no definite conceptions, we are compelled to speak of it either in dry, technical terms, or in the language of poetic fiction. . . . All the fantastic descriptions, characterizations, and paraphrases are either meta-

phorical or false. . . . Of music it is impossible to form any but a musical conception, and it can be comprehended and enjoyed only in and for itself.[4]

It is difficult to bring these two passages into conformity with one another. My own view is that the first is the one more likely to be dismissed as an unintentional lapse, being a familiar kind of volte face, produced in the heat of the moment. In an effort to make the representation of emotions in music, his major bugbear, seem monstrously implausible, Hanslick argues that contrary to common belief, it is *less* plausible even than the representation in music of natural phenomena (which, he might have added, is implausible enough). In so arguing, he has perhaps gone farther than he might have done, in a cooler moment, in the direction of admitting that the representation of natural phenomena in music is plausible at all.

Gurney was somewhat clearer on this point, and at least adumbrated something like the distinction I have drawn early on between musical pictures and musical representations. In music, he argued: "The suggestion of objects and events, the awakening in the mind of definite concrete images, may take place in two ways." The first way is roughly equivalent to what I have called musical picturing, and the "sounds like" cases of musical representation of the simpler kind, where "the actual sounds and motion of the music may perceptually resemble actual sounds and motions of other things."[5] The second more remotely suggests what I have been calling musical representation, particularly of the more complex kind, Gurney envisioning general agreement here only with the aid of title or text.

> These suggestions, however, remain in almost all cases extremely indefinite. . . . Given . . . the title, of course all who are the least interested in having an image at all will have the same image; but left to themselves they might each select a different one.[6]

Hanslick and Gurney, then, although not by any means friends of musical representation, particularly in its more extravagant manifestations, were not implacable enemies either. In any case, because of their preoccupation with musical expression—it is in reaction to that, after all, that their purism acquired its characteristic outline—they gave comparatively little attention to the nature of musical representation where its objects were other than the human emotions. That being the case, there is little in either author to be answered in defense of the kinds of musical representation I have been concerned with here.

Hanslick and Gurney certainly have been looked upon as providing a positive theory of the musical experience compatible with the denial of all forms of musical representation; and in that respect they have certainly provided aid and comfort to its critics. But we would have to look elsewhere, I think, for arguments really challenging to the views on musical representation expressed in the preceding pages. To such a challenge, in the recent philosophical literature, I shall therefore devote my attention.

◊ 3 ◊   In a recent article called "Representation in Music," Roger Scruton argues that "Music . . . is . . . an abstract art, with no power to represent the world."[7] His argument consists in laying out what he takes to be five necessary (but not sufficient) conditions for being an artistic representation, and in claiming that music does not meet some of them.[8] I am interested here only in answering the charge that music qua music cannot represent. So I will confine myself only to those criteria of representation adduced by Scruton that bear directly on that charge; and I shall not, therefore, spend time outlining Scruton's position in full.

The first condition on artistic representation, according to Scruton, is that the work be understandable only if the representation be perceived. In other words, the representational part of a truly representational work of art cannot be irrelevant to its aesthetic appreciation: it is a necessary condition.

> A man understands a representational work of art only if he gains *some* awareness of what it represents. His awareness may be incomplete, but it must be adequate. He may not see Masaccio's *Tribute Money* as a representation of a scene from the Gospel; but to understand it as a representation he should at least see the fresco as a group of gesturing men.[9]

A corollary of this seems to be, although Scruton does not mention it explicitly, that the representation in representational works be readily recognizable without verbal aids or esoteric knowledge; for one of his reasons for thinking music cannot be representational at all is the familiar claim that musical representation is never apparent, but always needs nonmusical props. "It is significant," he writes, "that, while a man may look at an untitled picture and know immediately what it represents, it is most unlikely that he should do the same with an untitled symphonic poem,"[10] However, the major argument against musical representation that emerges from this particular condition is that even what is called "representational" music can be understood, appreciated, or what you will, without ever recognizing the representational aspect. "To understand a representational painting, one must have some knowledge of the subject; but the same has never been honestly claimed for music."[11] And again: "One can understand a 'representational' piece of music without treating it as a representation, indeed, without being aware that it is supposed to be a representation at all."[12]

The claim that musical representation is never apparent and the argument against musical representation that it generates can both, at this point, be dismissed rather peremptorily. If, by "representations," are meant what I have been calling musical "pictures," then the claim is false; and if what I have been calling musical "representations" are intended, the claim is irrelevant. For musical pictures, insignificant though they may be in Western music, are as readily recognizable without verbal aids as any representational painting. (No one fails to recognize the bird songs in Beethoven's *Pastoral,* or, I believe, the steam engine in *Pacific 231.*) And musical representations, like the general's representation of the battle of Balaclava, a circuit diagram of your radio, or, for that matter, Picasso's *Guernica* or Mondrian's *Broadway Boogie-woogie,* although they require verbal instructions, are no less *representations* for that.

The argument that what we normally call musical representation is irrelevant to, unnecessary for a proper understanding of music, whereas recognition of representation in representational painting is a necessary condition for painterly understanding, requires careful consideration. Unlike the previous objection, it cannot be summarily dismissed.

To begin with, we must distinguish two versions of this argument which, it seems to me, are never properly separated by Scruton. Sometimes Scruton seems to be arguing that since we can *fully* understand representational music without knowing what subject is intended, or even being aware that we are hearing representational music at all, such music cannot be truly representational, since in truly representational art it would be ridiculous to suggest that we fully understand the work even though we have no idea what (or that) it represents. At other times, however, he seems to be making the weaker claim that, although we do not understand a piece of representational music fully when we do not know its subject, so little is lost that it cannot be a truly representational work; for in a truly representational work, if we did not know what was represented, we could hardly be said to understand the work at all, or if at all, only in the most minimal, and wholly inadequate way.

The claim that we can always *fully* understand a piece of representational music without knowing what (or that) it represents can easily be construed in ways that make it either trivially true or questionbeggingly false. Suppose I insist that if there is any one thing about a work that I do not know, I do not understand it *fully*. (How could I, since *full* knowledge seems to imply completeness?) In that case it follows trivially that I do not understand *La mer* fully unless I know what its subject is; but it also follows trivially, that I do not understand it fully if I do not know whether Debussy wrote out the string parts or the winds first, or what kind of ink he used in making the fair copy. The obvious retort is that the former kind of knowledge contributes to our *musical* understanding whereas the latter does not—but this lays a snare for our feet. For if I simply decide from the start that knowing the subject of a musical representation never contributes to our *musical* understanding properly so-called, it sounds very much as if I have just stipulatively defined "musical understanding" in such a way as to exclude all musical representation a priori. In other words, the question has been begged in favor of musical purism. I shall try to avoid the former snare, and the latter one, by adducing two examples that, it seems to me, are clear, unproblematic cases where those at least uncommitted to musical purism will readily admit that to be ignorant of the musical representation is not fully to understand (or appreciate) something very important and nontrivial about the *musical* character of the work.

There is a certain kind of chorale prelude in which Bach sets each line of the chorale melody in a markedly contrasting musical way, no real thematic germ being consistent throughout to connect the contrasting sections. These chorale preludes are, of course, purely instrumental compositions for organ; they are not settings of texts (in the usual sense), and bear simply the first line of the first strophe of the chorale melody as their title. In many cases, the material of the contrasting sections is musically unrelated. What material one section will have is not musically "implied" by anything that happens in the sections before: there is no thematic unity. But as soon as one looks at the *text* of the first strophe of the chorale, one knows immediately why the musical character of a section is what it is: it almost invariably represents or is expressive of some image in the text. For example, a peculiarly jagged, leaping, and percussive figure dominates the musical fabric of the second section of one of the chorale preludes on *Jesus Christus, unser Heiland* (Example 28).

EXAMPLE 28
Bach, Chorale Prelude (BWV 665), *Jesus Christus, unser Heiland*

Musically its presence is quite inexplicable in the sense that nothing that goes before makes use of it, or "implies" it in any way: there is no motivic connection (except for some obvious rhythmic continuity). It is only by knowing, through the text, that, in Schweitzer's words, it is "a representation of the strokes of God's wrath,"[13] that we can make *musical* sense of its appearance, and see the chorale prelude as a connected unit. (Bach's congregation, of course, knew these texts and melodies by heart, and could perceive the musical significance directly.)

A second and perhaps more familiar example of the same kind of thing occurs in Weber's *Invitation to the Dance*. It exhibits, to be sure, a perfect musical form: a slow introduction, a series of waltzes in the form of a rondo, and a brief return of the material of the introduction as a coda. But the musical material of the introduction and its return, are completely inexplicable in purely musical terms without Weber's program: "First approach of the dancer (measures 1–5); to whom the lady gives an evasive answer (5–9). His more pressing invitation (9–13); her acceptance of his request (13–16). Now they converse in greater detail; he begins (17–19); she answers (19–21). . .," and so on (Example 29). Anyone familiar with the Western musical tradition will immediately recognize the strangely disjointed thematic material of the introduction as characteristic not of an instrumental composition at all, but of an operatic recitative. It simply does not make any musical sense, does not "hang together" until one knows the program, and can see the alternating melodic fragments of the left and right hands as the conversation of the male and female dancers. (Indeed, had a program not been provided by the composer, it is a safe bet that many would have been by commentators.) It is not that any errors in harmony or counterpoint have been made. It is musically correct: a "well-formed formula." But it is musical hash, bits and pieces, until the program puts them together into a discursive sequence. It seems clear in the Weber, as in the Bach, that in a very proper sense of "musical," one cannot fully understand the musical structure without knowing the subject of the musical representation.

Unless one simply begs the question in favor of musical purism right from the start, the text of Bach's chorale and the program of *Invitation to the Dance,* give answers to *musical* questions of *musical* interpretation: questions that cannot be answered, in these cases, in terms of purely musical parameters. If I am puzzled by the entrance of a second subject in a fugue, and seek for its connection with what has gone before, my

EXAMPLE 29
Weber, *Aufforderung zum Tanz: Rondeau brillant,* Op. 65

puzzlement will perhaps be dispelled, my desire for musical continuity satisfied, when I come to perceive, or it is pointed out to me, that the second subject is an inversion of the first. Similarly, if I am puzzled by the entrance of the peculiarly jagged, leaping theme in the second section of *Jesus Christus, unser Heiland,* or the oddly fragmented thematic structure of the introduction to *Invitation to the Dance,* my puzzlement will perhaps be dispelled, my desire for musical continuity satisfied, when I come to perceive, or it is pointed out to me, that the jagged, leaping theme represents the "strokes of God's wrath" alluded to in the text, or that the alternating bass and treble phrases of Weber's introduction represent a conversation between a man and a woman. The *difference* is that what could be provided in the former case by reference to a purely musical concept, the inversion of a fugue subject, can be provided in the latter ones *only* by reference to a representational content. But in all cases, I am claiming, we are gaining *musical* understanding of musical works. (What else?) This, it seems to me, is sufficient to defeat Scruton's claim that since we can *always fully understand* representational music without knowing what it represents, music can never be properly representational.

Let me now turn, briefly, to Scruton's weaker and more conciliatory claim—briefly because once the stronger has been defeated, the weaker will, I think, have little appeal, since in principle it concedes to music representational features, and merely denies their aesthetic or musical significance. In its weaker form, it will be recalled, Scruton's argument seems to be that although we cannot understand a piece of representational music *fully* without knowing the subject of the representation, so little is lost in not knowing, that we cannot fairly call the music representational at all. The problem of course lies with the phrase "so little is lost." How much is "much"? How little "little"? And doesn't it matter at all whether we are talking about a musical composition in which there is a single incidental representation in three hours of music, or one that is built entirely around a program or title? Surely more is lost if—per impossible—I perceive the *Madonna della Sedia* as an abstract design, not a woman's face and figure, than if I fail to perceive that a "growling" figure in the orchestra represents the rolling away of a stone from a cistern in Beethoven's *Fidelio* (the only such piece of representation in the work, so far as I can remember). But to claim that my loss, in failing to perceive the representation in *Invitation to the Dance,* or in Bach's chorale preludes, is negligible and musically unimportant, seems to me to be indefensible, however defensible the claim might be in regard to other musical works. Do I lose more or less than if I saw Mondrian's *Broadway Boogie-woogie* without the title? For here is a case of representation in painting where all is *not* lost when the subject is not known. (Compare it with those works of Mondrian in a similar style that are untitled.) I will not belabor this point, for it seems to me clear enough that musical representation of the kind I have been discussing throughout this book cannot in all cases be dismissed as trivial or irrelevant to the *musical* understanding of the music of which it is a part. It would be folly to maintain that I really have full musical understanding of certain of Bach's chorale preludes if I do not know the texts of the relevant chorales—and folly, too, to maintain that I have a full musical understanding of *Invitation to the Dance* while totally ignorant of its title or program. That the importance of musical representation in some works is less than in others, and that its importance is less to the musical art than representation historically has been to the painterly one cannot deny. But that the latter difference in degree warrants the denial that music can ever, in any case, be *properly* described as functioning representationally seems to me wrong-headed, and without foundation. The distance separating musical representation (as I have been using that term) from representation elsewhere, whatever that distance is, is hardly great enough to warrant the claim that we are not dealing in music with the genuine article.

◊ 4 ◊   Another condition on artistic representation that Scruton believes music cannot fulfill is the condition that there be, in representation, a *medium*: "Representation requires a medium, and is understood only when the distinction between subject and medium has been recognized."[14] But in musical representation, Scruton insists, no medium can be located, and the distinction between subject and medium dissolves, at least where the subject represented is *sound*.

> When music attempts the direct "representation" of sounds it has a tendency to become transparent, as it were, to its subject. Representation gives way to reproduction, and the musical medium drops out of consideration altogether as superfluous. In a sense the first scene of *Die Meistersinger* contains an excellent representation of a Lutheran chorale. But then it *is* a Lutheran chorale. Similarly, the tinkling of teaspoons in Strauss's *Sinfonia Domestica,* and the striking of anvils in *Rheingold,* are not so much sounds represented as sounds reproduced, which in consequence detach themselves from the musical structure and stand out on their own.[15]

When music attempts to represent sound, "since there is nothing to music except sound, there ceases to be any *essential* difference between the medium of representation and the subject represented."[16]

It is important to notice to start with, that Scruton is talking here only about instances of music representing sounds: more or less what I have been calling musical "pictures," and musical representations of the "sounds like" kind. Nothing he says casts the slightest doubt on instances in which music represents (in my sense of the word) things other than sounds. When Bach represents the imitation of Christ, or Handel the exodus out of Egypt, the distinction between medium and subject is as clear as it is anywhere else, as we have seen (in Chapter V). No one takes Bach to be imitating the sound of the imitatio Christi (whatever that would be), or Handel the sound of the children of Israel escaping their Egyptian captivity. They are representing acts, or events, or "things" in sound. These are the subjects, sound—more properly, musical sound—the medium. And since these kinds of musical representations are far and away the most numerous, the most aesthetically interesting, the most musically significant, even if Scruton's argument held good for musical sound pictures and representations of the "sounds like" variety, it still would leave intact the main body of musical representation. However, it does not hold good even for those, as I will now try to show.

Scruton considers two kinds of case in which music might be said to represent or picture sounds: those cases in which the sounds to be represented or pictured are themselves music, and those in which they are nonmusical.

When music represents music, Scruton argues, it simply becomes what it represents, and thus the distinction between medium and subject dissolves. The representation of a Lutheran chorale in *Meistersinger* just *is* a Lutheran chorale. But although this may be true in some cases—the representation of late eighteenth-century divertimento music in *Don Giovanni* just *is* late eighteenth-century divertimento music[17]—it is not by any means true in all. As a matter of fact, it is not true of the example Scruton cites in the passage above. The Lutheran chorale in *Meistersinger* clearly is *not* a Lutheran chorale, at least if one means by that a Lutheran chorale as it might have been sung in a service during the period in which the events in *Meistersinger* are supposed to have taken place (or any other period, for that matter).[18] Nor is it an imitation of a chorale: that is the sort of thing harmony students do for practice, and Wagner would have gotten very low marks for his effort (from Beckmesser no doubt). But if the chorale in *Meistersinger* is neither a Lutheran chorale nor an imitation of one, what is it? Can there really be any doubt that the best way of describing it is as an imaginative, artistic representation of one? The subject is a Lutheran chorale as Wagner imagined it might have sounded in the historical period in which *Meistersinger* is set. The medium is musical sound—more precisely, nineteenth-century Wagnerian harmony, woven into the texture of the opera (Example 30).

To cite another instance, it seems to me that the most felicitous way of describing Mozart's *Musical Joke* (*Ein musikalischer Spass*, K.522), is as a musical representation of a divertimento composed by a second-rate composer and executed by incompetent musicians. What are the other possibilities? Surely it can't just *be* a divertimento by a second-rate composer, not just for the trivial reason that it was not composed by a second-rate composer, but because it is not second-rate: it has all the marks of Mozart's genius on it. Nor is it an imitation of one, at least not a very good imitation, for the music is splendidly written music and its subject second-rate stuff. A well-made chair cannot be a good imitation of an ill-made one (although it might be a good *representation*).

Furthermore, even if one were to disagree with me that the *Musical Joke* is splendidly written music, a comparison with the real second-rate music of Mozart's time, which he was lampooning, would instantly reveal that the *Musical Joke* is neither an imitation nor just another instance of the second-rate. For like any good satirist, Mozart has exaggerated, distorted, and put into bold relief the object of his raillery for the purpose of casting light on what it is about the music he is lampooning that is inept and clumsy. It is not possible for K.522 to be mistaken for a second-rate eighteenth-century divertimento. There is too much craft and distortion for that. In short, one simply cannot avoid the epithet "representation" in characterizing Mozart's caricature. Nothing else will do, and certainly not "just another example of the very thing pilloried." Where, then, would be the joke, or the art?

EXAMPLE 30
Wagner, *Die Meistersinger von Nürnberg*, Scene I

Perhaps it might worry some that both in the case of the Lutheran chorale in *Meistersinger,* and the *Musical Joke,* the medium and subject are the same "stuff": that is, music. If so, there is really no justification for the worry, as a simple example will illustrate. Suppose an Impressionist painter were to execute a still life with a bowl of fruit, a vase of flowers, and a seventeenth-century oil painting of the Dutch landscape school. The *medium* of the Impressionist painting is oil on canvass; the *subject* of part of the painting (that is, the Dutch landscape) is the same. Nor do the subject and the representation coalesce. The subject is a painting in one style; it is executed in quite another. Clearly, there is no logical problem in the painterly case. Why, then, should there be in the musical ones?

Moving on to the instances of music representing non-musical sounds, I think it must be granted that there is even less temptation to think the medium and the subject coalesce here than in the former instances. For if there is a temptation to think (falsely, I have argued) that the Lutheran chorale in *Meistersinger* just *is* a Lutheran chorale (since both subject and medium are music), there is no temptation at all, pace Scruton, to think that the sounds made in Beethoven's *Pastoral* just *are* bird songs (or replicas of them). Anyone who can't distinguish between a cuckoo or a nightingale, and musical "pictures" of them, notated in score, played *espressivo* on a platinum flute and ebony clarinet, had better listen again, and try to notate the sounds birds make in the well-tempered scale, in appropriate duple or triple meter. (One can, of course, just put bird sounds into a musical composition, as Respighi did; but that is another matter, and one swallow doth not the summer make.) Beethoven represented, or "pictured" (in my sense of the word), the "songs" of birds, but the "songs" of birds are not "songs." The subject is natural sounds, the medium musical ones.[19]

◊ 5 ◊   The final point I want to consider is Scruton's claim that "representation is . . . essentially propositional," whereas musical "representation" (so-called) cannot be. Scruton writes, of what he takes to be the propositional element in artistic representation:

> A representational work of art must express thoughts about its subject, and an interest in the work should involve an understanding of those thoughts. . . .Even in the most minimal depiction— say, of an apple on a cloth—appreciation depends on determinate thoughts that could be expressed in language without reference to the picture; for example: "Here is an apple; the apple rests on a cloth; the cloth is chequered and folded at the edge."[20]

Representational art, then, makes statements conveying at least minimal information about its subjects. Music, however, even in its so-called representational moments, cannot.

> If music is to be representational, then its subject must be not only picked out, but also characterized. But that requires a context, and in music the context seems to add no further precision to the "representational" parts. A certain passage in *Der Rosenkavalier* "imitates" the glitter of a silver rose. But what more does this passage say about the glitter except that it is a glitter (and even that may go unnoticed)?[21]

In the nineteenth century particularly, extravagant claims were made for the informational content and capabilities of music, perhaps inspired by the claims of Schopenhauer, never matched before or since, which made music out to be nothing less than philosophy in sound, revelatory of the ultimate nature of metaphysical reality. (Extravagant claims were made for *philosophy* as well.) I hardly think anyone is prepared to make such audacious claims today. If representational music is propositional, it is a limiting case; if it conveys information about its subject, the information is minimal. But if Scruton's own account of the propositional in artistic representation is to be credited, still life painting, which is surely a very paradigm of representational art, can only be regarded as a limiting case of the propositional, a minimal conveyor of information about its subject. And if music can come up to the standard of still life painting, it can hardly fall below the standard of representational art. It would seem that a sufficient condition for a representation being propositional is that its subject be describable. A still life of an apple resting on a checkered cloth expresses, according to Scruton, the following propositions: here is an apple; the apple rests on a cloth; the cloth is checkered, and so on. All these propositions amount to is whatever can be offered as a verbal description of the picture's subject: the subject is an apple; the apple rests on a cloth; the cloth is checkered. And that propositional condition can be fulfilled by any intelligible musical representation or picture as well, for any bona fide, intelligible, unproblematic musical representation or picture must, of course, have a subject at least minimally describable in words: "Here is a cuckoo; it sounds a descending major third." "These are the ten commandments; they are the foundation of (that is, underlie) our faith." These "propositions" have been expressed in music simply by virtue of the fact that the cuckoo, and the ten commandments as the foundation of the Lutheran faith, have both been successfully represented in music. For that matter, music can go beyond such minimal propositions, as where Bach, for example, makes a profound, informative statement of his view (or *a* view) of death by ending the *Crucifixus* of the B-minor Mass on that sublimely restful and untroubled G-major chord, after taking us, with agonizing chromatics, through various and remote minor tonalities. I will not claim, however, that musical representation ever gets much beyond the bare minimum in respect of what Scruton construes in painting as propositional content. But it does not fall below it, which is all I need claim for my own purposes. Indeed, it cannot fall below it, since, really, all the minimal claim to propositional content amounts to is what all representation posseses: a verbally expressible subject. Of course one might deny, as an article of faith, that any music has a subject expressible in words. That, however, would just beg the question of musical representation from the start.

CHAPTER IX

Music as Narration

◊ 1 ◊   To the average concertgoer, "musical representation" is a phrase that is likely to call to mind Berlioz, Liszt, and Richard Strauss; and, in particular, works that purport not just to "paint a picture" but to "tell a story." Narrative music, to be sure, is only a subclass of the representational kind. Nevertheless, it tends to loom large; and it would be a poor book on musical representation that did not attempt to deal with this controversial genre. That is the task I undertake in the present chapter, but here, as elsewhere in this study, my aspirations are modest. I have no intention of attempting an exhaustive analysis of narrative technique in music. Rather, I hope simply to lay bare some of the ways in which narration has been pursued as a musical goal in purely instrumental music: that is, music without a sung or spoken text.

The problem of musical narration lies, clearly, in the propositional poverty of the musical art. In the previous chapter I did not agree with Scruton about much; but I was forced to agree with his conclusion that the ability of music to express propositions is, if not nonexistent, at least limited in the extreme. Yet even the simplest narration seems to require a propositional content beyond the capacity of music to convey. Music cannot say that Jack and Jill went up the hill. It cannot say that Mary had a little lamb, and the failure must lie in the inability of music to express the appropriate propositional content even of such limiting cases of narration. Music is, for all intents and purposes, propositionally dumb. That is the problem of musical narration—and an insoluble problem it seems to be.

Yet we all know that storytelling in instrumental music has been attempted now and again, and examples of the genre hold a permanent place in the modern symphonic repertoire. What, then, does the composer do, under the guise of "narration," if it is not to tell a story? Or perhaps we have been over hasty in denying the power of narration to music—over restrictive, perhaps, in our notion of what narration is, and guilty of overemphasis in our insistence on the dependence of the narrative on the propositional.

In what follows, I shall not try to present an abstract philosophical analysis of narration in general, or musical "narration" in particular. Rather—what is more in the spirit of these reflections on musical representation—I shall examine two examples of musical storytelling with a view to revealing some of the actual techniques involved. I will leave it to the reader to decide whether this is bona fide narration or narration "in quotes," but in the process of analysis, I will provide at least some conceptual frames in which to view these musical techniques. We have already laid the necessary groundwork for that.

◊ 2 ◊   The earliest instances of musical narration that still hold any place in the modern repertoire are the *Biblical Sonatas* of Johann Kuhnau, J. S. Bach's predecessor as cantor of the Thomaskirche, Leipzig (1707–1722). These six *Biblische Historien* are in the form of keyboard suites or partitas. They were originally published by Kuhnau in 1700, and enjoyed considerable popularity in the early years of the eighteenth century, being reissued (from the same plates) in 1710, and again in 1725. Of the six, the best known is the first: "The Battle between David and Goliath" (*Der Streit zwischen David und Goliath*). This sonata will be the subject of my first narrative analysis.

Each of the *Biblical Sonatas* is prefaced by a rather baroque evocation of the story it is meant to tell, and each of the movements bears a title or description to indicate the incident of the story it depicts. Clearly, Kuhnau was quite well-aware of the limitations on the narrative powers of music, and made free (even excessive) use of the resources of language to supplement them. One might, at the outset, wonder why he felt it necessary, with such a familiar story as that of David and Goliath, not only to put descriptive titles to the individual movements of the sonata, but to tell the story in a preface as well. With the preface and music before one, the answer is quite clear; for the preface embodies the composer's vision of what the events depicted must have been like, an "interpretation" of the biblical text, if you like, and thus provides additional help in reading the representation in the music, as we shall see in a moment.

"The Battle between David and Goliath" consists of eight separate movements, each with a descriptive title. To get an overview of the narrative, I will lay out the plan of the sonata, with the titles and examples of thematic material where relevant, but with only as much comment of my own as is necessary to give a general notion of the composition. In the following section, once the music is before us in its broad outline, we can take a closer look at the details, and reach some analytical conclusions with regard to Kuhnau's narrative technique, and perhaps the technique of musical narrative in general.

The sequence of movements in "The Battle between David and Goliath" is as follows:[1]

1. *The boasting of Goliath (La bravate di Goliath).* From the purely musical point of view, this serves as a prelude or overture to the suite. The opening theme, suggesting the dotted rhythm of the French Overture, represents, according to Kuhnau, "the snorting and stamping of Goliath by means of the low-pitched and (on account of the dotted notes) defiant-sounding theme. . ."[2] (Example 31).

EXAMPLE 31
Kuhnau, "The Battle Between David and Goliath"

II. The trembling of the Israelites at the appearance of the giant and their prayer made to God (Il tremore degl' Israeliti alla comparsa del Gigante, e la loro preghiera fatta a Dio). This remarkable movement is in the form of a chorale prelude, the trembling of the Israelites represented by the accompanying eighth-note figure (a sort of slow "tremolo"), their fear and anguish by the minor key in combination with a pronounced chromaticism, and the prayer to God by the introduction of the Lutheran chorale, *Aus tiefer Noth schrei ich zu dir* ("From the depths I cry to thee"), in the treble, as a cantus firmus. I quote from the entrance of the first strophe (Example 32).

EXAMPLE 32

III. David's courage and his desire to blunt the pride of the frightening enemy, together with his confidence placed in God's aid (Il Coraggio di David, ed il di lui ardore di rintuzzar l'orgoglio del nemico spafentevole, colla sua confidenza messa nell' ajuto di Dio). The "objects" to be represented here being psychological rather than physical—courage, pride, fear, confidence—Kuhnau, as might be expected, does his illustrating in the expressive vein, representing David's courage, and, of course, his size relative to "il Gigante," with light, jaunty, "courageous" music. Apparently, the opening figure is meant to be David's leitmotiv, for it reappears, in altered form, in the following movement, as we shall see in a moment (Example 33).

EXAMPLE 33

IV. *The battle between one and the other and their contest (Il combattere fra l'uno e l'altro e la loro contesa).* This is the centerpiece of the sonata, and contains the dramatic moment where fortunes change. Kuhnau portrays the battle, naturally enough, with two musical figures "battling" one another: a heavy, percussive motive for Goliath (in the bass, needless to say), and a light, airy one (in the treble) for David, which turns out to be an inversion, in diminution, of part of David's leitmotiv of the previous movement (Example 34).

EXAMPLE 34

At measure 11, this musical texture is abruptly broken for the climactic denouement, in which Kuhnau represents the slinging of David's stone with rapid scales, and the fall of Goliath with a descending figure in the bass (Example 35).

V. *The flight of the Philistines who are hunted and slaughtered by the Israelites (La fuga de' Filistei, che vengono persequitati ed amozzati dagl' Israeliti).* A fugue—the flight of the Philistines represented by rapid scale passages, the Israelites' pursuit by the successive entries of the fugue subject, the parts "following" one another. As Kuhnau himself puts it: ". . .

EXAMPLE 35

vien tirata la selce colla frombola
nella fronte del Gigante.

The stone which he throws with his sling   casca Goliath
sinks into the forehead of the Giant.   *Goliath falls.*

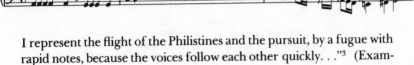

I represent the flight of the Philistines and the pursuit, by a fugue with rapid notes, because the voices follow each other quickly. . ."[3] (Example 36).

EXAMPLE 36

Nor is the pun on flight (*fuga*, in Italian) and fugue unintentional. As Johann Mattheson, for example, derived the term "fugue" in *Der vollkommene Capellmeister* (1739): "Such artworks are called fugues because one voice so to speak *flees* before the other, and such flight . . . in Latin is called *fuga*. . . ."[4]

VI. *The joy of the Israelites in their victory (La gioia degl' Israeliti per la loro Vittoria).* The Israelites' joy is represented, appropriately enough, by a joyous gigue-like dance in triple meter.

VII. *The music concert given by the women in honor of David (Il concerto Musico delle Donne in honor di Davide).* Kuhnau is obviously thinking here of I Samuel 18:6: "And it came to pass as they came, when David was returned from the slaughter of the Philistine, that the women came out of all cities of Israel, singing and dancing, to meet King Saul, with tabrets, with joy, and with instruments of music." The "tabret" is a small tabor, that is to say, a drum, which Kuhnau imitates in the bass with a characteristic beat, and the tonic-dominant of the Baroque timpani. The flourishes in the right hand are obviously trumpet fanfares, the trumpet being the invariable companion of the kettledrum in the eighteenth century (Example 37).

EXAMPLE 37

VIII. *The common rejoicing and the dancing and gaiety of the people (Il Giubilo commune, ed i balli d'allegrezza del Populo).* Thinking still of the dances of the women in I Samuel, only this time in a more stately form, Kuhnau ends the sonata and the story with what appears to be a minuet and trio, but with only a truncated return of the minuet.

◊ 3 ◊   With the general plan and some of the thematic material of the sonata before us, let us see if we can reach any conclusions about the narrative technique that it embodies.

To begin with—and this will hardly be surprising—Kuhnau relies heavily on the resources of language to tell his story. Had "The Battle between David and Goliath" been called simply "Sonata," and had there been no titles to the individual movements, not only would we have been unable to recognize the biblical story in Kuhnau's music, we would never even have suspected that this was anything but a piece of purely instrumental music (except perhaps for the rather disjointed character of movement III). But does it follow from this that the music does not do some of the storytelling? To answer this question we had better first see in specific terms just what the music *does* do. We have already developed some conceptual apparatus to facilitate this.

The music, it is clear, is meant by Kuhnau to illustrate some things: these illustrations are all of the kind I have called representations,

rather than pictures, since they are not recognizable without the aid of
text or title. They can be subdivided further into those that are and
those that are not of the "sounds like" kind. Thus, for example, the
representation of the tabret and trumpets in movement VII, are representations, in sound, of the sound of the trumpet and drum: not, of
course, recognizable as such without the aid of a text, but, like the representation of laughter in Cantata 31, or the buzzing of flies in *Israel in
Egypt*, clearly identifiable, after the fact, as "sounding like" their respective objects. Again, the concluding minuet is a representation in
sound, of dance music that, Kuhnau imagines, accompanied the dancing of the Israelite women. Unlike Handel, or later composers, he
makes no attempt to introduce "exotic" elements into his dance, modal
harmonies or scales, for example, to suggest the eastern or "primitive"
provenance of the events, but simply supplies a stately dance of his
own time, the "social" minuet. This has, to my mind, a kind of sublime
naiveté about it, much like that to be found in some medieval illuminations. Perhaps others will merely find it simple or silly, but whether silly
or sublime, dance represents dance, and dance sounds like dance
(however remotely). Of the other kind of representation, we find such
familiar instances as musical imitation used to represent folks following other folks (the fugue in movement V), the descending figure to
represent the fall of Goliath in movement IV, and the rush of thirty-
second and sixty-fourth notes in the same movement to represent the
slinging of David's stone. (A very similar figure is used by Handel, in
Saul, to represent the distracted King hurling his javelin at David.)

Kuhnau's musical representations, in addition, can be divided into
those that represent in a "graphic" manner and those that represent
"expressively." (Again, the distinction is familiar from what has gone
before.) That is to say, there are instances in which Kuhnau represents
what is going on by making his music expressive of some emotion or
mood that is part of the scene or event depicted. Thus, the clumsy, "gi-
gantic" pomposity of Goliath is represented by music expressive of the
clumsily pompous (movement I); the melancholy mood of the Israelites at the sight of Goliath by melancholy music (movement II); David's
courage by "eager," "confident" music (movement III); the Israelites'
joy over David's victory by joyful music (movements VI, VII, and VIII).

What this survey reveals, then, is that Kuhnau has made use of
pretty much the whole catalogue of representational techniques outlined in Chapter III. The question remains: Has he "told" the story of
David and Goliath? We are now, I think, closer to an answer—or, at
least, to all the answer I will attempt to give. What we must determine is

the relation of these representations to the story Kuhnau is attempting to tell.

◊ 4 ◊   I think it should be obvious, at this point, that we have one very good analogue for what Kuhnau has done with biblical narrative, in the illustrated novel, the difference, of course, being that in the case of Kuhnau's *Biblical Sonatas,* the text is accessory to the music, whereas, even where the graphic artist is a superior one, the illustrations in a novel are usually accessory to the text. What the illustrator does is to take a time-slice, an instant of the narrative, say, Ahab "shooting the sun" (in Chapter CXVII—"The Quadrant"—of Melville's *Moby Dick*) or Hugh Lofting's Doctor Dolittle feeling an elephant's pulse, and give us that slice of the narrative in frozen motion. And that, in effect, is how Kuhnau presents, in music, the story of David and Goliath. He cannot tell us of the events that brought David and the giant face to face. But he can illustrate a moment of the giant's boasting, or David's taunts, as the illustrator can show us the pregnant moment, whatever it may be.

To this it may well be responded that in one very crucial respect musical illustrations of narratives are very different from—and perhaps in this respect, at least, superior to—graphic ones. For music is, after all, a temporal art, and need not, therefore, confine itself to presenting instantaneous time slices. A musical movement, in reading or performance, is an "event," and events can be its subject. (Compare the well-known argument in Lessing's *Laokoön,* contrasting the temporal character and subject matter of poetry with the atemporal arts of painting and sculpture.)

The point is well-taken—which is not to say that music *cannot* present time-slices much in the way the literary illustrator does. Goliath's pomposity and David's courage are not "events" (not, by the way, because they are "psychological," but because they just happen not to be psychological "events"). Kuhnau simply illustrates the giant's pomposity and the boy's confidence by giving us "snapshots" of them: the music is simply an example of pomposity and confidence, nothing "happens" in it (except for purely musical "events"). Of course the music takes time to get from first measure to cadence, but it also takes time to scan an illustration from Rockwell Kent's *Moby Dick.* And as regards Kuhnau's illustrations of Goliath's pomposity and David's courage, musical time functions merely as scanning time—the time necessary to "take in" the plate: pomposity and courage in amber.

Nevertheless, musical temporality *can* function to "illustrate" temporal events; and for this function we possess in the silent film, a more felicitous model than the literary illustration. For *one* way of looking at some silent films is as narrative texts with *moving* illustrations.[5] We can, in other words, look upon the running titles of these films as the bearers of the story line, and what we see on the screen above them as moving illustrations of the crucial events in the narrative. But whereas the literary illustrator can only give us instantaneous time-slices, an Eisenstein or a Griffith can give us an edible slice of the temporal pie: not just the baby buggy on the brink, but in full career. Similarly, Kuhnau gives us not just David and Goliath toe to toe at the instant of the challenge, or Goliath caught by the illustrator's pen in mid-fall, but a *moving* picture, as it were, of the challenge, the conflict, the slinging of the stone, the fall and death of the Philistine. If Goliath's pomposity and David's courage are best seen as the illustrations for a novel, movement IV—*Il combattere*—I would suggest, has more the aspect of a scene from the silent cinema, with appropriate titles. For here Kuhnau makes use of the temporality of music to represent the temporality of events, not merely to provide the musical equivalent of the scanning of a still.

One more model for musical narrative might usefully be mentioned here, not so much for any advantage it might have over those already canvassed, but to point up a deficiency in narrative potential that it might be mistakenly thought is characteristic of musical illustration alone. I refer to the genre of narrative painting in general, and, in particular, to historical painting broadly conceived to include the religious and mythological.

Compare, for example, a painting of the *Martyrdom of Saint Sebastian*, showing just the martyred saint, but not the archers, or Peter Bruegel the Elder's *Landscape with the Fall of Icarus*, with Kuhnau's depiction of the battle between David and Goliath in movement IV. Surely, it might be argued, what makes a painter able to "narrate," and a composer unable to, is the fact, freely admitted throughout this study, that a "realistic" painting can be recognized for what it is, sans text or title, whereas except for a paltry few, for the most part utterly trivial examples, illustrational music cannot. There is the story of Saint Sebastian's martyrdom before us, in all of its gory detail: the martyr tied to his stake, the arrows protruding from his body. And here is the story of Icarus: the sun, the sea, the drowning aviator going down for the third time. After all, in narration, as elsewhere, hasn't it been rightly said that one picture is worth a thousand words? But where are David and Goliath in Kuhnau's illustration? Would one person in a thousand guess, without text or title, that their encounter is what is depicted here? Or that *any-thing* is?

But, of course, the *Martyrdom of Saint Sebastian* or the *Fall of Icarus,* as narrations or illustrations of historical events, are no more indepen-dent of narrative texts than are Kuhnau's *Biblical Sonatas.* The dif-ference is merely that in the former the narrative is "implied," it is "in the head" of the viewer, whereas in the latter the text is provided. What would I make of a *Martyrdom of Saint Sebastian* if I did not know the story? Is the figure on the post a man shot full of arrows or a man in an "arrow suit"?[6] And even if, as is likely, I take the figure of Saint Sebas-tian to be the victim of execution by bow and arrow, I am not very much closer to learning, from the picture, the story of Saint Sebastian. Similarly, Bruegel's *Fall of Icarus* can hardly *tell* the story in the full sense of the word. Are these two tiny legs our last view of the drowning flyer, or are they those of a vacationer out for a swim on a nice sunny day? (There's the sun, after all!)[7] In both cases, indeed in all such cases of historical painting, a narrative text is assumed, which the viewer is expected to know, and the title of the painting to call to consciousness. The painting is an illustration of a scene from that narrative text, and, needless to say, one of the tasks of the critic, art historian, and iconolo-gist, is to determine for us, if need be, because of the loss of a tradition to contemporary viewers, what the text is we must familiarize ourselves with to view the historical painting before us.

It seems reasonable to conclude, then, that given the commonsense distinction between telling a story and "illuminating" it, between, that is, a narrative and the illustrations of it, what Kuhnau's biblical "narra-tives" turn out to be are musical "illuminations" rather than musical "storytelling"—the illustration of the narrative, not the narrative it-self. Needless to say, it would be folly to generalize from one instance—and that, after all, of a composer who is hardly known to any but musi-cologists and a handful of harpsichord players. Furthermore, it might be argued, Johann Kuhnau, a composer not of the first rank, writing in a time when the "narrative" techniques of music were perhaps still in their infancy, can hardly be taken as the example to prove that "narra-tive" music cannot be "narrative" in the full sense of the word, but merely its illustrational embellishment.

To this objection I would answer, to start with, that I intend to make no generalizations at all about narrative music tout court, either from one instance or many. Nor, however, do I intend to let Kuhnau stand alone as an example of musical storytelling. Rather, I shall turn now to a case that no one can claim is in the backwaters of the genre, to, in fact, what many would consider the paradigm: Berlioz' *Symphonie fantastique*. To go from Kuhnau to Berlioz is, truly, to go from one universe to another. So much the better, for what I hope to show is that *plus ça change, plus c'est la même chose*.

◊ 5 ◊   The *Symphonie fantastique*, first performed in Paris, 5 December, 1830, is unquestionably one of the most controversial, as well as genuinely revolutionary works in the history of Western music. Its premiere, as Edward T. Cone remarks, in his critical edition of the score, "vividly brought to the attention of the public the fact that it was entering a new musical era."[8] Surely, one of the off-putting aspects of the symphony, to its first audiences, as well as audiences for a remarkably long time thereafter, was its purely *musical* daring.

For despite the many traditional and even eclectic elements of the symphony, despite its obeisance to classical formal procedures, despite the composer's insistence on his harmonic orthodoxy, this music *sounded* like no music ever before heard. The proof of its great originality is that today, almost a century and a half later, it still sounds like no other music; and not very long ago critics were still attacking it for its disregard of accepted procedures.

What concerns us, however, is not, of course, the purely musical aspects of Berlioz' style, but, rather, the "literary" ones, at least in so far as they can be considered separately; and here too *Symphonie fantastique* has been an object of contention.

The relationship between the program and the music of the *Fantastic Symphony* has been the source of as much discussion and controversy as the music itself. Is a familiarity with the program necessary to an understanding of the music? Or is it actually detrimental to the musical experience? Is the symphony viable as absolute music? Did Berlioz write the music to fit the program or vice versa? And so on.[9]

Whether the program of *Symphonie fantastique* is or is not necessary to its comprehension, and (what may amount to the same thing) whether or not the symphony is viable as pure music, are questions that do not concern me, at least in so far as they are understood to be questions specifically about Berlioz' work. And in so far as they are questions about program or illustrational music in general—that is to say, questions about whether text or title is *ever* necessary for the comprehension of music—I have answered such questions already, in the affirmative, in the previous chapter. As to the historical question of whether, in the case of *Symphonie fantastique*, the music or the program came first, it has no direct bearing on the nature of what resulted, one way or another, namely, a symphony that purports, with the help of a text, to tell a story. Another question, however, regarding the history of the work's composition, or, rather, its various revisions at Berlioz' hands, is of some interest in what follows, and must be gone into at least briefly.

The history of *Symphonie fantastique*, and its program, both before and after the premiere, is a tangled tale which Edwart T. Cone admirably unravels in his critical edition of the score. To oversimplify a bit for present purposes, there would appear to be two clearly distinguishable versions of the work, differing not only in musical particulars, which need not concern us, but in programmatic ones, which must. In brief, the version that Berlioz performed in 1830 was to be accompanied by a printed text outlining the story the symphony was meant to tell. In a footnote to the Avertissement that precedes this program, Berlioz insisted, as he did when the first edition of the score was published in 1845, that the narrative text be considered an essential part of a correct performance. "The distribution of this program to the audience, at concerts where this symphony is to be performed, is indispensable for a complete understanding of the dramatic outline of the work."[10] The first version of *Symphonie fantastique*, then, consists of a musical score (with titled movements) *and* an accompanying narrative text to be perused by the listener as a prerequisite for a satisfactory audition of the piece.

Early on, however, Berlioz was also contemplating, and subsequently composed, a sequel to the *Symphonie fantastique* called *Lelio, or the Return of Life,* a dramatic monologue (monodrama) with musical accompaniment. It was intended as the second half of concerts in which *Symphonie fantastique* was to be the opening work. But he also, apparently, continued to think of the symphony as a separate entity in its own right, performable without *Lelio.* And this in turn led to a rather interesting volte face in which he essentially removed the programmatic text (but *not* the titles) from the symphony, when it was performed alone, that is, sans *Lelio.* Thus, in later editions of the score, the Avertissement reads in part:

If the symphony alone is performed in a concert, . . . one can [if necessary] even dispense with distributing the program, keeping only the titles of the five movements. The symphony by itself (the author hopes) can afford musical interest independent of any dramatic purpose.[11]

The remark is not altogether single-minded, as it suggests at first that the narrative is to be dispensed with *only* if necessary, whereas I detect in the conclusion a very strong plea for the *Symphonie fantastique* as "pure" instrumental music—with titles to the movements, to be sure; but *that*, after all, was no more than Beethoven had ventured in the *Pastoral* which, nevertheless, was accepted as a genuinely symphonic work for all of that. Thus, if I am right about Berlioz' conclusion, we have a *second* version of the *Symphonie fantastique*, about the same (for our purposes) in its purely musical particulars, but denuded of its narrative text.

Now when two versions of a musical work are extant, questions naturally arise. Which is the definitive version? Which is better? (A later version is not necessarily definitive, as the composer may have produced a revision for a performance under less than optimal conditions. Nor need the definitive version necessarily be the better. Many people, myself included, prefer the first version of Mozart's G-minor Symphony (K. 550), the one without clarinets, although Mozart obviously thought the later revision definitive.) Such questions, however, need not perturb us. It suffices to observe that there are, extant, two versions of *Symphonie fantastique*, and that the earlier contains, as part of the work, a narrative text the music is meant to embody. Needless to say, *that* is the version I will be concerned with here, better or not, definitive or not, in my discussion of musical narration, and the version I will always have in mind when I refer to *the Symphonie fantastique*.

◊ 6 ◊   The *Symphonie fantastique* has five movements: like Beethoven's Sixth, an expansion of the usual four-movement form. The movements are titled, respectively: Dreams, Passions (*Rêveries, Passions*); A Ball (*Un bal*); In the Country (*Scène aux champs*); March to the Scaffold (*Marche au supplice*); Dream of a Witches' Sabath (*Songe d'une nuit du sabat*). It is also necessary, for what follows, to give the reader a clear idea of the narrative program that Berlioz originally thought indispensable to a proper appreciation of the music. I reproduce it below, in the definitive early version, as published with the first edition of the score in 1845.[12]

PART ONE

REVERIES—PASSIONS

The author imagines that a young musician, afflicted with that moral disease that a well-known writer calls the *vague des passions*, sees for the first time a woman who embodies all the charms of the ideal being he has imagined in his dreams, and he falls desperately in love with her. Through an odd whim, whenever the beloved image appears before the mind's eye of the artist it is linked with a musical thought whose character, passionate but at the same time noble and shy, he finds similar to the one he attributes to his beloved.

This melodic image and the model it reflects pursue him incessantly like a double *idée fixe*. That is the reason for the constant appearance, in every moment of the symphony, of the melody that begins the first Allegro. The passage from this state of melancholy reverie, interrupted by a few fits of groundless joy, to one of frenzied passion, with its movements of fury, of jealousy, its return of tenderness, its tears, its religious consolations—this is the subject of the first movement.

PART TWO

A BALL

The artist finds himself in the most varied situations—in the midst of *the tumult of a party*, in the peaceful contemplation of the beauties of nature; but everywhere, in town, in the country, the beloved image appears before him and disturbs his peace of mind.

PART THREE

SCENE IN THE COUNTRY

Finding himself one evening in the country, he hears in the distance two shepherds piping a *ranz des vaches* in dialogue. This pastoral duet, the scenery, the quiet rustling of the trees gently brushed by the wind, the hopes he has recently found some reason to entertain—all concur in affording his heart an unaccustomed calm, and in giving a more cheerful color to his ideas. He reflects upon his isolation; he hopes that his loneliness will soon be over.—But what if she were deceiving him!—This mingling of hope and fear, these ideas of happiness disturbed by black presentiments, form the subject of the Adagio. At the end one of the shepherds again takes up the *ranz des vaches*; the other no longer replies.—Distant sound of thunder—loneliness—silence.

PART FOUR

MARCH TO THE SCAFFOLD

Convinced that his love is unappreciated, the artist poisons himself with opium. The dose of the narcotic, too weak to kill him, plunges him into a sleep accompanied by the most horrible visions. He dreams that he has killed his beloved, that he is condemned and led to the scaffold, and that he is witnessing *his own execution*. The procession moves forward to the sounds of a march that is now sombre and fierce, now brilliant and solemn, in which the muffled noise of heavy steps gives way without transition to the noisiest clamor. At the end of the march the first four measures of the *idée fixe* reappear, like a last thought of love interrupted by the fatal blow.

PART FIVE

DREAM OF A WITCHES' SABBATH

He sees himself at the sabbath, in the midst of a frightful troop of ghosts, sorcerers, monsters of every kind, come together for his funeral. Strange noises, groans, bursts of laughter, distant cries which other cries seem to answer. The beloved melody appears again, but it has lost its character of nobility and shyness; it is no more than a dance tune, mean, trivial, and grotesque: it is she, coming to join the sabbath.—A roar of joy at her arrival.—She takes part in the devilish orgy.—Funeral knell, burlesque parody of the *Dies irae, sabbath round-dance*. The sabbath round and the *Dies irae* combined.

◊ 7 ◊   Here, then, is the story that Berlioz proposes to "tell" in music. And a quick comparison with the stories Kuhnau is concerned with in the *Biblical Sonatas* reveals the palpably obvious fact that whereas Kuhnau's stories are of "external" events mostly, Berlioz' is, to a large extent anyway, an "internal" narrative: a series of "inner," "psychological" events. That is to be expected, of course, given the preoccupations of the Romantic movement with the life of feeling and thought. Thus, in the first version of the program, three out of the five movements are wholly concerned with the inner life of the artist: his reveries and passions (first movement), and his opium dream (movements four and five). And, indeed, in the later versions of the program, Berlioz transports the whole story into the artist's (now specifically a *musician's*) consciousness, imagining right from the start of the symphony that the protagonist is the victim of an hallucination.

A young musician of a morbidly sensitive temperament and fiery imagination poisons himself with opium in a fit of lovesick despair. The dose of the narcotic, too weak to kill him, plunges him into a deep slumber accompanied by the strangest visions, during which his sensations, his emotions, his memories are transformed in his sick mind into musical thoughts and images.[13]

The flight to the subjective in later versions of the program, may have been motivated by a number of considerations, but principally, no doubt, by the desire to make a case for the *Symphonie fantastique* as pure instrumental music in its own right—an effort, as we have seen, supported also by Berlioz' relegating of the printed program to an ad libitum status: thus the retreat to what had always been the favored domain of music, the inner life of feeling, with all of its vagaries. As Cone observes, "It is possible, then, that the new program was his way of telling the audience: 'Look, don't take all this too seriously; it's only a dream. The main thing is the music.' "[14] Remember too that Berlioz, as we saw in Chapter VII, favored the view that musical representation comes down to musical expressiveness, thus making the subjective, so often identified with the emotive, the ideal object of musical representation. Even "pure," programless, nonrepresentational music can be expressive, after all. So if Berlioz tells us, essentially, "The program isn't really necessary, *and* it only recounts a succession of feeling-states (in a *musician*'s consciousness!) by a succession of expressive sounds, *which is exactly what pure music often amounts too anyway*," he has more or less collapsed representational music into pure music, thus establishing the right of *Symphonie fantastique* to be taken as, first and foremost, a *musical* work.

Be all that as it may, however, I have chosen the early version of the *Symphonie fantastique* for my specific purposes; and whatever status its later incarnations may have, *it* remains musical narration in its most unabashed form. And what I hope to convince the reader of is that although its subject matter, and musical "vocabulary" are worlds apart from Kuhnau's, the "narrative" technique is essentially the same: that is to say, the illustration of a narrative, not the narrative itself. Let us first, then, look at the narrative line from a distance, to see how the plan of the symphony as a whole reflects it; and then look in detail at one of the more "narrative" movements—the third, *Scène aux champs*—which serves as the traditional symphonic "slow movement." (To do more would exceed the bounds of the present study.)

The five movements of the *Symphonie fantastique* represent five discrete stages in the life of an artist of rather delicate sensibilities who has, the program tells us, fallen in love at first sight, in the literal sense of that phrase: that is to say, by merely seeing the object of his love once. Each of these stages, it should be noted, is a time-slice rather than, as in the case of some of Kuhnau's narrative illustrations, static instants in the story. Thus throughout Berlioz makes use of the temporal character of music to illustrate events, real or imagined, in the artist's life. The model best suited, then, to Berlioz' "narrative" technique is the cinematic one. But representing events in time by musical "events" in musical time was not, as we have seen, unknown to Kuhnau; so the difference here is one of degree, not of kind. Nor should the fact that many of the events Berlioz depicts are "mental events" create any problems, or reveal any great musical disanalogies between Berlioz and Kuhnau. Perhaps there may be some who harbor metaphysical scruples of one kind or another about the concept of a "mental event," but at least at the level of common sense there appear to be no grounds for such scruples, and I shall remain, I hope, well within the bounds of common sense.

The first movement, Reveries, Passions, is a dimly recognizable, though much altered, sonata-allegro, with the traditional symphonic slow introduction. It represents, according to the program, the violently changing moods of the distracted lover; and these shifting moods are easily recognizable in the alternating expressive qualities of the music as it shifts from major to minor, diatonic to chromatic, and from one tempo or pulse to another, in a nervous style quite characteristic of such emotional vulcanism, irrespective of the originality of the musical style that is so distinctively Berlioz'.

The first theme of the sonata-allegro is the celebrated idée fixe (Example 38). Its "logical" peculiarity is worth noting, although it raises no particular problem for our understanding of musical representation. Berlioz tells us in the program: "Through an odd whim, whenever the beloved image appears before the mind's eye of the artist it is linked with a musical thought whose character, passionate but at the same time noble and shy, he finds similar to the one he attributes to his beloved." The musical theme, then, which begins the sonata-allegro, and which recurs in every other movement of the symphony, is a representation *not* of the beloved, but of a recurring musical phrase in the artist's head, which phrase is, in turn, a representation of the character of the beloved through its expressiveness: both being passionate, noble, shy. It is, then, a representation, and, at the same time, like the Lutheran chorale in *Meistersinger*, a musical representation of imaginary music. And, of course, in its periodic recurrence in the symphony, it represents an experience of the protagonist that most of us have had at

EXAMPLE 38
Berlioz, *Symphonie fantastique, Rêveries, Passions*

one time or another: the maddening tune running through the head
that cannot be quelled. It is, then, a logical briar patch; but, after all, in
any one of its representational manifestations, a fairly straightforward
example of the genre: a musical picture of music, an expressive representation of the beloved, and a structural analogue to the psychological phenomenon known as the idée fixe.

Standing in place of the classical minuet, or the scherzo, is the second movement, A Ball, a clearly recognizable song and trio, in the
shape of a waltz, with the idée fixe prominent in the trio. Representationally it is equally "traditional" and straightforward. The waltz represents the kind of dance music we are to imagine the protagonist would
have heard at the ball; and the idée fixe in the trio represents, of
course, the persistent return to the artist's consciousness of the maddening tune and the "beloved image [which] appears before him and
disturbs his peace of mind." Like the first movement, it is a representational time-slice, depicting the party (waltz), and a "mental event"
(trio), which interrupts the artist's perception of the proceedings.
However, here *external events* (the party) as well as internal ones (the
return of the idée fixe and the image of the beloved) are represented.

In the Country, an *adagio*, forms the traditional symphonic slow
movement. It occurs after the "scherzo" or "minuet," rather than before, which is not the usual practice; but, again, Berlioz has

Beethoven's precedent, in the Ninth. This, as I said, is the most directly and unabashedly illustrational of the movements. But as I shall be examining its illustrational elements in more detail in a moment, I will not linger over them here, and move quickly on to the two final movements.

Schumann, in an attempt to force the *Symphonie fantastique* into the traditional four-movement mold, argued that: "If we look at the five movements in relation to one another, we find that they comply with the traditional succession, except for the last two, which, however, as two scenes of a dream, seem to form a single whole." His conclusion was that "the last two constitute the final Allegro."[15] This seems to me to be a needless concession to the traditional four-movement symphony in the attempt to prove orthodoxy, given that we not only have Beethoven's precedent for the five-movement form, but for the five-movement form *specifically* as an illustrational symphony, the *Pastoral* being at once Beethoven's *only* five-movement symphony and the *only* one to possess a "program." My own view is that the fourth movement, March to the Scaffold, might best be seen as a second "scherzo," much like the second minuet in the classical divertimento. (It is, after all, a "dance" movement, as is the first.) The last movement, Dream of a Witches' Sabbath, then, stands alone as the symphony's proper finale. And if one is looking for classical precedents, it is not without interest that Berlioz' finale is especially rich in contrapuntal, particularly fugal, development, including a full-blown double "fugato"; for the fugal finale was a well-known feature of the classical symphony and string quartet, the finale of Mozart's Jupiter being the most famous, but not by any means the only example.[16]

As for the representational elements of the last two movements, they are more or less straightforward. The protagonist, in an opium-induced dream, sees himself marched to the scaffold (fourth movement), to the strains of a marche funèbre: "At the end of the march," Berlioz tells us, "the first four measures of the idée fixe reappear, like a last thought of love interrupted by the fatal blow." The sound of the blade's fall is obvious enough (Example 39).

The finale is, for the most part, a musical picture of clamor, confusion, cacophony, general bedlam (and is, on that account, one of the things that has given Berlioz his entirely unjustified reputation for bluster, bombast and overblown orchestral noise). "Strange noises, groans, bursts of laughter, distant cries which other cries seem to answer," all can be heard quite easily in the music, with the help, of course, of Berlioz' verbal description. The "Dies Irae" the somewhat melodramatic late medieval chant, is introduced to suggest that the

Example 39

Berlioz, *Symphonie fantastique, Marche au supplice*

hero is witnessing (in his dream) his own funeral. The text is a traditional part of the Requiem Mass. And its textual reference to the Last Judgment further reinforces the impression of horror and confusion that Berlioz wishes to give (see Chapter I, Example 4).

This, then, is the general outline of Berlioz' narrative, for the most part more dynamic than Kuhnau's, illustrating the temporal progression of inner and outer events with the temporal progression of musical "events" in musical time. But, as we have seen, cinematic, "moving" musical illustration was not unknown to Kuhnau; so what we have here, to repeat, is not a difference in kind of technique, but merely a different mix of the same technical procedures.

A swift overview, however, may leave the reader with the feeling that justice has not been done to the unique and original in Berlioz' musical illustrationism. So let us now look more closely, as I said we would, at the slow movement of the *Symphonie fantastique* before drawing any precipitous conclusions.

◊ 8 ◊   The *Scène aux champs* is nature music; and I do not think there can be much doubt that Beethoven's *Pastoral* is the principal exemplar, particularly the *Szene am Bach*, and *Gewitter, Sturm*; its bird calls and thunderstorm find clear echo in Berlioz' musical landscape, as does a certain (to me at least) ineffable Beethoven sound (which others, I am sure, can find the proper technical words for). Berlioz' little "pastoral" begins with a duet for English horn and offstage oboe, representing "two shepherds piping a *ranz des vaches* in dialogue" (Example 40).

EXAMPLE 40
Berlioz, *Symphonie fantastique, Scène aux champs*

The next clearly recognizable "event" begins at measure 67 with a series of answering bird calls, in the flute, oboe, and clarinet. Berlioz does
not mention them specifically in the program, but they are unmistakable to the ear, particularly if one recalls the ones explicitly identified
as such in the *Szene am Bach*. (Compare, too, the "answering" wind passages in "Forest Murmurs" in the second act of *Siegfried*) (Example 41).

The pastoral tranquillity of the movement, so reminiscent of
Beethoven's Sixth, is broken at measure 83 with a heightening of chromaticism and the beginning of an ominous crescendo, reinforced at
figure 41 with an insistently repeated figure of "seriousness" in the 'cel-
los, basses and bassoons (Example 42). It clearly represents "these
ideas of happiness disturbed by black presentiments. . . ." But on another, external level it represents, I am certain, a thunderstorm, the
aftermath of which forms the coda of the movement—"distant sound
of thunder—loneliness—silence." The climax of this at once inner and
outer storm—a nature allegory if you will—comes with an orchestral
tutti at measure 106, subsides at 109, the musical weather clearing at

EXAMPLE 41

113 with a rising figure in the woodwinds, and a sunny cadence in F major (Example 43).

The closing section of the movement brings a return of the first, dialogue theme, in the English horn—but this time, significantly, not answered by the oboe: the shepherd's call elicits no reply. And in the background, the monologue of the English horn is interrupted by the distant thunder of four timpani (tuned to F, B-flat, C, and A-flat, the percussionist specifically directed by Berlioz to use sponge-headed sticks). "One of the shepherds takes up his simple tune again, the other no longer answers. The sun sets—distant sound of thunder—loneliness—silence" (Example 44). Again, I think, it is clear that we have representation taking place on two levels. Externally, it is the shepherd, unanswered by his companion, threatened by distant thunder; internally, the hero, rejected, and overcome by "stormy emotions." Berlioz refers to the two characters represented by oboe and English horn as "shepherds"; but only the one represented by the English horn, the "tenor" of the double-reed family, is referred to as "he," and it hardly seems unwarranted to assume that the oboe, the "soprano" of the double-reeds, represents a shepherd*ess*. Is the shepherd "rejected," or does the absence of the shepherdess' response merely

EXAMPLE 42

EXAMPLE 43

Example 44

signify that she has taken shelter from the storm? In either case, the unanswered call and distant thunder are an allegory for the hero's "rejection" (hardly real, as the beloved does not know he exists) and his inner turmoil, and if anything besides the purely musical separates Berlioz' "narration" from Kuhnau's, it is this literary sophistication on the part of the former, that gives layers and depths to his representations. There are no layers or depths to David and Goliath. (But we should be careful here not to attribute this to any lack of sophistication on the part of Baroque composers in general. Bach, for example, is a composer who luxuriates in the musical allegory and double entendre.)

A detailed look, then, at Berlioz' "narrative," which is to say, illustrational technique, reveals no logical or musical disanalogies with the illustrational techniques canvassed in the preceding chapters of this book, or the "narrative" technique of his Baroque predecessors. What it does reveal, which is hardly surprising, is a depth of sophistication in "literary" and "psychological" matters, a preference for the "inner" over the "outer," the "state of mind" over the "state of nature," multiple levels over single ones, double meanings over literal ones, allegory over simple story line, only to be expected in a "literary" composer plying his trade in the high tide of the Romantic movement, of which he was a principal figure. But amidst all of this subtlety we look in vain for anything in the music beyond the illustration of a narration, carried forward (as in Kuhnau's *Biblical Sonatas*) by a narrative text. And, indeed, Berlioz himself gives his imprimatur to just that interpretation of musical "narration": that is to say, the illustration of a text. In a notice printed in *Figaro* (May 20, 1830), Berlioz (in Cone's summary)

> tries to explain his approach to symphonic music by invoking the French opéra comique with its alternation of song and spoken dialogue. The opera composer determines which episodes, scenes, and emotional states in his drama are expressible in music; these he sets as numbers, connecting them with dialogue ("texte parlé"). In the same way, Berlioz has chosen [in *Symphonie fantastique*] certain situations from the artist's life that have musical possibilities ("ce qu'elles ont de musical"); these have become the movements of his symphony. And just as the operatic dialogue leads into the numbers ("amener des morceaux"), explaining their meaning and motivating their expression, so Berlioz's program introduces each movement in turn.[17]

I have invoked the model of silent cinema with subtitles to convey the nature of *temporal* musical illustrations, that is, illustrations of events in "moving" musical pictures. But the musical play with spoken dialogue—opéra comique in France, Singspiel in Germany, ballad opera in England—will serve to convey the same idea, except for the fact that whereas in the opéra comique the accompanying text is heard (unless you are reading the score), in the silent cinema, as in the program symphony, it is read. The basic idea, however, is the same: a story told in words and illustrated in music. Berlioz is my own best witness in this regard, then. He no more claims to be able to "tell" the story of the *Symphonie fantastique* without the written text, than Rockwell Kent could "tell" the story of *Moby Dick* without Melville's novel, or Griffith *Birth of a Nation* without subtitles. That makes them all "illustrators." To call them "mere" illustrators is to suggest an evaluation of their work quite at odds with mine, and irrelevant, anyway, to my present concerns, but, for that matter, one might call many a great English novelist a "mere" storyteller, with equal insensitivity. I mean, as I have said often enough, to stay clear of such normative questions. Berlioz, in the *Symphonie fantastique,* is an illustrator; "mere" or not is a question I leave for others.

◊ 9 ◊   Here, then, are two examples—paradigms, it seems fair to say—of musical narration, from widely separated periods in musical history, but periods, nonetheless, in which illustration and "narrative" were of particular interest to composers of the first rank. What we find in these two cases, is that musical narrative comes down to musical illustration of a narrative text, much in the manner, I have suggested, of an illustrated novel, or in the way silent cinema can be thought to illustrate a subtitle with a "moving" picture of an event in progress.

Two questions now become pressing. Can we generalize from two instances? And, generalizable or not, can we remove the quotation marks from around musical "narration"; that is to say, is the musical illustration of a narrative text itself a *narration* in the proper sense of that word, or is ordinary discourse correct in distinguishing here, as it does, between a *narration* and an *illustration* of it, which is only "narration" loosely speaking?

As for generalizing from two instances, I am content not to generalize at all. I don't think it needs any argument to convince that both the *Biblical Sonatas* and *Symphonie fantastique* are not isolated examples of the kind of "narration" they exemplify. And I make no claim that their "narrative" techniques exhaust the possibilities, any more than I need claim that the illustrative techniques I have canvassed in this book exhaust the possibilities of musical illustration, either past or future.

Whether musical "narration" of the kind I have discussed here is narration properly so-called, or narration in a loose, extended sense, is, it seems to me, either a trivial question of no intrinsic interest at all, or a profound question about the nature of narrative in general, the answering of which would carry us well beyond the bounds I have set for myself in the present study. It is a trivial question if it is merely a semantic quibble. We certainly refer to Eisenstein's "narrative technique," meaning to include, of course, both the pictures and the titles, just as we say that in the edition of *Moby Dick* illustrated by Rockwell Kent, the artist helps to "tell the story." And it is a matter of no interest to me at all whether one uses "narrative technique" and "tell the story" in this liberal way, or insists that we reserve those descriptions for narrative texts (that is, texts written in natural languages), and call the pictures, moving or not, *illustrations of* the narrative story or text. It is equally immaterial, needless to say, whether we call Kuhnau's *Biblical Sonatas* and *Symphonie fantastique*—the musical parts, that is—musical "narrations" or "illustrations" of the narrative text, just as long as their limitations are recognized; just as long as we realize how powerless music is to "tell a story" in the absence of a narrative text. Berlioz may have made more extravagant claims for music's power of description than we are comfortable with today. But he was hardly deluded as to the reliance of the *Symphonie fantastique,* qua narrative, on the programmatic text: "it is precisely in order to fill in the gaps which the use of musical language unavoidably leaves in the development of dramatic thought," Berlioz wrote in *Figaro,* "that the composer has had to avail himself of written prose to explain and justify the outline of the symphony."[18]

The deeper question involves digging into the nature of narrative itself, with a view towards determining necessary and/or sufficient conditions (if any there be), and then, in turn, determining whether music, qua music, can fulfill them. That, no doubt, is a profound, and profoundly interesting philosophical task, but it goes well beyond what can be undertaken here. So if the former question can be dismissed as too trifling, the latter must be dismissed, for the present anyway, as too philosophically dense and ramified. We must rest content, then, with the modest conclusion that at least some exemplary cases of musical narration are best understood as illustrations in sound of a narrative text; and that "musical narration" had best remain quarantined in quotation marks until narration in general is better understood by the philosophical practitioner.

CHAPTER X

How to See It in Music
(Without Losing Your Respectability)

◊ 1 ◊　In a way this study has been a defense of music as, at least in part, but not by any means wholly, a representational art; not a defense in the traditional sense of an attempt to convince people that representational music is a good thing, or an artistic goal worthy of pursuit, but, rather, a defense simply in the sense of an answer to the charge that music cannot, properly speaking, ever be a representational art. It has been, in other words, an attempt to explain how music can, and indeed has, represented things in the world. It was not my purpose to urge a musical aesthetic upon practitioners of the art or upon those whose profession it is to analyze and evaluate music past and present. But the fact that it has been a defense at all may raise some musical eyebrows and recall a great many "interpretations" of the instrumental masterpieces which have, we all would say with a considerable sigh of relief, passed quite justifiably out of the realm of accepted critical practice and polite musical company. For, it might be argued, in defending the representational powers of music, have I not opened the door again to those infernal asses who must find a story in Beethoven's piano sonatas, and pictures in *The Well-Tempered Clavier*, and to those teachers, devoid of all musical intelligence, who impart "musical appreciation" to their young prisoners by encouraging them to freely associate as a substitute for listening, thus transforming Beethoven's Fifth into Rorschach's First?

The short way with such objections is simply to reply that here, as anywhere else, we have a right to distinguish between valid and invalid interpretations. It is a valid interpretation of *Pacific 231* to read it as a representation of a steam locomotive; it is an invalid interpretation of *The Art of the Fugue* to read it as a representation of the Leibnizian Weltanschauung.[1] To defend the claim that music can be representational no more opens the critical floodgates to representational interpretations of any music you like, than the claim that narratives can have more than one layer of meaning implies that *Winnie the Pooh* is an allegory of the dark night of the soul.

To this strategy two related objections can be anticipated: that interpretations of works of art are at least problematic, and perhaps even
irretrievably "subjective," across the board, and, therefore, the distinction between valid and invalid interpretations comes to nothing; or,
less ambitiously, that although there may be grounds for distinguishing between valid and invalid interpretations of some kinds, in some of
the arts, whether or not music represents this, that, or the other thing
is one of those instances where there are no grounds at all for distinguishing between acceptable and unacceptable ascriptions (for, after
all, music is quintessentially "such stuff as dreams are made on," the
subject of reverie, the stimulus unparalleled of "free fantasy"; and if
music is capable of representation at all, there is nothing to say that *The
Art of The Fugue* does not represent the Leibnizian Weltanschauung, or
the architecture of the Gothic cathedral, or anything else it might
evoke in the listener's overactive imagination).

As to the first objection, I think it can be fairly dismissed from consideration here, for in a very real sense it is irrelevant to the *particular*
difficulties that are (mistakenly, I think) thought to surround the concept of musical representation. The possibility that artistic interpretation across the board might be an epistemically suspect endeavour
is a problem for *all* characterizations, descriptions, evaluations, of artworks beyond the most innocuous and trivial; it is not a special problem for pictorial or representational interpretations of music. Thus it
is fair to assume, for the purposes of this study, that artistic interpretation is an intellectually respectable activity, with objective ground rules
of some kind or other whereby interpretations can be separated into
the acceptable and unacceptable, the valid and invalid, the true and
false, or whatever the favored dichotomy might be. If artistic interpretation fails across the board, then, indeed, musical representation fails
along with it—but so too does the whole enterprise of art criticism, music criticism, literary criticism, in fact all hope of talking intelligibly to
one another about works of art. Such skepticism is a worthy opponent
of the philosopher of art; but not his business when he has taken up
the special tasks of the "philosopher of music."

The second objection, however, the "philosopher of music" must
deal with; for it makes a claim *specifically* about *musical* interpretations,
to wit, that those that construe music pictorially or representationally
are, *unlike* other kinds of interpretations, hopelessly "subjective" or
"relative"—in other words, without agreed upon standards whereby a
correct illustrational ascription can be accepted, and an incorrect one
dismissed. I intend to deal with this objection in the following empirical way. It seems to me reasonable to assume that if illustrational as-

criptions to music are like other bona fide interpretational claims in the
arts, two things must be true of them: first, that it be possible to "discover" new, unobvious, and unforeseen illustrational interpretations
of music that are valid and defensible; and second, conversely, that it
be possible, and defensible, to throw out new, unforeseen, unobvious
illustrational interpretations of music that are wholly idiosyncratic.
That being so, what I intend to do in what follows is to exhibit a real example of each case: that is to say, an example of a newly discovered
(for me) illustrational interpretation, along with a defense of its validity; and an example of what I take to be an invalid illustrational interpretation, along with a demonstration of its invalidity. In so doing, I
hope to convince the reader that illustrational interpretations of music
are defended and defeated with the very same kinds of arguments that
other artistic interpretations call forth; that just as one can "discover" a
literary interpretation of a text not before thought of, one can "discover" a musical illustration not before heard; finally, that one can, in
the usual ways, be convinced that what purports to be such an illustrational "discovery" is, in fact, a case of "reading in" rather than "reading
out," and hence unacceptable. I will conclude from this procedure that
my defense of musical representation does not open the critical
floodgates to "free association" or impose bizarre pictorial or narrative scenarios on "pure" instrumental music, where we all agree they
do not belong, under the assumption always that artistic interpretation
is a rational exercise. What I *cannot* convince the reader of in this way is
that the process of artistic interpretation is a rational exercise, for that
is a task of a philosophy of criticism, not a philosophy of music, which
must only content itself with showing that in this respect music is at
least not *worse off* than her sister arts.

◇ 2 ◇   I go on now to a very simple but, I hope, convincing case of
illustrational "discovery" in music. Part II of Haydn's oratorio, *Die
Jahreszeiten, Der Sommer,* begins with a brief instrumental prelude
whose languid, drooping chromaticism describes the dog days, specifically, die Morgendämmerung. It is followed by a recitative for Lucas
(tenor) and Simon (bass), setting the scene of a drowsy summer morn-
ing. Simon sings:

> Des Tages Herold meldet sich;
> Mit frohem Laute rufet er
> Zu neuer Tätigkeit
> Den ausgeruhten Landmann auf.

His recitative is introduced by an instrumental interlude with a distinctive, even somewhat eccentric passage in the oboe, repeated twice (Example 45).

What does this passage in the oboe represent or picture? Or is it not illustrational at all? If it is not, what musical sense can be made of it? It has no echo in what follows, nor presentiment in what has gone before. It thrusts itself out of the musical fabric and disappears without a trace after one more appearance. Here, one would think, is one of those obvious places where some representational or pictorial raison d'être is absolutely required, beyond the purely musical parameters, to make the music *musically* comprehensible. Yet, at least on first reflection, the text seems to yield no obvious clue as to what Haydn's representational

EXAMPLE 45
Haydn, *Die Jahreszeiten,* Part II

intentions, if any, might have been. Nor does the music itself, unaided by the text, strike us in any pictorial way, as, say the cuckoo calls in the *Pastoral* might have done.

Another avenue to the text is open to us, however. The libretto of *The Seasons*, by Baron van Swieten, is based, as is well-known, on James Thomson's poem of the same name, and the latter gives us a fruitful hint. Who, or what, is van Swieten's "Des Tages Herold"? The verse of Thomson's, on which this passage is obviously based, reads:[2]

> Roused by the Cock, the soon-clad Shepherd leaves
> His mossy cottage, where with *Peace* he dwells;
> And from the crowded fold, in order drives
> His flock, to taste the verdure of the Morn.

Clearly, then, "Des Tages Herold" must refer to the barnyard rooster. That being van Swieten's intention, it would be natural to assume that the peculiar oboe passage in question is a representation, of the "sounds like" kind, of the crowing cock. Can this hypothesis be further substantiated?

As we have seen, a representation of the "sounds like" kind need not, indeed seldom does, suggest to the listener, sans text or title, what is being represented; but it must be recognizable when the text or title is known. No one would guess that the rapid violin figuration in "He spake the word," and the unison tutti passage in the Sonata of Cantata 31 represent, respectively, the buzzing of insects and the sound of laughter. But after the texts are known, we get the point: we *hear* the resemblance. Is such the case with our problematic oboe passage? It is, I think, in two rather striking respects.

To begin with, the extremely quirky beginning of the phrase, quite unaccountable in itself as a musical theme, is immediately seen (with Thomson's verse in mind) as a musical representation of "cock-a-doodle-do" (more or less) (Example 46).

EXAMPLE 46

"cock-a-doodle-doodle-do"

And the almost equally eccentric chromatic descent (by the way, a piece of glittering virtuosity on the three-keyed oboe of Haydn's day) can be understood as the only musical way, commensurate with high classical sensibility, available to Haydn, of representing the *glissando* characteristic of so many bird calls. (Recall Mozart's strictures against the composer ever letting musical representation overstep the bounds of art.) Haydn certainly knew enough English, after two trips to the British Isles, to have read and understood Thomson's poem in the original language. Put this fact together with the easy success of reading the oboe passage as a musical representation of the rooster's crow, and I think such an illustrational interpretation well-nigh unassailable. Heard in this way, the passage slips into place as just another of the nature illustrations in which *The Seasons* abounds, and no longer protrudes from the musical texture. Discovering the representational character of the figure solves the aesthetic problem of its musical eccentricity as no consideration of purely musical parameters seems able to do. Unless, then, some defeating circumstance should come to light forcing us to reject this representational interpretation, it would seem to me to be a secure part of our construal of Haydn's musical text, albeit, perhaps, not an overwhelmingly important one.

Let this stand, then, as an example of how one might make bona fide, defensible discoveries of representational elements in music not heretofore perceived. What, now, of their opposite numbers: the unjustified, fanciful, pseudo-discoveries? Those, I think, are the more disturbing, as they raise the spectre of all of the Romantic excesses epitomized by the programizing, in the nineteenth century, of Beethoven's piano sonatas, quartets and symphonies. To these abominable practices I now must turn my attention.

◊ 3 ◊   Imagine that the following representational gloss were offered for the Prelude in C-minor from Book I of *The Well-Tempered Clavier*.

"The rustling sixteenth-note figure, in both the right and left hands, that pervades the entire piece, represents the rustling of the dry autumn leaves in the cold October wind. The feeling of chilling, autumnal foreboding and desolation is reinforced by the dark key of C minor (Example 47).

EXAMPLE 47
Bach, Prelude in C-minor, *The Well-Tempered Clavier*, Book I

At measure 28 *(Presto)* the tension heightens, reinforced by a pedal point: the wind has now attained the proportions of a gale, the leaves, detached from the branches by its fury, fall to the ground, their descent represented by the descent of the rustling sixteenth-note figure in the treble and bass (Example 48).

EXAMPLE 48

The gale subsides at measure 34 *(Adagio)*; but in a last burst of fury (measure 35, *Allegro*) completely denudes the trees of their remaining leaves, their fall again marked by a descending figure in the music (Example 49). And thus is completed the annual autumnal tragedy of vegetable destruction, with only the merest hopeful hint of the vernal rebirth to come on the cadence in C major."

It is easy to anticipate the completely justified revulsion that would be evoked in anyone of musical taste and the least appreciation for *The*

Example 49

Well-Tempered Clavier by the above piece of fanciful nonsense, were it offered seriously as a reading of the C-minor Prelude. But as exaggerated and overblown as it is—purposefully so, of course—it is far outstripped in that regard by many an example of "serious" musical interpretation, and a feeling of revulsion can hardly do duty for an argument to show that such an interpretation is wide of the mark. Worse still, if what I have said in the preceding chapters, in defense and explication of musical representation, is true, the case for the above interpretation seems, at least on first reflection, to be distressingly strong. So before we attempt to dispatch it, we had best know the worst; it will do us no good to knock down a straw man when there is a real one standing in his shadow.

To start with, our illustrational interpretation of the C-minor Prelude has just what every bona fide representation of the "sounds like" kind seems to have: a perceived resemblance, once the text or title (or interpretation, in this case) is known, between the sound being represented and the sound doing the representing. We may never have noticed the resemblance of sound between the sixteenth-note figure and the rustling of leaves in the wind before it was suggested in our illustrational interpretation; but once the suggestion is made, we hear the analogy (particularly if the piece is played on the harpsichord, which has a more "rustling" sound than the piano).

Second, the fall of the leaves, which our interpretation asks us to hear towards the close of the composition, fulfills another requirement of representational music that we have established, namely the isomorphism between what is represented and what musically represents it, where the representational property of the music is what I called, in Chapter IV, a "structural" one. Thus, in the present instance, the downward path of the musical notes describes a downward path isomorphic with the downward path of the leaves; and the descriptions of both the line and the leaves as "falling" are univocal—"falling," in other words, is used literally and synonymously.

Thirdly, the expressiveness of the music—its somber, chilly character—when perceived as a representational property, seems to exemplify the technique of representation as expression that we discussed at some length in Chapter VII, thus giving further reason to believe that the interpretation we are offered is not as unfounded as we might first have thought, at least if what I have said about the representational use of expressiveness in music has any validity (and clearly we are operating here under the assumption that it has).

Finally, the whole musical form of the C-minor Prelude—its overall plan—conforms perfectly with the literary interpretation of it that we are now considering. It is a little "cinematic narration," like Kuhnau's depiction of David killing Goliath, and represents, as a musical event in time, the little story that the interpretation asks us to hear in it. The rustling of the leaves, the growing intensity of the storm, cessation, the final trickling down of the leaves that remain, the hint of optimism at the end in the close on the tonic major, all are reflected in the music, in the appropriate time-sequence. And why not? The interpretation after all has been carefully tailored to fit the artistic facts (as any interpretation naturally would be). The whole thing fits together; there are no loose ends.

But surely I have not succeeded in convincing anyone, least of all myself, that Bach's prelude represents any of this maudlin, puerile stuff, and if anything I have said about musical representation implies that this interpretation, and ones like it, must be valid, then so much the worse for what I have said. I would much prefer to discard it all than to sanction with it such a travesty of the C-minor Prelude. Fortunately, however, we need not make a choice between accepting the interpretation or rejecting the defense of musical representation that has been given in these pages. I believe that, on the contrary, rejection of the former and acceptance of the latter are perfectly consistent one with the other. But that must be argued for.

◊ 4 ◊   It is clear, I think, that the C-minor Prelude fulfills *some* conditions for musical representation of rustling leaves and the rest. I have avoided calling them necessary conditions—they certainly are not sufficient ones—because I do not want to suggest that the kinds of musical illustrations I have explicated are the only kinds there might be, or their inner workings the only ways of doing the business. Better, then, to call them simply conditions frequently encountered in musical illustrations, and frequently responsible for making these musical illustrations work. The question now before us is why they don't make the Prelude in C-minor work as a representation of rustling and falling leaves; or, in the particular form we want to ask the question here—which is crucial—why does their presence not make an illustrational interpretation of the C-minor Prelude a valid one?

Let us recall what invited us to seek an illustrational interpretation for the little oboe passage in *The Seasons,* discussed earlier, and what made us content with the interpretation we settled on. What invited us to seek an illustrational interpretation in the first place was that we could not make sense of the passage on purely musical grounds. *Any* interpretation, I would urge, begins with a question, a problem, a perplexity. One does not "interpret" the crystal clear, the obvious, the unproblematical, and in music, we are driven to seek a representational or pictorial answer to a problem in those instances where, for one thing, a purely musical one will not suffice, or is not available at all, and where we have some at least prima facie reason for believing representational or pictorial features might be present. This is just the situation we found ourselves in with regard to the passage for oboe that introduces Simon's recitative. It is idiosyncratic, distinctive, odd, eccentric; and its character is explained neither by what comes before it in the music, nor by what comes after: it can be seen neither as a transformation of, or counterpoint to, any musical figure that has preceded it, nor as a new figure to be worked on musically in what follows. All of the usual strategies for explaining its musical significance in purely musical terms fail, and the context in which the figure is placed surely suggests, even demands, that an illustrational interpretation be sought. The presence of the text alone might suffice; but in addition, the instrumental interludes of accompanied recitatives are traditionally motivated more by the text than by purely musical considerations. Add to this the fact that musical illustrations of a very obvious kind abound in *The Seasons,* and an illustrational interpretation of the passage becomes not just a possibility but an absolute necessity.

So much, then, for what impels us to seek for an illustrational interpretation. What satisfies us about the one we have found? Three very obvious things: it fits the facts; no other interpretation of a more obvious kind does; and the context is one in which the kind of interpretation given seems to be indicated (if that is not just another way of fitting the facts). Specifically, it accounts for an eccentric musical figure by showing how it represents an image in the text; there is no more obvious, that is to say purely musical, explanation for the presence of the figure. The presence of the text and titles, and the ubiquity of obvious musical illustrations throughout the work constitute a context in which a representational interpretation is not only not out of place, but positively demanded. In short, the interpretation removes the perplexity which gave rise to it without leaving any others to resolve in its place. It satisfies.

Compare this outcome with that of the interpretation proposed for the C-minor Prelude. I shall argue that in the latter case not one of the symptoms of a satisfactory interpretation alluded to above, is present.

The attempt to provide an illustrational interpretation for the oboe passage in *The Seasons* is set in motion by perplexity. It is an attempt to answer a question: Why *this* peculiar chromatic passage *here*? There is no such perplexity about the C-minor Prelude. What sort of an explanation would one be looking for if one asked, about the first measure of the prelude, Why just *this* "rustling" sixteenth-note figure *here*? It might simply be that one wanted to know what made this theme occur to Bach. And perhaps, indeed (though I seriously doubt it), it *was* suggested to him by the rustling of leaves. But even if that were the case, that would not make it a *representation* of the rustling of leaves. Nor is this kind of question a question about the music. It is a question about Bach's mental processes, to which, we can be sure, we will never be able to give an answer. It has nothing to do with the interpretative question, Why *this* funny oboe passage just *here*?

Clearly, there *is* no answer to the question, Why just *this* "rustling" sixteenth-note figure *here*?, anything like our answer to the question about the oboe passage. This is the *beginning* of a textless piece of apparently pure instrumental music in a two-volume collection of apparently pure, textless instrumental compositions bearing only the title "prelude" or "fugue." One might, of course, be asking for a demonstration that the C-minor Prelude is related thematically to what has gone before or will come after, as, for example, I might ask why *this* particular Contrapunctus of *The Art of the Fugue* has *this* particular subject, and be given the answer that it is the mirror inversion of the main theme, or something else of the kind. But it is generally agreed that there is no unifying theme in *The Well-Tempered Clavier*. Each piece is a self-contained unit, and there does not seem even to be any thematic relationship between a given prelude and its fugue, so there can be no such answer to the question about the C-minor Prelude. It is, indeed, close to a nonsensical question. An instrumental composition may begin with any theme you like. It is what *follows* that can be queried, and explained in terms of what began. The opening of the C-minor Prelude is no more in need of interpretation than would the opening of a piano sonata by Haydn be, if he had begun it with the same chromatic passage that is so in need of interpretation where it stands in *The Seasons*.

Had Bach titled the prelude *Autumn Memories*, then the question, Why just *this* "rustling" sixteenth-note figure *here?* would make sense. The title would, of course, raise the question of whether the music might be representational, and the answer, it represents the rustling of leaves in the cold October wind, might lay to rest our perplexity about whether there were some relationship between the opening figure and the title, and if so, what it might be. But in the absence of such a literary or poetic title, there is no perplexity whatever for an illustrational interpretation, or any *other,* for that matter, to lay to rest.

Granted, it will be replied, that the opening of the C-minor Prelude neither requires, nor admits of any accounting, what follows, however, surely does. And mightn't that accounting be a representational one? That an accounting is in order no one would wish to deny. That one in terms of representation is called for, or required, however, is quite false. For everything that happens in the C-minor Prelude after Bach makes his opening musical gesture is completely comprehensible in terms of purely musical structure and "syntax."   The figure itself is spun out according to well-known harmonic, contrapuntal, and melodic principles; nor does the *Presto* or *Adagio* require literary or narrative justification, since Bach simply uses accepted and familiar methods of structuring musical climax and relaxation, quite characteristic of a particular kind of seventeenth- and eighteenth-century keyboard style. The gradual winding-down of the piece is in no more need of poetic interpretation than what has gone before, being a release of musical tension, as the *Presto* was an intensification of it; and the ending in C major again has a purely musical function, namely, the accomplishing of a fuller, more reposeful close than would have resulted from a minor cadence (although there is nothing, I think, "inevitable" about this particular piece having a major as opposed to a minor cadence). In a word, whatever perplexity might be raised by the progress of Bach's prelude is dissipated by *purely musical* considerations. And so the first, most basic requirement of an illustrational interpretation, some perplexity over the music not resolvable in some more obvious (that is to say *musical*) way is not met.

But if the most basic condition of an interpretation, perplexity, puzzlement, a question, is lacking, it is hard to see how any of the rest can follow. If an interpretation answers no question, solves no problem, can it "fit the facts"? What facts would it fit? If I have a genuine difficulty with a work of music, an interpretation will resolve it for me by calling my attention to features of the work I may have missed, or by redescribing features with which I may already be familiar in such a way as to bring to them a significance and (therefore) an intelligibility they did not have for me before. If I do *not* have a question, there can be no answer, and in such a case an interpretation becomes a gratuitous appendage that can really describe nothing about the work, fits no facts. The unwanted interpretation of Bach's C-minor Prelude does indeed mention things about the work that truly exist in it: the "rustling" sixteenth-note figure, the descent of the musical line in the *Presto,* the major cadence. It asks us, however, to reinterpret them as representational features for the purpose of "explaining" their presence. But as their presence already has a completely adequate explanation in terms of purely musical parameters, a further explanation can be no explanation at all, can call attention to no new aspect of the work, can reveal no new "inner workings," cannot, in other words, fit any facts, for there are no facts for a gratuitous explanation to fit. If there is no gap in an explanatory chain, another explanation cannot reveal, either by reference or reinterpretation, a missing link. In this sense, the illustrational interpretation of the Prelude in C-minor fails to fit the facts, for the work fails to have the illustrational facts about which the interpretation speaks.

Now it may, perhaps, be felt that there is a certain sense in which our "autumnal" interpretation of the C-minor Prelude fits the facts, where another such interpretation might fail. For, after all, the prelude does have certain features that can be heard in the way the "autumnal" interpretation requires, whereas the C-major Prelude, say, does not; and another interpretation might not even achieve *that.* The sixteenth-note figure does sound something like rustling leaves; the descending line can be heard as a representation of their falling; the musical events do fall out, temporally, in tandem with those in the little story that our interpretation embodies. In *that* sense, our interpretation fits the musical facts, whereas another might simply find no echo at all in the music, as the "autumnal" interpretation would not in the C-major Prelude. Or, to put it another way, the C-minor Prelude could have, by virtue of its musical features, represented the rustling of leaves in the autumn wind, had Bach chosen to do so by, perhaps, titling it *Autumn Memories,* or even fitting it with running heads, as Kuhnau did in the "Battle Between David and Goliath": "Here the leaves are blowing in the wind; here they fall," and so on. Whereas it simply could not, in its present musical form, represent any number of other things one could think of, as the C-major Prelude could not represent the events recounted in the "autumnal" interpretation.

A flesh-and-blood example might bring the point home more vividly, while also reminding the reader that representation may sometimes occur, as it were, after the musical fact. Consider the following excerpt from the *Componimenti Musicali* of Gottlieb Muffat (1690–1770) (Example 50).

EXAMPLE 50
Muffat, *Componimenti Musicali,* Suite IV

Were I to suggest that the "leaping" figure represented the cosmic elements—earth, air, fire, water—in their primal motions, I might be praised for my imagination, but hardly for my insight; my interpretation would be greeted with no less incredulity, certainly, than the one offered for Bach's prelude. But Handel remembered well this passage when he came to set Dryden's *Ode for St. Cecilia's Day.*[3] In fact he lifted it bodily for recitative accompaniment to the lines:

> The tuneful voice was heard from high:
> Arise, ye more than dead.
> Then cold and hot and moist and dry
> In order to their stations leap,
> And Music's power obey.

EXAMPLE 51
Handel, *Ode for St. Cecelia's Day*

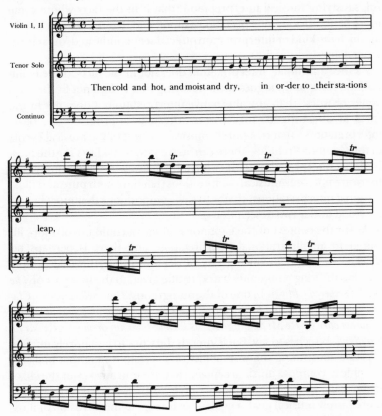

And there, in Handel's work, the very same notes do indeed represent what they could not in Muffat's, by virtue of the "potential" for musical representation that Muffat's music possessed. In this limited sense of fitting the facts, then, the "autumnal" interpretation of the C-minor Prelude, and an "elemental" interpretation of Muffat's Fantasia fit the facts; but not in the sense in which a true theory fits the facts—and it is the latter sense that we require to validate an illustrational interpretation.

The "autumnal" interpretation of Bach's C-minor Prelude, then, bakes no bread: it answers no question, solves no riddle, because there is no question to answer or riddle to unravel. And because it fills no explanatory gap, it fits no facts, not because it is deficient in some way, but simply because there are no facts for it to fit. That being the case, I think we can dispatch fairly quickly the final two criteria for a successful, satisfying musical interpretation: that it fit the facts where some more basic, obvious interpretation cannot; and that the context be one in which the kind of interpretation offered seems indicated, or, at least, is not contraindicated.

As the "autumnal" interpretation does not fit the facts, there being no facts for it to fit, it goes without saying that it does not fit the facts better or worse than any alternative interpretation: it does not fit the facts at all. Indeed, just *because* there is another, more basic interpretation—that is, a purely musical account of the musical events in the C-minor Prelude—there can, as we saw, be no facts for the illustrational interpretation to fit (which, by the way, does not imply that there are not some musical compositions that have both pure and illustrational interpretations: that is to say, compositions that must be understood under two descriptions).

As for the context of the C-minor Prelude, it could not be more ill-suited to an illustrational interpretation, and there is perhaps no quicker, or more convincing way of demonstrating this than simply quoting the long, eminently baroque title given to the first part of *The Well-Tempered Clavier*, in one of the autographs: *Das wohltemperirte Clavier oder Praeludia und Fugen durch alle Tone und Semitonia sowohl tertiam majorem oder Ut Re Mi amlangend, als such tertiam minorem oder Re Mi Fa betreffend.* Which is to say, Bach intends the work to be a purely musical exercise, illustrating the workability of a certain tuning that makes it possible to compose music acceptable to the ear in any key of the chromatic scale, in major or minor, from C to B. It is hard to imagine a more purely musical goal, a goal more foreign to the intrusion of illustrational, literary, or programmatic elements; and to emphasize further the purely musical nature of the work, Bach chooses for the individual compositions one of the "severest" forms in which the eighteenth-century composer could work, namely, the fugue, and the form with the most non-descript, non-descriptive title of all, the laconic "Prelude." In other words, the individual compositions that make up *The Well-Tempered Clavier* are called either "Fugue," or, essentially, "The thing that comes before (in this case) the fugue," that is, "Prelude." Can one think of more arid soil in which to plant illustrational interpretations than this? Isn't it as clear as anything at all in the world of art can be that Bach *intended* there to be no pictorial, representational or programmatic elements in *The Well-Tempered Clavier?*

At long last, then, we have arrived at the question of *intention*, and the reader might well wonder why it has taken so long. Would it not have been more effective, instead of chipping away bit by bit at the implausibility of the "autumnal" interpretation rather to have simply knocked it over at a blow by arguing that as Bach could not possibly have intended the C-minor Prelude to be a representation of autumn leaves rustling in the cold October wind, that cannot be what it represents; further, that as Bach could not possibly have intended it to represent anything at all, no representational interpretation of it can possibly be valid? As a matter of fact, I *do* believe that lack of intention, *of itself,* defeats a representational interpretation (although presence of intention does not, of itself, support one). But the well-known controversial nature of intention as a critical category makes it good tactics to have other, intention-independent grounds for being able to reject such unwanted illustrational interpretations as the "autumnal" interpretation of the C-minor Prelude. Nevertheless, the subject of intention in interpretation is important enough to make a separate consideration of it in illustrational interpretations, both desirable and necessary; although, as we shall see in a moment, since for all practical purposes, determining intention or its lack is parasitic, in the case of representation, on just the criteria we have been discussing, it turns out to be of no real use to the critic, one way or the other, in determining the presence or lack of illustrational elements in music.

◇ 5 ◇   Consider the following two possible, though admittedly unlikely, scenarios: (a) I discover a letter from Haydn to Baron van Swieten to the effect that he (Haydn) never intended the oboe passage in *The Seasons* to represent a bird call, or anything else, but merely intended to show off the facility in playing chromatic scales of the great oboist Friedrich Ramm. (b) I discover a letter from J. S. Bach to his son, Carl Philipp Emanuel, to the effect that he (J. S.) intended the C-minor Prelude to represent autumn leaves rustling in the cold October wind, the memory of which he carried with him from his childhood in Eisenach.

Now the fact is that, as Wimsatt and Beardsley long ago observed in their much discussed essay on intentions in criticism, the intentions of artists are seldom documented in any other way than in their artworks themselves; or, in other words, usually the *only* evidence we have of what an artist intended to do is a work of art that successfully does it— and what a work of art does is defined for us by what we take to be the valid interpretations of it. That is to say, we almost always must go from interpretation to intention rather than the other way around, simply as a practical matter, if for no other deeper reason of logic.

"One must ask how a critic expects to get an answer to the question about intention. How is he to find out what the poet tried to do? If the poet succeeded in doing it, then the poem itself shows what he was trying to do."[4]

The very best evidence we have—and in all likelihood could ever possibly have—for Haydn's intention to represent the crowing of the cock in the chromatic passage for oboe is that interpreting it that way works. The very best evidence we have—and in all likelihood could ever possibly have—for Bach's lack of intention to represent the rustling of autumn leaves in the cold October wind (or anything else) in the C-minor Prelude is that interpreting it that way does not work, is contraindicated by the Prelude, and by the larger work of which it is a part.

If, per (almost) impossibile, we did discover a letter by Haydn, explicit enough to convince us that he did not intend to represent anything with the chromatic passage in the oboe, that would indeed, *of itself*, be enough to defeat any claim to representation. That is simply a consequence of the "logic" of the concept of representation: it is an "intentional" concept in the sense that I cannot represent unintentionally, although I can unintentionally make something that might (mistakenly) be taken for a representation, just as the winds and the tides can make a piece of driftwood appear to be a representation of a human figure, say, by virtue of its having a strikingly "human" shape. (There is a tree on the campus of Vassar College called, for very obvious reasons, the Venus tree.) But the driftwood, not being a product of intentional human agency, is not a representation in fact, nor is Haydn's passage for oboe a representation of a crowing cock if unintended, no matter how like a bird call it might accidentally be.[5]

But if, again per (almost) impossibile, we should find incontrovertible documentary evidence of J. S. Bach's intention to represent the "tragedy of falling leaves" in the C-minor Prelude, we should not, at a single stroke, have discovered that that is truly what is represented there. For along with being an "intentional" concept in the sense explained, representation is also a "success" concept as well, which is to say, a certain modicum of success is required beyond the intention to represent, to make the intended representation a representation in fact. Urmson observes, "while it is necessary that A should be intended to resemble B for it to be a representation of B, it is also necessary that some minimum degree of resemblance should be achieved."[6] Or, more neutrally, to avoid putting such great weight on the presence of resemblance in representation, *some* success of some unspecified kind, beyond the mere intention to represent, is required to do the job.

It appears, then, that although discovering the intention to represent is not sufficient to validate a representational ascription, it is, nevertheless, always evidence in favor, intention to represent being a necessary (though not sufficient) condition for representation; and discovering intention not to represent, or not to represent some particular thing, is *decisive* evidence against, in the first case, representation across the board, and in the second, representation of that particular thing.

Whatever the force of intention in other critical contexts, it is considerable in the representational ones. The catch is, however, that for all practical purposes, intention as an indication for or against representational ascriptions is utterly impotent, except in the most unusual circumstances, such as we imagined above in the form of letters by Haydn and Bach. For, as we have seen, the fact is that we seldom have any evidence of an artist's intention outside of the work of art itself; and this is true, pari passu, of the composer's intention to represent. The intention not to represent in music may be decisive against a representational interpretation. But it is a delusion to think that this might save one from the dreary task of deciding, by examination of the music itself, with all the vagaries and uncertainties that that implies, whether or not it is representational. In almost all cases, the only evidence we have for the composer's intention to represent is that a representational interpretation of the music works. So we cannot be saved from the hard work of interpretation by the evidence of lack of intention: it is only by interpretation that intentions are divined. The thing is rather like concluding, as Locke does in Book IV, Chapters 18 and 19, of the *Essay Concerning Human Understanding*, that revelation is a direct source of knowledge. Does this mean that we then have a shortcut by which we can bypass the burdensome task of rational inquiry, with all of *its* vagaries and uncertainties? By no means. Reason cannot be so disdained, for "consult it we must, and by it examine, whether it be a *Revelation* from God or no. . .,"[7] on pain of a regress ad infinitum whereby a revelation's claim to its status is verified by yet another revelation claim, and so on. There are no "revelations" to be had for determining representational properties through direct knowledge of composers' intentions, that somehow bypass the process of interpretation. Reason about music we must: here, as elsewhere, there is no royal way.

◊ 6 ◊   If what I have written in the preceding chapters of this book comes anywhere near the truth about musical pictures and representations, then it would appear that many of the skeptical doubts with regard to music's illustrational powers have no basis in argument or fact. And to that extent, hearing it, seeing it, or even tasting, touching, and sniffing it in music, are respectable ways of responding, *just so long as the musical text supports the illustrational interpretation,* whatever it may be. If, further, what I have said in the present chapter comes anywhere near the truth about how we can establish that an illustrational interpretation is warranted, and, perhaps more important, how we can establish that it is *not,* the respectability of illustrational interpretations need not lead to the acceptance of the kind of "free association" that seems to sanction *anything* in the music that the Romantic imagination spews forth. We need not be committed to a storybook interpretation of *The Well-Tempered Clavier,* or A. B. Marx's effusions over Beethoven's Op. 81a: "Soul picture, which brings before the mind the Parting—let us assume of two lovers; the deserted—let us assume again sweetheart or wife—and Reunion of the Parted Ones."[8]

What, finally then, has been shown? Certainly not that there are no devastating arguments against musical representation waiting in the wings. Nor has it been argued—certainly not shown—that music is a representational art, if by that one means an art essentially, primarily, or even *importantly* representational. My musical nature, as a matter of fact, is drawn strongly to the antirepresentational thesis, not because I think it is true, but, rather, because I think it is an extremely useful falsehood. For so strong is the urge, in the West, to give music a subject, a literary content, a philosophical message, that a proper mean can only be struck, it would seem, by aiming at the opposite, formalist extreme. Whatever its usefulness, however, a falsehood it remains, and it is the philosopher's part to expose it. This will comfort those whose common sense and musical experience tell them that music sometimes *is* a picture or a representation, no matter what the musical purist may tell them to the contrary. But the purist will, perhaps, be somewhat reassured by my final conclusion, which is that when one knows *only* what a musical composition might picture or represent, one doesn't know so very much.

Pictures, Representations, and Hearing-in

My purpose in writing *Sound and Semblance* was to counter the more common skeptical arguments concerning the possibility of musical representations. The idea was not to present a general account of representation in the arts, and then show that music, at times, is representational within the requirements of the theory. I had no such theory when I wrote the book, nor do I have one now. Rather, I was trying to show that, given a set of fairly uncontroversial, presystematic beliefs about what constitutes representation, Western art music, at least since the high Renaissance, presents bona fide examples of it, as so construed.

Since the publication of *Sound and Semblance*, a great deal of extremely fruitful theorizing has been published on the general question of what representation is. None of it has compelled me to call into doubt any of my major conclusions about musical representation. But one author in particular has made some deeply insightful remarks about representation in music, having direct relevance to my distinction between musical "pictures" and musical "representations" that, although not, I think, wildly inconsistent with the main outline of my position, invite comment in this new edition of my book.

In her essay "Music as a Representational Art," Jenefer Robinson writes, "According to Kivy's theory in *Sound and Semblance,* all but a few musical pieces [that are illustrational] are 'representations' rather than 'pictures' of the world. . . . I think that the present essay can usefully be thought of as a theoretical underpinning for Kivy's distinction where his 'pictures' correspond to my 'depictions' and his 'representations' to my 'descriptions.'"[1]

This characterization does not seem to me to be quite right, although I have no quarrel with Robinson's distinction between "depictions" and "descriptions." For I do not think that her distinction cuts exactly along the same seam as mine: to be specific, although all of what I call musical "pictures" fall on the side of what Robinson calls "depictions," some of what I call musical "representations" do so as well. To see this, we will, of course, have first to understand exactly what the distinction is, on Robinson's view, between "depictions" and "descriptions."

Robinson explores, in her essay, two theories of pictorial representation. According to the *semantic* theory, associated closely with the name of Nelson Goodman: "Pictures are characters in pictorial symbol systems, just as words are characters in linguistic symbol systems (i.e. languages) and what a picture represents, like what a word denotes, is a function of what character it is in what symbol system" (169). Thus, on this view, pictures represent the world as natural languages do. That is to say, they describe it. "Pictures, then, always characterize or ascribe qualities to something" (170). In her essay, "describe" is defined by Robinson "in this very general sense of characterizing: in this sense words, pictures and even pieces of music may all 'describe' the world" (170).

But on Robinson's view—and I share it in this regard—the semantic theory has serious difficulties, the major one, for our own purposes, being its failure to accommodate our rather firm intuition "that even if pictures do characterize the world, they cannot be purely conventional symbols like words" (171); for "we have a strong inclination to say that pictures do 'match' appearances to one degree or another" (173).

To capture this intuition Robinson invokes the concept of "seeing-in," which Richard Wollheim has developed in successive stages over a period of some twenty years.[2] In his most mature statement of the concept, Wollheim writes, "Seeing-in is a distinct kind of perception, and it is triggered off by the presence within the field of vision of a differentiated surface. Not all differentiated surfaces will have this effect, but I doubt that anything significant can be said about exactly what a surface must be like for it to have this effect. When the surface is right, then an experience with a certain phenomenology will occur, and it is this phenomenology that is distinctive about seeing-in."[3]

Seeing-in, as Wollheim conceives of it, is not tantamount to the experience of representation, for "I can see something in surfaces that neither are nor are believed by me to be representations":[4] for example, seeing things in clouds or in ink blots. Nevertheless:

Representation can be explained in terms of seeing-in, as the following situation reveals: In a community where seeing-in is firmly established, some member of the community . . . sets about making a surface with the intention of getting others around him to see some definitive thing in it: say, a bison. If the artist's intention is successful to the extent that a bison can be seen in the surface as he has marked it, then the community closes ranks in that someone who does indeed see a bison in it is now held to see the surface correctly, and anyone is held to see it incorrectly if he sees, as he might, something else in it, or nothing at all. Now the marked surface represents a bison.[5]

Following Wollheim, Robinson describes artistic seeing-in as "a special kind of visual experience whereby one is simultaneously aware both of a painted surface or medium and of a particular object, scene or event which seems phenomenologically to be 'behind' or 'in' the painted surface or medium" (173). And with the concept of seeing-in in hand, Robinson now can amplify the semantic theory of representation in such a way as to capture the intuition, lost in a pure semantic construing of representation, that pictures "match" appearances. From the semantic theory we retain, on Robinson's view, the insight that representations characterize or ascribe. "The seeing-in theory does not contest the semantic theory's claim that pictures describe the world as predicates do. . . . If, however, we augment the semantic theory with the requirement that whatever is represented by a picture must be seen in that picture, we will, I think, arrive at a more adequate account of representation" (174). The concept of seeing-in will do duty for the intuition of picture-matching appearance, and will, in the bargain, help distinguish between "naturalistic" and "nonnaturalistic" representations. "The seeing-in view claims that we must be able to *see* a woman *in* any picture that depicts a woman, whether that picture be naturalistic or nonnaturalistic. The difference between a naturalistic and a nonnaturalistic picture of a woman is that the woman (i.e. the paint-woman) which we see in a naturalistic picture looks like a woman, whereas the nonnaturalistic paint-woman looks less like a woman because 'she' is distorted in some way" (175). A further and, for our purposes, more important implication of the seeing-in view is that "it is crucial to representation that an *individual* be represented (a dancer, a woman) and not just a set of qualities (grace, charm, dynamism, etc.). That is because what is represented in a picture must be seen in the picture and only individuals (objects, persons, events, etc.) are appropriate objects of seeing-in" (176).

With this last implication in hand we can now distinguish between what Robinson calls "representational" and "nonrepresentational" painting. A representational painting "represents," "depicts"; a nonrepresentational one "suggests," "describes." "In the language of the 'seeing-in' theory, a picture suggests rather than depicts some object if we can see in the picture certain features that might belong to an object of that sort but not enough of those features to enable us to see such an object in the picture" (177).

This rough overview of Robinson's general account of representation gives enough of the basic materials to enable us to take in, in summary fashion, her basic position with regard to the particular case of musical representation. In view of what has gone before, the central question to be answered with regard to music must be Is there a "hearing-in" experience comparable to the "seeing-in" experience that is so essential to pictorial representation? Summarizing in her own words Robinson's answer:

> With a few exceptions, music does *not* satisfy the hearing-in requirement and so, even though it can and does "describe" or characterize the world, it rarely if ever represents or depicts it in the way that pictures do. In particular . . . (1) . . . with some exceptions, we cannot hear any individual in a piece of descriptive music, (2) . . . the title or other verbal label accompanying a piece of descriptive music can and normally does determine what in particular is being described by the music, and (3) . . . musical descriptions function much more like descriptive *nonrepresentational* paintings than like representational paintings. In short, music can *describe* but only rarely *represents* the world (184).

I might begin the evaluation of Robinson's three conclusions, as they apply to my own position, by observing that I am in essential agreement with the second and the third. Given *her* terminology, both seem to me to be completely consistent with my views in *Sound and Semblance*. The second is, indeed, explicitly stated by me in my distinction between musical "pictures" and musical "representations." The third is implied, if not stated, and, given the differences in our terminologies, is altogether in accord with both the letter and the spirit of my book; for I take it that the third conclusion is to the effect that *most* of what I call musical "illustrations" are what Robinson calls musical "descriptions" rather than what she calls "depictions" or "representations." Given her terminology, I concur. But, as we shall see, on the question of how much is "most"? there is disagreement, since I believe there are far more cases of bona fide hearing-in than Robinson wants to allow.

The real, substantive issue between Robinson's and my views devolves on her first conclusion and its possible relation to her second. And again, to begin with at least, it seems a matter of degree. Robinson says that "with some exceptions, we cannot hear any individual in a piece of descriptive music." Well, in letter, given Robinson's terminology, I might be able to agree with her that there are far fewer real instances of hearing individuals in what I call musical "illustrations" than in painting. But I gather that I would allow significantly more cases than Robinson; and, more important, I demur with regard to the word "exceptions," which seems to suggest that where hearing individuals in music does occur, it is a kind of anomaly rather than (as I believe) a well-founded phenomenon.

Let me first broach the possibility of a connection between Robinson's first and second conclusions. Is Robinson claiming that if a title or text is required to determine what is being described by a piece of music, then it follows merely from that that we cannot hear any individual in the music? If she were claiming that—and if that claim were true—then much of the music I call "representational" would not be what Robinson calls "representational" but what she calls "descriptive." It would also follow that Robinson would be correct in characterizing what I called "pictures" as what she calls "depictions" and what I called "representations" what she calls "descriptions." For the way I drew the line between musical "illustrations" that are "pictures" and those that are "representations" is exactly as between those musical "illustrations" that do not and those that do require a text or title to determine what is being illustrated.

I will not try here to answer the exegetical question whether

Robinson maintains that requiring a text or title is sufficient for ruling out the possibility of hearing an individual in music or seeing one in the visual arts. I believe it is not, shall so argue, and leave it an open question whether Robinson would agree.

The basic reason why I do not think that requiring a text or title defeats hearing an individual in a medium is that seeing- (or hearing-) in is, as Wollheim says, simply a certain phenomenological experience: "When the surface is right, then an experience with a certain phenomenology will occur, and it is this phenomenology that is distinctive about seeing-in." It seems to me that sometimes a "surface," be it a visual or an aural one, is such that seeing or hearing an individual in it can occur only with the help of a text or title to "fix" the image. But the image, once so fixed, may well achieve just that "certain phenomenology . . . that is distinctive about seeing- [or hearing-] in." There is no point in trying to establish this a priori. If I can convince, it must be with examples, and I must appeal to the listener's experience. So let me try to establish my conclusion a posteriori with a pair of musical cases in point.

Both my examples come initially from Robinson, but I amplify them along the way. Robinson says that "what we hear in a piece of descriptive music is not an individual but only a set of qualities. . . . For example, you can hear the whirring of the spinning wheel in *Gretchen am Spinnrad[e]*, the surge of the sea in *La Mer*." Although we can hear the whirring and the surging, however, "we cannot hear any *individual* in the music, such as a spinning wheel, a sea" (185).

But is this the case? I think it must be granted straightaway that because of how our sense organs have evolved, we are able to (and do) gain far more information about the external world by sight than by sound. Obviously, therefore, I usually form a far clearer, more detailed, more replete picture of a spinning wheel or a sea by looking than by listening, and, a fortiori, through a visual rather than a musical representation. And since being able to *individuate* in a representation must surely be a function, in large measure, of the information conveyed, the visual arts of representation have a clear, imposing, and uncontested advantage in this regard over the art of music.

But this advantage notwithstanding, I think Robinson seriously underestimates the ability of music to present individuals for "hearing-in." And I can best show this, I think, in amplifying her two examples, *Gretchen am Spinnrade* and *La mer*, by contrasting them with two other musical representations of the same objects. For by seeing how two other musical representations of these objects present such distinctively different instances of them, we can come to see that we have, indeed, been presented in each case with an *individual*, at least within some minimal set of conditions for individuality, not merely "a set of qualities."

Compare Schubert's spinning wheel, in *Gretchen am Spinnrade*, with Haydn's, in the spinning scene of *The Seasons*. How different they are: Schubert's full of passion and *Angst*, Haydn's quite tranquil. It is odd that Robinson should insist that "we cannot hear in it [i.e. Schubert's music] *Gretchen's* spinning wheel" (185). For it *is* driven, clearly, by the hand of the very character whose rest and peace have been forever shattered by sexual passion and love, while Haydn's are driven (it is a sewing circle) by maidens of "pure" heart and prerevolutionary contentment.[6]

Compare next *La mer*, let us say the opening, calm sections of the first movement, with Mendelssohn's *Fingal's Cave*. Now it strikes me with even greater force here than in the case of Haydn's and Schubert's spinning wheels that we are being presented with two starkly contrasting "objects" of representation whose comparison helps to bring our attention to the individuality of each. Debussy's seascape is of a calm, gentle, sunny strand; Mendelssohn's gives us a dark, ominous, brooding vista. I find in these works ample opportunity for hearing-in of a very vivid kind, although I do not pretend to be able to characterize my "hearings-in" in the detail one might muster if these were, rather, "seeings-in," and works by Manet and Delacroix.

It is well to differentiate, at this juncture, two ways in which individuals represented in musical works, or any other art works, might be distinguished from one another. One way is *stylistically*. Thus, Haydn's spinning wheels are Classical, Schubert's Romantic; Mendelssohn's sea Romantic, Debussy's Impressionist (although I believe that is an unfortunate way of describing Debussy's music). A second way I will call, for want of a better term, *objectively*. Thus, the object represented in Mendelssohn's *Fingal's Cave* is a brooding, turbulant sea, whereas the object of his *Calm Sea and Prosperous Voyage* is (at least in the slow introduction) a calm and unperturbed one.

But the style of representation is the same: namely, Mendelssohn's distinctive Classical-Romantic one.

Now a reasonable question might be raised here about how much of the *difference* in the musical representations of things like spinning wheels, oceans, brooks, laughter, thunderstorms, and so on are really differences in the objects of representation and how many merely (*merely?*) differences in style of representation. And if the differences are only in style, not in "content," then perhaps it seems plausible to argue that for all of the "differences" between (say) Haydn's spinning wheel and Schubert's, or Mendelssohn's sea and Debussy's, they do not make for the hearing of individuals in the music, as the hearing-in theory requires, but, as Robinson insists, merely descriptions of whirring or motion or whatever, differentiated, to be sure, but by the styles of the descriptions and nothing in the objects.

To a degree the point is well taken, but not as a blanket condemnation of hearing-in in what I call musical "representations." Doubtless, there is little to distinguish one musical thunderstorm from another except style. It is Classical noise or Romantic noise, Beethoven noise or Berlioz noise, but with no recognizable meteorological difference. Perhaps this is true of many other musical illustrations as well. But I believe it would be a serious mistake to think it true of all, or that cases where hearing individuals does occur are negligible or anomalous. That the cases I adduced are members of a significant and populous class, not singularities, cannot be argued for here, indeed, cannot be *argued* for at all. What is needed, rather, is the multiplying of real musical examples. That is a task for another time and place.

But assuming (as I do) that I am correct in may claim that hearing individuals in music, and (so) hearing-in, does occur in what I call musical "representations" frequently enough to constitute a well-founded phenomenon, let me, in conclusion, return to the question with which I began: Does Robinson's distinction between musical depictions and musical descriptions have the same extension as mine between musical pictures and musical representations? She says that it does. I will contend that it does not.

What I call musical "pictures" presents no problem. They are depictions, on Robinson's view, and I am happy to acquiesce in that characterization of them. It is what I call musical "representations" about which there is dispute.

Musical representations are of two kinds: those that represent sounds and those that represent things, ideas, events, and so forth that cannot be heard. It is uncontroversial, I think, that musical representations of what cannot be heard cannot be examples of hearing-in, since what I cannot hear I cannot, a fortiori, hear-in. I have no quarrel with Robinson's calling them "descriptions" rather than "depictions" or "representations." Musical representations of sounds, however, fall into two categories. There are those that do and those that do not manage to present individuals for our perception, and, by consequence, those that do and those that do not present a "surface" enabling the hearing-in phenomenology. Again, it seems unobjectionable to call those musical representations of the "sounds like" kind that do not facilitate hearing-in, after Robinson, "descriptions" rather than "depictions" or "representations." Those, however, that do achieve the hearing-in phenomenology—on my view a significant number—deserve to be thought of as full-blooded representations or depictions, as Robinson understands those terms. Thus, to draw the obvious conclusion, Robinson's "representations" or "depictions" do not have the same extension as my "pictures"; rather, they spill over into my "representations," some of which are, but some of which are not, mere "descriptions" but bona fide examples of hearing-in.

Finally, I think Robinson is dead right to have perceived that Wollheim's concept of seeing-in would have been useful in helping to spell out what I had to say about musical illustrations in *Sound and Semblance*. In my view, though, it would have had, as I have said, the role not of making clear my distinction between musical pictures and musical representations, but rather of making out a distinction with regard to musical representations themselves: between those that do and those that do not facilitate the hearing-in phenomenology—a distinction which, I should add, I had not even thought of at the time. The concept of seeing-in had, indeed, been adumbrated by Wollheim before my book was completed, and I was familiar with it. But the first mature and elaborated formulation, in the second edition of *Art and Its Objects*, for some reason evaded my notice. In its earliest form, the phrase "seeing-in," so far as I can remember, had not even appeared. And nothing in that earliest formulation seemed suggestive to me for my own work. Indeed, it was Robinson's essay, more even than the mature version of seeing-in in Wollheim's *Painting as an Art*, that made me see the relevance of the concept. I am happy now to give it its due, and to give Robinson hers.

Notes

NOTES TO I

1. *Aristotle's Treatise on Poetry*, trans. Thomas Twining (London, 1789), p. 65.
2. *Aristotle's Theory of Poetry and Fine Art*, trans. S.H. Butcher (4th ed.; New York: Dover, 1951), p. 7.
3. Aristotle, *Politics*, trans. Benjamin Jowett, in *The Basic Works of Aristotle*, ed. Richard McKeon (New York: Random House, 1941), p. 1311.
4. "On the Different Senses of the Word, Imitative, as Applied to Music by the Antients, and by the Moderns," the second of *Two Dissertations* which introduce Twining's translation, p. 48.
5. Ibid., p. 46.
6. Ibid., p. 48.
7. *The Corded Shell: Reflections on Musical Expression* (Princeton: Princeton University Press, 1980), chapters II and IV, passim.
8. Twining, *Aristotle*, pp. 44–45.
9. James Harris, *Three Treatises: the First Concerning Art; the Second Concerning Music, Painting, and Poetry; the Third Concerning Happiness* (3rd ed.; London, 1772), p. 55. For a useful review of such theories in Britain, see James S. Malek, *The Arts Compared: An Aspect of Eighteenth-Century British Aesthetics* (Detroit: Wayne State University Press, 1974).
10. It survives, regrettably, in much of the theoretical writing that surrounds the birth and maturation of the newest art. The search in film theory for the "essentially cinematic" still goes on in spite of the Enlightenment experience, much to its own confusion.
11. Harris, *Three Treatises*, pp. 55–56.
12. Ibid., p. 58.
13. Ibid.
14. Ibid., pp. 65–67.
15. Ibid., p. 69.
16. Another way of looking at the matter, suggested by Kendall Walton, is to construe the pervasiveness of the convention and our (subliminal) familiarity with it as *making* the drawing *look like* a dog in motion. This would have the virtue—if it is one—of avoiding the common notion that the resemblance relations are natural and convention-free. But these are deep waters, and for our purposes nothing hangs on the question; for the main point, which is that Harris fails sufficiently to recognize the role convention plays in representation, is

made under either interpretation, and is, indeed, made with even greater force under the latter.

17. *Aristotle's Treatise on Poetry*, trans. Twining, p. 70. I have used Twining's translation here because it is close in time to Harris' work and can, therefore, be assumed to be close to the way Harris would have understood the passage. Harris, *Three Treatises*, pp. 80–81.

18. Aristotle, *The Poetics*, trans. W. Hamilton Fyfe, Loeb Classical Library (Cambridge: Harvard University Press; London: William Heinemann, 1953), p. 5. But compare the more recent translation of G. M. A. Grube, which reverts to the old rendering of μίμησιζ: "The epic, tragedy, comedy, dithyrambic poetry, most music on the flute and on the lyre—all these are, in principle, imitations. They differ in three ways: they imitate different things, or imitate them by different means, or in a different manner." Aristotle, *On Poetry and Style*, trans. G. M. A. Grube (New York: Bobbs-Merrill Library of Liberal Arts, 1958), p. 3.

19. *The Poetics*, trans. W. Hamilton Fyfe, pp. 4–5n.

20. For a careful examination of the wide variety of things that were meant by μίμησιζ in the writings of Plato and Aristotle, see Richard McKeon, "Literary Criticism and the Concept of Imitation in Antiquity," *Critics and Criticism*, ed. R. S. Crane (Chicago: University of Chicago Press, 1957).

21. Cf. *Republic*, Book III (397), where Plato talks about the *narrator* who will "think nothing too low for him, so that he will attempt, seriously and in the presence of many hearers, to imitate everything without exception, . . . claps of thunder and the noise of wind and of hail, and of wheels and pulleys, and the sounds of trumpets and flutes and pipes and all manner of instruments; nay even the barking of dogs, the bleating of sheep, and the notes of birds. . ."; trans. John Llewelyn Davies and David James Vaughan (London: Macmillan, 1950), p. 90.

Notes to II

1. *Source Readings in Music History: From Classical Antiquity through the Romantic Era*, ed. Oliver Strunk (New York: Norton, 1950), p. 867.

2. Johann Adam Hiller, "Abhandlung von der Nachahmung der Natur in der Musick," *Historisch-kritische Beyträge*, ed. Friedrich Wilhelm Marpurg, I (1754), p. 533. My translation.

3. Nelson Goodman, *Languages of Art* (New York: Bobbs-Merrill, 1968), p. 38.

4. Ibid., p. 37.

5. Ibid., p. 39.

6. See his *Born to Sing* (Bloomington: Indiana University Press, 1973).

NOTES TO III

1. Nelson Goodman, *Ways of Worldmaking* (Indianapolis: Hackett, 1978), p. 106.
2. Boris Schwarz, *Music and Musical Life in Soviet Russia, 1917–1970* (New York: Norton, 1973), p. 85.
3. Ibid.
4. André Pirro, *L'Esthetique de Jean-Sebastien Bach* (Paris: Libraire Fischbacher, 1907).
5. Albert Schweitzer, *J. S. Bach,* trans. Ernest Newman (New York: Macmillan, 1950).
6. Ibid., vol. II, p. 41
7. *Beethoven: Letters, Journals and Conversations,* trans. and ed. Michael Hamburger (Garden City: Doubleday Anchor Books, 1960), p. 99.
8. *Letters of Mozart and His Family,* trans. Emily Anderson (London: Macmillan, 1938), vol. III, p. 1144.
9. André Pirro, *J. S. Bach,* trans. Mervyn Savill (New York: Orion Press, 1957), p. 104. This short biography of Bach is not to be confused with the longer treatise of 1907; and the translation, by the way, leaves a great deal to be desired.
10. Henry S. Drinker, *The 389 Chorales of J. S. Bach, with English Texts* (Association of American Choruses, Choral Series No. 1, 1944), p. 131.
11. I owe this point to Alan Tormey.
12. On this, see *The Corded Shell,* chapter VI, section 4; and Wilson Coker, *Music and Meaning: A Theoretical Introduction to Musical Aesthetics* (New York: Free Press; London: Collier-Macmillan, 1972), pp. 42–45.

NOTES TO IV

1. J. O. Urmson, "Representation in Music," *Philosophy and the Arts,* ed. Godfrey Vesey (London: Macmillan, Royal Institute of Philosophy Lectures, Vol. VI, 1971–1972).
2. Ibid., p. 134.
3. Ibid., pp. 138–139.
4. Ibid., pp. 139–140.
5. Joseph M. Williams, "Synaesthetic Adjectives: A Possible Law of Semantic Change," *Language,* 51 (1976), p. 461. I am grateful to Ted Cohen for calling my attention to Williams' article.
6. Ibid., p. 463.
7. Ibid. Italics mine.
8. John Burnet, *Early Greek Philosophy* (4th ed.; London: Adam and Charles Black, 1930), pp. 133–134.

9. "Having of a long time experienced certain ideas, perceivable by touch as distance, tangible figure, and solidity, to have been connected with certain ideas of sight, I do upon perceiving these ideas of sight forthwith conclude what tangible ideas are by the wonted . . . course of Nature like to follow" (45). *Berkeley's Philosophical Writings,* ed. T. E. Jessop (London: Thomas Nelson, 1952), p. 7.

10. Williams, "Synaesthetic Adjectives," p. 463. The figure is reproduced from Williams.

11. Ibid., p. 464.

12. Ibid., pp. 464–465.

13. Ibid., p. 463.

14. *Philosophical Investigations,* trans. G.E.M. Anscombe (New York: Macmillan, 1953), p. 216^e. On this, see Cora Diamond, "Secondary Sense," *Proceedings of the Aristotelian Society,* 63 (1966–1967).

15. Gilbert Ryle, *The Concept of Mind* (New York: Barnes and Noble, 1949), p. 16.

16. *Philosophical Investigations,* p. 216^e.

17. Ibid.

18. *The Blue and Brown Books* (New York: Harper Torchbooks, 1965), pp. 136–137.

19. *Philosophical Investigations,* p. 216^e.

20. Stephen Toulmin, *Reason in Ethics* (Cambridge: Cambridge University Press, 1968), p. 10.

21. Williams, "Synaesthetic Adjectives," p. 464.

22. *The Corded Shell.*

23. On this, see Philip Alperson, " 'Musical Time' and Music as an 'Art of Time,' " *Journal of Aesthetics and Art Criticism,* 38 (1980).

24. Henri Bergson, *The Creative Mind: A Study in Metaphysics,* trans. Mabelle L. Andison (New York: Philosophical Library, 1946), p. 14.

25. Urmson, "Representation in Music," p. 140.

26. *Harvard Dictionary of Music,* ed. Willi Apel (Cambridge: Harvard University Press, 1951), p. 349 (in the article "Imitation").

27. Urmson, "Representation in Music," p. 144.

28. Sigmund Freud, *The Interpretation of Dreams,* trans. James Strachey (New York: Avon Books, 1972), p. 265.

29. Ibid., pp. 441–442.

NOTES TO V

1. This is not, by the way, an experience reserved for the virtuoso. I speak as an amateur, but have, I believe, achieved that kind of physical intimacy with the instrument I play.

2. Karl Geiringer, *The Bach Family: Seven Generations of Creative Genius* (New York: Oxford University Press, 1954), p: 153.

3. Malek, *The Arts Compared,* p. 96.
4. Adam Smith, "Of the Nature of that Imitation which takes place in what are called the Imitative Arts," *Essays on Philosophical Subjects* (London, 1795), p. 133.
5. Ibid., p. 136.
6. Ibid., p. 137.
7. Ibid
8. Ibid., pp. 137–138.
9. Ibid., p. 138.
10. Ibid., p. 140.
11. Ibid., pp. 145–146; italics mine.
12. Ibid., p. 149. On this, see Peter Kivy, "Charles Darwin on Music," *Journal of the American Musicological Society,* 12 (1959); and "Herbert Spencer and a Musical Dispute," *The Music Review,* 23 (1962).
13. Ibid., p. 152. Smith alludes here to the first three lines of Milton's *At a solemn Musick*: "Blest pair of Sirens, pledges of Heav'ns joy,/Sphear-born harmonious Sisters, Voice and Vers,/Wed your divine sounds, and mixt power employ."
14. On this, see *The Corded Shell,* chapter III. By the time Smith was writing, this was a rather old-fashioned view; but in this, as in many other things musical, the British were a bit behind the times.
15. Smith, "Of the Nature of Imitation," pp. 159–160.
16. Ibid., pp. 163–164.
17. Ibid., p. 154.
18. Ibid.
19. Urmson, "Representation in Music," p. 136.
20. John Locke, *An Essay Concerning Human Understanding,* ed. Peter H. Nidditch (Oxford: Clarendon Press, 1975), p. 405 (III, ii, 1 and 2).
21. Ibid., p. 407 (III, ii, 6).
22. Jonathan Bennett, *Locke, Berkeley Hume: Central Themes* (Oxford: Clarendon Press, 1971), pp. 1–2.

Notes to VI

1. Nelson Goodman, *Languages of Art,* p. 232.
2. Ibid., p. 132.
3. Ibid., p. 135.
4. Ibid., p. 136.
5. Ibid., p. 140.
6. Ibid., p. 148.
7. Ibid., pp. 148–149.
8. Ibid., p. 150.
9. Ibid., pp. 152–153.
10. Ibid., p. 173.

11. Ibid., p. 178.
12. Ibid., pp. 184–185.
13. Ibid., p. 5.
14. Ibid., p. 22.
15. Ibid., pp. 225–226.
16. Ibid., pp. 225–226.
17. Ibid., p. 120n.
18. Stuart Hampshire, *Two Theories of Morality* (London: Oxford University Press, 1977), pp. 1–2.
19. Goodman, *Languages of Art*, p. 185.
20. See V. A. Howard, "On Representational Music," *Nous*, 6 (1972).
21. Leonard Meyer, "Exploiting Limits: Creation, Archetypes, and Style Change," *Daedalus*, 119 (1980), p. 194.
22. Arthur Danto, *The Transfiguration of the Commonplace: A Philosophy of Art* (Cambridge: Harvard University Press, 1981), p. 47. Danto talks mostly of the visual arts, but makes it evident that he thinks his views cut across the boundaries.
23. Ibid., p. 83.
24. Howard, "On Representational Music," p. 52.

NOTES TO VII

1. Quoted in the pocket edition of the score (Paris: Editions Salabert, n.d.). My translation.
2. Vincenzo Galilei, *Dialogo della musica antica e della moderna* (1581), trans. Oliver Strunk, *Source Readings in Music History*, ed. Strunk, p. 317.
3. Paul Oskar Kristeller, "The Modern System of the Arts," *Journal of the History of Ideas*, 12 (1951) and 13 (1952).
4. Charles Batteux, *Les beaux arts reduits à un même principe* (Paris, 1747). My translation.
5. Ibid., p. 270.
6. Ibid., p. 277.
7. See, for example, my "What Mattheson said," *The Music Review*, 34 (1973); and *The Corded Shell*, chapters III and V.
8. Hiller, "Nature in Music," p. 536. My translation.
9. Jean-Jacques Rousseau, *A Dictionary of Music*, trans. William Waring (London, n.d.), p. 199 (in the article "Imitation").
10. *Beethoven: Letters, Journals and Conversations*, p. 53.
11. Edward T. Cone, *The Composer's Voice* (Berkeley and Los Angeles: University of California Press, 1974), p. 83.
12. Ibid., pp. 83–84n.
13. Ibid., p. 84.
14. J. W. N. Sullivan, *Beethoven: His Spiritual Development* (New York: Vintage Books, 1960), p. 38.

15. Ibid., pp. 34–35.
16. For my own view of the matter, see *The Corded Shell*, pp. 22–23, 29–33, et passim.
17. Ibid., especially chapters V–VIII.
18. Alan Tormey, *The Concept of Expression: A Study in Philosophical Psychology and Aesthetics* (Princeton: Princeton University Press, 1971), chapters IV and V.

NOTES TO VIII

1. Section 51: *Von der Einteilung der schönen Künste.*
2. The best attempt recently to extract the "philosophy" from Hanslick's little volume is Malcolm Budd, "The Repudiation of Emotion: Hanslick on Music," *British Journal of Aesthetics*, 20 (1980), pp. 29–43.
3. Eduard Hanslick, *The Beautiful in Music*, trans. Gustav Cohen (New York: The Library of Liberal Arts, 1957), p. 36.
4. Ibid., p. 50.
5. Edmund Gurney, *The Power of Sound* (London: Smith, Elder, 1880), p. 349.
6. Ibid., p. 350.
7. Roger Scruton, "Representation in Music," *Philosophy*, 51 (1976), p. 273.
8. Cf. Richard Kuhns, "Music as a Representational Art," *British Journal of Aesthetics*, 18 (1978), pp. 120–125.
9. Scruton, "Representation," p. 273.
10. Ibid., p. 277.
11. Ibid., p. 280.
12. Ibid., p. 279.
13. Schweitzer, *J. S. Bach*, vol. II, p. 73.
14. Scruton, "Representation," p. 273.
15. Ibid., p. 283.
16. Ibid.
17. I am really giving this example to Scruton as a gift; for, truth to tell, even here there is a subtle distinction between Mozart's "representation" of eighteenth-century divertimento music and the genuine article. Don Giovanni's dinner music departs from its models in all sorts of subtle ways, to accommodate its theatrical function, and does not have an exact counterpart in any extant eighteenth-century divertimento that I know of.
18. Since the plot of *Meistersinger* revolves around events in the later life of Hans Sachs (1494–1576), we must imagine the period of the events to be in the second or third quarter of the sixteenth century; and so it is a Lutheran chorale of that period that the chorale in *Meistersinger* most likely "represents." I strongly suspect that Wagner was

not acquainted with any examples of Protestant church music of this period, but this is irrelevant to the question.

19. Actually, Charles Hartshorne thinks bird songs are "songs" and birds "musicians," as I have had occasion to mention previously. On this, see his *Born to Sing,* especially pp. 35–37. But this should cause no problem, except that bird songs, if Hartshorne were right, would turn out not to be a felicitous example of nonmusical sound.

20. Scruton, "Representation," pp. 274–275.

21. Ibid., p. 276.

NOTES TO IX

1. I follow here the "popular" practical edition of Margery Halford (Port Washington: Alfred Publishers, 1976).

2. Ibid., p. 4.

3. Ibid.

4. Johann Mattheson, *Der vollkommene Capellmeister,* trans. Ernest C. Harriss (Ann Arbor: UMI Research Press, 1981), p. 693.

5. Cf. Rudolf Arnheim, "A New Laocoon: Artistic Composites and the Talking Film," *Film as Art* (Berkeley and Los Angeles: University of California Press, 1957): "the opera is an almost entirely musical form, and the dialogue is limited more or less to the task of the printed 'titles' in silent movies" (p. 222). Let me add that I do not think this trivializes the art of Eisenstein, Griffith, et al., for it does not follow from what I am suggesting that the text is more aesthetically significant than the celluloid. But here is not the place to offer an essay in the aesthetics of the silent cinema.

6. This delicious suggestion was made by Jay Bachrach.

7. Cf. Arthur Danto's discussion of *The Fall of Icarus* in *The Transfiguration of the Commonplace,* pp. 115–120.

8. Hector Berlioz, *Fantastic Symphony,* ed. Edward T. Cone (New York: Norton Critical Scores, 1971), p. 13. I follow Cone's edition of the score throughout.

9. Ibid., p. 18.

10. Ibid., p. 21n. The quotation is from the program as published in the first edition of the score in 1845.

11. Ibid., p. 31.

12. Ibid., pp. 23–25, trans. Edward T. Cone.

13. Ibid., pp. 31–33.

14. Ibid., p. 35.

15. Robert Schumann, "A Symphony by Berlioz," in Cone's edition of the symphony, p. 228.

16. I am not suggesting that Berlioz was familiar with the more obscure practitioners of the fugal finale, such as Michael Haydn. But he cer-

tainly knew Mozart's last symphony, the third Razumovsky quartet, is likely to have known the fugal finale of Mozart's G-major Quartet, and might even have known, too, the fugal finales of Haydn's earlier Op. 20.

17. Berlioz, *Fantastic Symphony*, ed. Cone, pp. 27–28.

18. Ibid., p. 28, trans. Cone.

NOTES TO X

1. For a "Leibnizian" interpretation of Bach, see Edward E. Lowinsky's "Taste, Style, and Ideology in Eighteenth-Century Music," *Aspects of the Eighteenth Century,* ed. Earl R. Wasserman (Baltimore: Johns Hopkins Press, 1965). I take this as a representational interpretation of music that is "off the wall." Others may disagree. (Obviously Lowinsky does.)

2. James Thomson, *The Seasons, The Poetical Works* (Leipzig: Bernhard Tauchnits, 1853), p. 45. And compare the standard English performing translation of *The Seasons* which seems to follow Thomson's poem, rendering "Des Tages Herold" as "The crested harbinger of day," the "crest" obviously being an allusion to the cock's comb (in, for example, the Kalmus miniature score, p. 85).

3. On Handel's notorious "borrowings," see, Sedley Taylor, *The Indebtedness of Handel to Works of Other Composers* (Cambridge: Cambridge University Press, 1906); and P. Robinson, *Handel and His Orbit* (London: Sherratt and Hughes, 1908).

4. William K. Wimsatt, Jr., and Monroe Beardsley, "The Intentional Fallacy," reprinted in *Philosophy Looks At the Arts,* ed. Joseph Margolis (New York: Charles Scribner's Sons, 1962), p. 92.

5. For a dissenting view of representation as a nonintentional, "natural" phenomenon, see Dennis W. Stampe, "Toward a Causal Theory of Linguistic Representation," *Contemporary Perspectives in the Philosophy of Language,* ed. Peter A. French, Theodore E. Uehling, Jr., and Howard K. Wettstein (Minneapolis: University of Minnesota Press, 1978). For an answer, see *The Corded Shell,* pp. 64–66. There seems little reason for going into the question here, as nothing really turns on it for present purposes. Even if Stampe were right that intention is not a necessary condition for representation, it would have no adverse effect on my position, since I have given grounds independent of intention for rejecting putative, but unwanted representational interpretations. It is, of course, inevitable that we should ask *why,* if representation really does, as I believe, imply intention to represent, this is indeed the case. One very powerful answer to this question has been spelled out in some detail by Nicholas Wolterstorff in his *Works and Worlds of Art* (Oxford: Clarendon Press, 1980), where an elabo-

rate theory of "world projection" as human action is presented. I have no answer of my own, nor do I want to endorse Wolterstorff's. But I do think it valid, and important, to distinguish in this regard between something's *being* a representation and something's being able to be used, or being able to function as one in human society. Natural objects are frequently "representations" in the latter, attenuated sense, but not (as a matter of logic) in the former, literal one. That at least is what ordinary usage, for whatever that is worth as evidence, suggests to me.

6. Urmson, "Representation in Music," p. 134.

7. Locke, *Essay Concerning Human Understanding*, ed. Nidditch, p. 704 (IV), xix, 14).

8. Quoted in Alexander Wheelock Thayer, *The Life of Ludwig van Beethoven* (Carbondale: Southern Illinois University Press, 1960), vol. II, pp. 143–144. "But unfortunately for the writer," Thayer adds, "Beethoven's manuscript bears these inscriptions in his own hand: 'The Farewell, Vienna, May 4, 1809, on the departure of His Imperial Highness, the revered Archduke Rudolph'; on the Finale: 'The Arrival of His Imperial Highness the revered Archduke Rudolph, January 30, 1810.' " Here, then, is one of those rare occasions where an independent determination of the composer's intentions settles an interpreter's hash instantaneously, and with no interpretational work.

NOTES TO AFTERWORD

1. Jenefer Robinson, "Music as a Representational Art," in *What Is Music?: An Introduction to the Philosophy of Music*, ed. Philip Alperson (New York: Haven, 1987), p. 192n (hereafter cited parenthetically by page number in the text).

2. See Richard Wollheim, "On Drawing an Object," reprinted in *Art and the Mind* (Cambridge: Harvard University Press, 1974); "Seeing-as, Seeing-in, and Pictorial Representation," *Art and Its Objects* (2d ed.; Cambridge: Cambridge University Press, 1980); *Painting as an Art* (Princeton: Princeton University Press, 1987), chap. 2.

3. Wollheim, *Painting as an Art*, p. 46.

4. Ibid., p. 47.

5. Ibid., p. 48.

6. The "sentiments" are prerevolutionary. The work, of course, is not.

Bibliography of Works Cited

Alperson, Philip. " 'Musical Time' and Music as an 'Art of Time.' " *Journal of Aesthetics and Art Criticism*, 38 (1980).

Apel, Willi. *Harvard Dictionary of Music*. Cambridge: Harvard University Press, 1951.

Aristotle. *Aristotle's Theory of Poetry and Fine Art*. Translated by S. H. Butcher. 4th ed. New York: Dover, 1951.

————. *Aristotle's Treatise on Poetry*. Translated by Thomas Twining. London, 1789.

————. *The Basic Works of Aristotle*. Edited by Richard McKeon. New York: Random House, 1941.

————. *On Poetry and Style*. Translated by G. M. A. Grube. New York: Bobbs-Merrill Library of Liberal Arts, 1958.

————. *The Poetics*. Translated by W. Hamilton Fyfe. Loeb Classical Library. Cambridge: Harvard University Press; London: William Heinemann, 1953.

Arnheim, Rudolf. *Film as Art*. Berkeley and Los Angeles: University of California Press, 1957.

Batteux, Charles. *Les beaux arts reduits à un Même principe*. Paris, 1747.

Beethoven, Ludwig van. *Beethoven: Letters, Journals and Conversations*. Translated by Michael Hamburger. Garden City: Doubleday Anchor Books, 1960.

Bennett, Jonathan. *Locke, Berkeley, Hume: Central Themes*. Oxford: Clarendon Press, 1971.

Bergson, Henri. *The Creative Mind: A Study in Metaphysics*. Translated by Mabelle L. Andison. New York: Philosophical Library, 1946.

Berkeley, George. *Philosophical Writings*. Edited by T. E. Jessop. London: Thomas Nelson, 1952.

Berlioz, Hector. *Fantastic Symphony*. Edited by Edward T. Cone. New York: Norton Critical Scores, 1971.

Budd, Malcolm. "The Repudiation of Emotion: Hanslick on Music." *British Journal of Aesthetics*, 20 (1980).

Burnet, John. *Early Greek Philosophy*. 4th ed. London: Adam and Charles Black, 1930.

Coker, Wilson. *Music and Meaning: A Theoretical Introduction to Musical Aesthetics*. New York: Free Press; London: Collier-Macmillan, 1972.

Cone, Edward T. *The Composer's Voice*. Berkeley and Los Angeles: University of California Press, 1974.

Danto, Arthur. *The Transfiguration of the Commonplace: A Philosophy of Art*. Cambridge: Harvard University Press, 1981.

Diamond, Cora. "Secondary Sense." *Proceedings of the Aristotelian Society*, 63 (1966–1967).

Drinker, Henry S. *The 389 Chorales of J. S. Bach, with English Texts.* Association of American Choruses, Choral Series No. 1, 1944.

Freud, Sigmund. *The Interpretation of Dreams.* Translated by James Strachey. New York: Avon Books, 1972.

Geiringer, Karl. *The Bach Family: Seven Generations of Creative Genius.* New York: Oxford University Press, 1954.

Goodman, Nelson. *Languages of Art.* New York: Bobbs-Merrill, 1968.

———. *Ways of Worldmaking.* Cambridge: Hackett, 1978.

Gurney, Edmund. *The Power of Sound.* London: Smith, Elder, 1880.

Hampshire, Stuart. *Two Theories of Morality.* London: Oxford University Press, 1977.

Hanslick, Eduard. *The Beautiful in Music.* Translated by Gustav Cohen. New York: Library of Liberal Arts, 1957.

Harris, James. *Three Treatises: the First Concerning Art; the Second Concerning Music, Painting, and Poetry; the Third Concerning Happiness.* 3rd ed. London, 1772.

Hartshorne, Charles. *Born to Sing.* Bloomington: Indiana University Press, 1973.

Hiller, Johann Adam. "Abhandlung von der Nachahmung der Natur in der Musick." *Historisch-kritische Beyträge.* Edited by Friedrich Wilhelm Marpurg. Vol. I. Berlin, 1754.

Howard, V. A. "On Representational Music." *Nous,* 6 (1972).

Kant, Immanuel. *Kritik der Urteilskraft.* Berlin, 1790.

Kivy, Peter. "Charles Darwin on Music." *Journal of the American Musicological Society,* 12 (1959).

———. *The Corded Shell: Reflections on Musical Expression.* Princeton: Princeton University Press, 1980.

———. "Herbert Spencer and a Musical Dispute." *Music Review,* 23 (1962).

———. "What Mattheson said." *Music Review.* 34 (1973).

Kristeller, Paul Oskar. "The Modern System of the Arts." *Journal of the History of Ideas,* 12 (1951) and 13 (1952).

Kuhnau, Johann. "The Battle between David and Goliath." Edited by Margery Halford. Port Washington: Alfred Publishers, 1976.

Kuhns, Richard. "Music as a Representational Art." *British Journal of Aesthetics,* 18 (1978).

Locke, John. *An Essay Concerning Human Understanding.* Edited by Peter Nidditch. Oxford: Clarendon Press, 1975.

Lowinsky, Edward E. "Taste, Style, and Ideology in Eighteenth-Century Music." *Aspects of the Eighteenth Century.* Edited by Earl R. Wasserman. Baltimore: Johns Hopkins University Press, 1965.

McKeon, Richard. "Literary Criticism and the Concept of Imitation in Antiquity." *Critics and Criticism.* Edited by R. S. Crane. Chicago: University of Chicago Press, 1957.

Malek, James S. *The Arts Compared: An Aspect of Eighteenth-Century British Aesthetics*. Detroit: Wayne State University Press, 1974.

Mattheson, Johann. *Der vollkommene Capellmeister*. Translated by Ernest C. Harriss. Ann Arbor: UMI Research Press, 1981.

Meyer, Leonard. "Exploiting Limits: Creation, Archetypes, and Style Change." *Daedalus*, 119 (1980).

Mozart, Wolfgang Amadeus. *Letters of Mozart and His Family*. Translated by Emily Anderson. 3 vols. London: Macmillan, 1938.

Pirro, André. *L'Esthetique de Jean-Sebastian Bach*. Paris: Libraire Fischbacher, 1907.

————. *J. S. Bach*. Translated by Mervyn Savill. New York: Orion Press, 1957.

Plato. *Republic*. Translated by John Llewelyn Davies and David James Vaughan. London: Macmillan. 1950.

Robinson, P. *Handel and His Orbit*. London: Sheratt and Hughes, 1908.

Rousseau, Jean-Jacques. *A Dictionary of Music*. Translated by William Waring. London, n.d.

Ryle, Gilbert. *The Concept of Mind*. New York: Barnes and Noble, 1949.

Schwarz, Boris. *Music and Musical Life in Soviet Russia, 1917–1970*. New York: Norton, 1973.

Schweitzer, Albert. *J. S. Bach*. Translated by Ernest Newman. 2 vols. New York: Macmillan, 1950.

Scruton, Roger. "Representation in Music." *Philosophy*, 51 (1976).

Smith, Adam. *Essays on Philosophical Subjects*. London, 1795.

Stampe, Dennis W. "Toward a Causal Theory of Linguistic Representation," *Contemporary Perspectives in the Philosophy of Language*. Edited by Peter A. French, Theodore E. Uehling, Jr., and Howard K. Wettstein. Minneapolis: University of Minnesota Press, 1978.

Strunk, Oliver, ed. *Source Readings in Music History*. New York: Norton, 1950.

Sullivan, J. W. N. *Beethoven: His Spiritual Development*. New York: Vintage Books, 1960.

Taylor, Sedley. *The Indebtedness of Handel to Works of Other Composers*. Cambridge: Cambridge University Press, 1906.

Thayer, Alexander Wheelock. *The Life of Ludwig van Beethoven*. 3 vols. Carbondale: Southern Illinois University Press, 1960.

Thomson, James. *Poetical Works*. Leipzig: Bernhard Tauchnitz, 1853.

Tormey, Alan. *The Concept of Expression: A Study in Philosophical Psychology and Aesthetics*. Princeton: Princeton University Press, 1971.

Toulmin, Stephen. *Reason in Ethics*. Cambridge: Cambridge University Press, 1968.

Urmson, J. O. "Representation in Music." *Philosophy and the Arts*. Edited by Godfrey Vesey. Royal Institute of Philosophy Lectures, vol. VI. London: Macmillan, 1973.

Williams, Joseph M. "Synaesthetic Adjectives: A Possible Law of Semantic Change." *Language,* 51 (1976).

Wimsatt, William K., Jr., and Beardsley, Monroe. "The Intentional Fallacy." *Philosophy Looks at the Arts.* Edited by Joseph Margolis. New York: Charles Scribner's Sons, 1962.

Wittgenstein, Ludwig. *The Blue and Brown Books.* New York: Harper Torchbooks, 1965.

————. *Philosophical Investigations.* Translated by G. E. M. Anscombe. New York: Macmillan, 1953.

Wolterstorff, Nicholas. *Works and Worlds of Art.* Oxford: Clarendon Press, 1980.

Index

Library of Congress Cataloging-in-Publication Data

Kivy, Peter.
   Sound and semblance : reflections on musical representation : with
a new afterword by the author / Peter Kivy.
      p.   cm.
   Reprint, with new preface and afterword. Originally published:
Princeton, N.J. : Princeton University Press, c1984.
   Includes bibliographical references and index.
   ISBN 0-8014-9946-1 (pbk.)
   1. Music—Philosophy and aesthetics.   2. Music—Theory.
I. Title.
ML3845.K59   1991
781.1'7—dc20   91-55159